TIPTIONARY™

TIPTIONARY™

MARY HUNT
THE PUBLISHER OF CHEAPSKATE MONTHLY™

ILLUSTRATED BY JOEL BARBEE

BROADMAN & HOLMAN PUBLISHERS
Nashville, Tennessee

1-56865-548-7

Published by Broadman & Holman Publishers, Nashville, Tennessee
Acquisitions and Development Editor: Vicki Crumpton
Page Design: Anderson Thomas Design
Typesetting: Desktop Miracles

Dewey Decimal Classification: 640
Subject Heading: TIME MANAGEMENT / PERSONAL FINANCE

CONTENTS

ACKNOWLEDGMENTS

This project would never have been completed without the tireless efforts of some very special people.

To Cathy Hollenbeck, my colleague, assistant, and friend, who's worked so closely with me from day one that we now think alike (how scary is that?): Thanks for becoming the quintessential tip evaluator, tip organizer, and tip coordinator. Now I have a tip for you: Sleep will do wonders for those glazed eyes.

Many thanks to Sandy Carlsen, Mary Ann Woirhaye, and Kelly Woirhaye, who assisted with the huge task of typing basic tip information into the computers. Here's a tip: Take a ten-minute break each hour to do carpal-tunnel-syndrome-prevention exercises. I need to know your wrists are in tip-top condition, because I feel a whole new generation of tips coming on.

And finally, I want to give special acknowledgment and thanks to Gwendolyn Hunt who, in her eighth decade of life, has become so proficient in computer skills that she single-handedly input more than half of the data that was eventually required to complete this book: You are an amazing typist and a wonderful person. I love you very much for giving me the best tip of my life the day you said, "You need to meet my son."

INTRODUCTION

I didn't actually set out to become a tip aficionado. But that's exactly what's happened since the day I began publishing *Cheapskate Monthly* newsletter and invited readers to share with me their best money- and time-saving tips.

Three or four fascinating tips came pouring in those first few months (two or three more than I expected); and because they were great, I shared them with my *Cheapskate Monthly* readers. The more tips I published in subsequent months, the more readers responded with new and better tips. In time I began to go out of my way looking for tips and was amazed at how many turned up. I'm not sure if I was more attracted to the tips or the tips to me (sometimes I feel like a tip magnet), but the result is clear: I love tips because I can read a tip, digest it quickly, mentally file it for future use, move on to the next one, and never get bored.

Before long, tips began arriving at my office faster than I could figure out what to do with them. I couldn't throw them away. And because of the way they arrived (and still do)—printed on napkins; buried in the recesses of long, detailed letters; salvaged on snippets torn from newspapers; phone, fax, and E-mail messages—I had a logistical challenge from the very start.

I was able to stick with a simple filing system for about three days until I discovered a much easier method: Piling took hardly any time at all. And piles began to grow at an unprecedented rate into what I would eventually name Mt. Tip.

I knew I was headed for trouble the day I spent hours searching for one wonderful tip I knew was in there somewhere. And that's the day I conceded that either I had to find a way to move mountains or call a rubbish-removal contractor. I couldn't go on living like this.

My idea was to computerize and arrange alphabetically the tips worth saving and have my own personal tip directory right at my keyboard-poised fingertips. That rather selfish idea lasted for a few days but soon gave way to the idea of making a Tip Directory (I've learned to pay attention when ideas become capitalized) available to my *Cheapskate Monthly* readers. One glance around the room confirmed that this job would far exceed my self-publishing limitations. I got to thinking that if it was possible to sort, evaluate, test, purge, input, and boil all of this down to some kind of searchable format, it might be nice to make the results available to a few more people than just the ones I know—like the entire English-speaking world.

Meet Broadman & Holman Publishers. All I had to do was whisper the word *Tiptionary* to my editor, Vicki Crumpton, and the best publishing team in the world was mobilized into action.

The idea accepted, the contract signed, the deadline short, I found myself paralyzed by one tiny question: Where do I start? Enter husband Harold, who came to my rescue with one powerful computer database that would do everything I dreamed it should, and then some.

And so one day not so very long ago the process actually began. Now, many hundreds of hours later, the monster that nearly overtook my office and my life has been harnessed, tamed, and reduced to something I find wonderfully entertaining and surprisingly educational.

Tiptionary is a fabulously fun collection of tips—short, to-the-point suggestions for ways to do things cheaper, better, and faster. Some of the best tips you will read have completely unknown origins because they've been passed from generation to generation, and someone along the line sent it my way. Some tips were left out because they turned out to be nothing more than myths—legends people believe with all their hearts, but when put to the test, they failed.

One tip that was rejected had to do with bread and wallpaper. No foolin'. The tip was to discard the crust from a piece of bread, wad it up into a tight dough ball, and use it like an eraser to clean dirt and marks from wallpaper. I tried it and "erased" with all my might, but that little dirty spot on my wallpaper would not budge. I threw the bread-ball in the trash, grabbed my bottle of Soilove (page 347), and took care of that smudge in a flash.

Some entries were discovered quite by accident. I think of the woman who wrote to me so excited that since her husband started dumping his denture-soaking liquid into the commode each morning, she no longer needed to scrub the toilet on Saturday. Bingo! A great household tip (page 135).

Surely there's a long story that goes along with the tip you'll read on page 283. It arrived on a postcard without a return address or signature, simply a postmark from somewhere in Alaska: "Have your head examined before you attempt to build your own home. Unless you are a developer or professional contractor, you are in for a few surprises, not the least of which is that it will take twice as long as promised and cost twice as much as estimated."

The criteria for whether a tip made it into *Tiptionary* was fairly simple: If it didn't insult my intelligence, included a reasonable expectation that it saved time or money, and provoked anything close to *Wow! What a great idea*—it was in. That means you won't be reading any tips that tell you to brush and floss your teeth, because we're smart and we already know we should do that every day. But floss a turkey? Now that's a great tip (page 101). Or floss that winter coat? You'll be glad you did (page 257)!

You're about to learn that there are many different ways to accomplish goals. And that's good, because if you need to polish the copper in your kitchen and you don't have any lemons on hand but you do have a jug of vinegar, you'll be able to get the job done without running to the store to spend money needlessly (page 196). When there's more than one way to achieve the same result, *Tiptionary* will give you choices.

And now to answer the question you will ask if you haven't already: No, I do not do everything recommended in *Tiptionary*. There's not a person on the face of the earth that could do all of these things in a single lifetime, nor would I want to. Some of the tips are just not applicable to my life. And some won't apply to your life either.

Think of *Tiptionary* as a grand smorgasbord loaded with every kind of delicacy you can possibly imagine—even some things you can't. As you pass by, look at everything, consider most things, and fill your plate with those that suit your taste. You might want to bring along a highlighter and Post-it Notes in case you get a hankering to make notes.

The best thing about *Tiptionary*, just like your favorite smorgasbord, is that you can come back again and again and again!

Mary Hunt
Garden Grove, California
1997

FAMILY

BEAUTY & GROOMING

Astringent
Instead of purchasing an expensive brand-name astringent for use in your skin-care regimen, use witch hazel, an old standby that has been recommended by skin professionals for decades. It's available over the counter at any drugstore and performs equally well to any brand of astringent, no matter how expensive.

Barrettes
Use isopropyl rubbing alcohol to remove buildup of hairspray from hair barrettes. Some megahold hairsprays cause metal barrettes to tarnish. In the future, allow hairspray to dry completely before putting in barrettes.

Blush correctly
To find the right blush, check the color of your skin after exercising and try to match that color. Blush should add a healthy glow, not introduce a foreign color.

Bracelet assist
Here's an easy way to put on a bracelet without assistance. Place the bracelet across the top of your wrist and secure one end to the inside of your wrist with a piece of tape. Now that the bracelet isn't slipping around it should be easy to close the clasp.

Buff nails
Buff your fingernails rather than polish them because it's a quicker and cheaper way to groom nails. Apply a bit of petroleum jelly as a buffing compound, which will also soften cuticles.

Cologne
Refrigerate your cologne, and it can last up to 2 years. If a fragrance is exposed to heat, air, or sunlight, it immediately begins to change.

Cosmetic samples
Before purchasing a new cosmetic or skin-care product in a department store, request a sample that you can use for a few days before making a decision.

Cosmetics, economy line

If you love a particular high-priced cosmetic line, inquire as to the name of their economy line. For example, Lancome (available in department stores) also produces the L'Oreal line (available in any drugstore). You can call the customer service department of your favorite line to inquire, or take a look at a book titled *Don't Go to the Cosmetics Counter without Me,* (Paula Begoun, Beginning Press, 1994) to learn more of this kind of insider information.

Cosmetics (opened) shelf life

According to the cosmetics industry, liquid foundation that has been opened can be used for up to 2 years or until it begins to separate. Toss face powder and eye shadow after 3 years or if they become dry and "cakey." Lipstick is OK for 3 years, but discard it if oil beads up on the sides of the product. Replace mascaras and liquid eyeliners every 3 months because they are prime targets for bacteria.

Cosmetics (sealed) shelf life

Stock up on cosmetic and grooming items when they are on sale. Most sealed cosmetics have a shelf life of 3 to 4 years, so take advantage when your local drugstore has a great sale. But no matter how great the bargain, don't buy beyond your ability to use within a reasonable period of time.

Deodorant alternative

Rubbing alcohol is an effective deodorant for both underarms and feet because it kills odor-causing bacteria, dries quickly, and becomes odorless. Apply in a fine mist from a spray bottle or with a cotton ball.

Earring allergic reaction

If earrings leave your lobes sore, chances are you are allergic to nickel silver, which is an alloy in many types of jewelry. With clear nail polish, coat the earring post and back or clasp and all parts that come in contact with your skin. Only surgical steel and platinum contain no nickel silver; even 14- or 18-karat gold earrings can contain some of this alloy to which many people are highly sensitive. You will need to reapply the polish after several wearings.

Earring back replacement

If you lose the back piece of a pierced earring, cut the eraser from a pencil and insert it on the post for a temporary fix.

Elbows

Elbows get lots of wear and tear, and they really show it. Here's the perfect way to give them the attention they deserve: Cut a lemon in half and rest an elbow in each section for at least 10 minutes. (Sure, you'll look ridiculous and that's why you're not going to do this in the middle of an important meeting or while sitting in church.) The lemon juice will actually remove the stains that make elbows look dirty. Jump in the shower, do the regular stuff, and then use those lemon halves to do a final body scrub. Towel dry, follow with lotion, and you'll think you've just visited an expensive spa.

Exfoliant

Mix ½ to ⅔ cup granulated sugar with the juice of 1 whole lemon to form a paste. While showering, invigorate your skin with the paste. Rub heels and elbows with the inside of the lemon rinds. This costs 12 cents per treatment. A comparable brand-name product costs $25 for a 4-ounce jar.

Eye makeup remover

Use a no-tears type baby shampoo to remove eye makeup. Ophthalmologists encourage contact lens wearers to do this to reduce protein buildup on their lenses. Apply with a cotton swab in a brushing motion while holding eyelid taut. Rinse thoroughly.

Face-lift

Here's how to give yourself an instant "face-lift" and beauty treatment: Mix 1 teaspoon each of baking soda and olive oil to form a slightly thick paste. Gently massage it into your skin, rinse well, and then pat dry.

Facial in a tube

Use Preparation H to firm small wrinkles and fine facial lines. It sounds gross at first, but think about it: The product shrinks delicate tissue. This really does work very well, so just get into the habit of using it every night. And try not to think about the rest.

Facial mask

Use milk of magnesia for a soothing facial mask. Spread it on your face, being careful to stay away from eye area. Leave on for 30 minutes, rinse off with warm water, and pat dry.

Facial scrub

Baking soda mixed with a tiny bit of water makes an excellent facial scrub.

Foot spritz

Spritz feet and inside of shoes with rubbing alcohol in a spray bottle. It's very refreshing and eliminates foot odor.

Hair coloring not just for men

One lady we know colors her gray hair with a popular product, Just for Men. It produces identical results, is half the cost, and lasts twice as long as a similar product manufactured for women.

Hair conditioner

Slather mayonnaise liberally on your hair. Wrap your hair in plastic wrap or a small plastic bag and heat with a hair dryer. Leave on for 30 minutes. Shampoo and rinse well.

Hair control

The combination of lemon, which closes the hair cuticle, and lime, which is slightly emollient, helps break up static electricity and puts an end to flyaway hair. Mix 1 teaspoon lemon juice, ½ teaspoon lime juice, and 1 cup water. Mix together and pour into a plastic spray bottle. Spritz onto clean, damp hair. Do not rinse. Style as usual. Keeps well up to 5 days in the refrigerator.

Haircuts

Learn to cut the kids' hair. Ask someone who's really good at it to teach you, or get a step-by-step video. It's not difficult, but learn well. We don't want any goofy-looking kids out there.

Hair detangler

Dilute a teaspoon or two of liquid fabric softener in a glass of warm water to make a hair detangler for after shampooing. It will leave hair soft and smelling great.

Hair dye alternative

As a color pickup for drab brown hair, rinse it with strong, stale coffee. Then rinse with cool water.

Hair residue remover

Mix 1 tablespoon dry baking soda with the amount of shampoo you normally use for 1 hair washing, and shampoo your hair with the mixture. This removes residue buildup and leaves hair shiny and bouncy. Repeat about once a month. This is a cheap substitute for very expensive commercial products that do the very same thing.

Hairspray buildup

To remove stubborn hairspray buildup and to control dandruff, mix 1 package lemon Kool-Aid with 2 quarts warm water (don't add sugar). Wet hair and pour the mix through. Work well into hair, leave on for several minutes, and follow with your regular shampoo procedure. The citric acid is the key ingredient.

BEAUTY & GROOMING

Hairspray clogs

Ordinary rubbing alcohol will unclog the spray nozzle of a hairspray container that even hot water has not been able to unclog. Just dip the nozzle into the rubbing alcohol, allow to sit for a few minutes, wipe off, and spray.

Hair treatment

A typical hair salon will charge $25 to $35 for a special treatment to remove a buildup of minerals, conditioners, sprays, mousses, and gels. Here's a cheap alternative one professional hairdresser we know uses on her own hair: Wash hair with a gentle shampoo, and rinse in cool water. Towel dry hair. Saturate hair with apple cider vinegar (not white vinegar because it's too harsh). Wrap hair in a plastic cap or plastic wrap, and heat with a blow dryer for 10 to 15 minutes. Rinse hair thoroughly, and shampoo again.

Herbal bath

There's nothing like a relaxing, naturally scented bath to revive a tired mind and body. Fill a piece of cheesecloth with fresh rosemary, tie it up with string, hang the bag from the faucet, and fill the tub.

Lipstick palette

Don't waste the last ½ inch of lipstick in the tube. Do what professional makeup artists do. Using an orange stick or other clean implement, transfer all of the product from the bottom of the lipstick tube into one compartment of a compartmentalized medication container (the kind with a little compartment for each day of the week, available at the drugstore for less than $2). Use a lipstick brush to apply. As you accumulate other colors, fill the rest of the compartments, and soon you will have a portable lipstick palette.

Makeup pencils

Long lipliner and eyeliner pencils are awkward to use and don't fit into today's smaller handbags. Solution: Break one in half; sharpen both pieces. Now you have 2 manageable pencils for the price of 1.

Makeup remover

Use baby wipes to remove makeup. They're made for sensitive skin and won't cause dryness or irritation.

Mascara

If you use an eyelash curler, do so before applying mascara. Otherwise, lashes could stick to the curler and break.

Mascara

Don't use waterproof mascara on a regular basis. It's hard on the eyelashes.

But water-soluble types really smudge, especially in sweltering heat. Here's a reasonable compromise: Use a waterproof version on lower lashes only, because that's where smudges originate.

Midday pickup

Use a cosmetic sponge to soak up some of your favorite after-bath splash. Put the sponge in a small, resealable plastic sandwich bag, and toss it in your purse or briefcase. Now you can freshen up before an important meeting or at the end of a long and tiring day.

Nail fix

Tea bag paper can mend a broken nail instantly and easily. First cut paper to fit the nail, then coat with clear nail polish.

Nail polish

Keep the top of a nail polish bottle from sealing shut by spraying non-stick vegetable spray on a cotton swab and wiping it around the neck of the bottle before closing it.

Nail polish

Never shake nail polish before using. Shaking whips bubbles into the product, which will cause chipping later. Instead, turn bottle upside down, and gently roll it between your palms.

Nail polish fix

Smudge your polish while giving yourself a manicure? Not a problem. Do what the professionals do: Put a drop of polish remover on the pad of your thumb, and rub it lightly over the smudge until the spot is smooth. Reapply polish.

Nail polish prep

Scrub your fingernails with white vinegar, rinse, and dry completely. Now apply your nail polish. It will adhere better and last longer.

Pearls

Pearls that are worn often are subject to a dirty buildup of hairspray, perfume, and dirt. To clean even the finest pearls, rub them gently with a soft cloth drenched in rubbing alcohol.

Perfume overdose

When you overdo it with your perfume, saturate a cotton ball with rubbing alcohol to use where you put the perfume. The alcohol will cut the scent without altering it.

Petroleum jelly

Apply a small amount of petroleum jelly to your skin nightly. It's a natural moisturizer and is especially effective on extra dry areas like elbows, heels, and knees.

Razor sharp

If you are careful to dry your razor after each use, it will stay sharp much longer than if you simply use, rinse, and leave it.

School of beauty

Take advantage of the inexpensive beauty services available at a local school of cosmetology. Students are carefully supervised, conscientious, and eager to please. Be nice but firm about your expectations and desires. If you're a bit nervous, try a low risk procedure like a wash and style or manicure. The advanced students who will be graduating soon are very qualified. The savings are fantastic because basically you'll pay only for the materials, not labor.

Shampoo

Don't be a shampoo snob. In a 1992 *Consumer Reports* test of 132 brand-name shampoos, the lowly cheap brands from the supermarket rated just as high as the pricey salon brands.

Shampoo, half-price

Read the instructions on most shampoo bottles: Apply, lather, rinse, repeat. Stop "repeating," and your shampoo will last twice as long.

Skin-care products

A reader asked a doctor friend what he learned during his dermatology rotation concerning expensive skin and facial cleansing products. He informed her that the best products are not the most expensive. Dermatologists recommend Dove or Lever 2000 for cleansing and Lubriderm lotion for moisturizing. Both products are sold over the counter at any drug and most grocery stores.

Soap slivers

Put leftover pieces of soap in a mesh produce bag to make an effective scrubber for feet, elbows, and hands. If the bag is fairly large, fold or cut it down to a delicate, dignified size.

Soft hands

Keep a pump dispenser of hand cream in the kitchen. When you're washing dishes, use it before putting on rubber gloves, and you'll get a quickie hand softening treatment while you work.

Sunless tan

Smooth baby oil onto skin and allow it to penetrate before applying sunless tanning lotion to achieve a more even, lighter tanning effect, especially on elbows and feet.

Tarnish-free silver

To keep silver jewelry tarnish-free and shiny, slip it into a small zippered storage bag when it is not being worn. Before zipping the bag closed, squeeze out as much air as possible.

Tired feet

Freshen tired feet and soften skin easily and quickly: Add 4 tablespoons of baking soda to 1 quart of warm water. Pour into a large container, and let your footsies soak in it for 10 minutes.

Towelettes

Keep towelettes and baby wipes moist by storing the container upside down.

Visit the men's department

Buy men's toiletries if you have a choice when it comes to unscented deodorant, shaving foam, and hair colorings, for example. Products manufactured specifically for men are significantly cheaper ounce for ounce. Go figure.

CLOTHING & SHOES

Accessorize
Well-chosen accessories can turn the same basic dress or suit into 4 or 5 different looks.

Big Ts for little people
Buy a 3-pack of all-cotton, white T-shirts to use as pajamas or beach cover-ups for small children. Select a size large enough so the bottom edge is just below those cute little knees.

Boot stretch
If you have boots that are too snug, try this: Place a strong plastic bag (test first to make sure it is watertight) in the boot, and fill the bag with enough water to fill the cavity. Tie the bag closed, and place the whole thing in the freezer. As the water freezes it will expand and will stretch the boot at the same time. This technique will work well for shoes too.

Boys' clothes for little girls
Revamp little boys' clothes for your little girl by sewing lace around the hems, necklines, and sleeves. Use fabric paint to draw little hearts and flowers around the necks of solid-colored shirts and "onesies."

Boys' department
To cut down on clothing costs for girls and young women, shop for T-shirts, shorts, jackets, and other accessories in the boys' and men's departments.

Buttons
A button hanging by a few threads can be rescued by wrapping a narrow strip of cellophane tape around the threads to hold them until they can be reinforced.

Button security
Buttons on new clothes often fall off after just one wearing and washing. Before you wear a new item, cover the thread on each button with clear nail polish or a drop of superglue. Just be careful not to get any on the fabric.

Classic is timeless
Buying classic clothing is a money saver. What's "in" today looks ridiculous

tomorrow. Buy timeless, simple clothes, maintain one weight, and you will reduce your clothing expenditures. Classic pieces for the wardrobe all tend to work together too.

Clothing swap

Arrange a clothing swap with friends. Ask everyone to bring at least 5 items in good condition that no longer fit, flatter, or meet their needs. One person's disaster could be your delight.

Collar and cuff turn

Save money on men's dress shirts. If the collar or cuffs wear out first, take the shirt to a dry cleaner or tailor (or learn to do it yourself) and have them turned. It will cost about $5 to $10, which of course is much less than the cost of a new shirt.

Consignment stores

Consignment shops are everywhere these days and are a wonderful source for previously owned clothing. These shops are many cuts above a thrift store and offer wonderful merchandise for a fraction of the original retail. Look for specialty consignment stores just for kids. And don't think of yourself only as a buyer, but also a seller. Typically you will share 50/50 with the store's owner when your items sell. Call ahead to learn of the store's policies regarding the condition of garments they will accept and other guidelines.

Coordinate

Select and stick to a basic wardrobe color scheme so you can mix and match to create more outfits with the classic clothes you have.

Debit merchandise

Make friends with the managers of your favorite stores, and you might be able to tap into a gold mine. Ask if their "debits" or used merchandise are available for sale. These are the items that have been returned for one reason or another but cannot be put back on the floor or returned to the manufacturer. Typically these items are sold for pennies on the dollar.

Dry-cleaned garments

It is advisable to air just-dry-cleaned garments for 24 hours on a porch or elsewhere outdoors before wearing them. This will allow any residual chemicals to evaporate.

Dry cleaners

Despite statements denying responsibility, the minute a dry cleaner takes possession of your garment, he is legally bound for any damages that may occur. Keep all receipts in case something goes wrong, and work with the dry cleaner to come up with a mutually satisfying compromise. If you cannot find a solution, contact your state's Consumer Protection Office.

Dry cleaner sales
Ask your dry cleaner or neighborhood repair shops to let you know when they have unclaimed goods for sale. This is a great way to find terrific clothing bargains.

Dry cleaning in the car
When taking clothes to the dry cleaner, be careful not to leave them in the car or the trunk of the car for any length of time, especially if they're stained. This is particularly important in hot weather, when the heat in the car may bake in the stain, making it difficult, if not impossible, to remove.

Dry-clean only
Think twice—or three times—before deciding to buy something that says "dry clean only." This kind of expensive maintenance will double or even triple the cost of a garment over the years.

Find a good tailor
Someone skilled at alterations can take in, let out, take up, let down, and redesign any classic and well-made garment.

Fraying collars
Use an old electric razor to "shave" the collars of men's cotton oxford dress shirts when they begin to pill. Men's neck whiskers chew up collars, and the "shaving" actually helps to slow the wearing out process. They come out looking like new, literally.

Handbag repair
Don't throw out that handbag, backpack, or piece of luggage because of a broken strap, tear, or busted zipper. Have these items repaired at your local shoe repair shop. You'll be amazed at the low cost and high quality service you'll receive on the repair of all kinds of things, even belts, gloves, bags, etc.

Hangers affect fabrics
Don't store clothing on wooden hangers. Over time, the acid in the wood can react with the fabric. Wire hangers aren't much better. Pad all nonplastic hangers with unbleached muslin or cotton.

Heel shields
Protect high heels from wear and tear by having your shoe repair shop cover them with heel shields, a thin

protective plastic wrap that goes around the heel. If they get scuffed, they are easy to remove and replace.

Hemline
When you lengthen a garment and want to get rid of the original hemline, dampen a washcloth with white vinegar, place it on the crease line, and just iron the crease away. The vinegar odor will dissipate quickly. This works well on new clothing. With older clothing, results will vary, but for best results, let down the old hem and clean the garment according to the care label before ironing.

High maintenance
Think twice about leather, suede, and silk. They are lovely but very expensive to maintain.

Hosiery
Fine hosiery and panty hose will be easier to put on and less prone to snags and tears if you slip on a pair of latex or vinyl gloves before starting the process.

Ink stains
Aerosol hairsprays, because they contain a high concentration of acetone, will remove some ballpoint ink stains from clothing. Try this: Hold a rag under the fabric to blot the ink that comes through on the other side, then aim and spray. Remember this tip when you're at the office and get an ink stain. Someone will usually have hairspray and the key to beating an ink stain is to get at it as quickly as possible.

Jeans
To soften new jeans, place them in a sink filled with cold water and a cup of liquid fabric softener. Let the jeans soak overnight, then wash as usual.

Label solution
If back-of-the-neck labels cause irritation, don't cut them out. That just produces a scratchy raw edge or a lump, and removes important care information you'll need in the future. Instead cover them with iron-on bonding tape.

Less lacing
When first lacing up kids' new shoes, tie knots in the laces after the first 2 holes have been threaded, so your child can't pull them out accidentally.

Men's T-shirts
Ladies, buy men's white T-shirts to wear under jackets. They're cheap, easy to dye or trim, machine washable, and quite fashionable.

Mothball odor
Remove mothball odor from clothing by placing it in the dryer with a couple of fabric softener sheets. Run on the "air only" setting for 15 minutes.

Outlet shopping
Try on more than one size when shopping at outlets. Think about it: All of these items landed in this store for some reason, one of which might be that they were mislabeled.

Pants hanger
Put a piece of self-adhesive weather stripping on the bar of a hanger to keep slacks from slipping off.

Panty hose
To keep small holes in panty hose from turning into nasty runs, rub a glue stick over the hole. It's less sticky and works better than nail polish.

Panty hose longevity
According to the Morton Salt Company, your panty hose will last longer and be less prone to snagging and running if you perform this little longevity trick before you wear them for the first time: Mix 2 cups of salt with 1 gallon of water, and immerse panty hose in the solution. Soak for 3 hours. Rinse in cold water, and drip-dry. Apparently one of the properties of ordinary table salt is that it toughens fibers. That's true for panty hose and broom bristles.

Panty hose trick
Instead of throwing away a pair of panty hose with a run in one leg, wait for a second pair in the same shade to run, also in one leg. Then simply cut off the "injured" legs about 6 inches below the crotch. Wear both one-legged panty hose at the same time. Yes, you'll be wearing 2 panty tops, but that will simply create the equivalent of industrial-strength, control-top panty hose, for which most of us would pay a premium. To make use of this technique more often, always buy the same brand, style, and color of panty hose to avoid the embarrassment of LDCS (legs of different colors syndrome).

Perspiration stains
"Dry-clean only" garments that are stained with perspiration should be taken to the cleaners as soon as possible. The longer the salts from perspiration remain in the fabric, the greater the chance of permanent damage.

Pilling on sweaters
To remove pills from a sweater, stretch the sweater over a flat surface

and shave it lightly with an ordinary electric razor. Shavers sold for this purpose are not nearly as effective as the real thing.

Recycle

Instead of having your children wear their siblings' hand-me-downs, trade with neighbors or friends who have children of the same sizes. The kids get a new look, and the price is right.

Redye

Redye navy and black cotton T-shirts and turtlenecks—even stretch pants—with Rit Dye when they start to fade. You'll be able to get a few more seasons out of items you might have considered too far gone.

Remove smoke odors

To remove smoky odors from clothes, fill the bathtub with the hottest water available. Add 1 cup white vinegar. Hang garments above the steaming water and close the door.

Remove smoke odors

To remove cigarette odor from a blouse, skirt, or pair of pants, place a dryer softener sheet on the hanger with the garment; cover with a plastic bag. The cigarette odor will be gone by morning.

Repair and reap

Repair, resole, and reheel shoes. You can easily double or triple the life of a good pair of shoes with simple repairs. Even expensive sneakers and athletic shoes can be resoled and repaired at some shops using new techniques and products. Check with your local shoe repair or sporting goods store to see if they offer this service yet.

Replacement guarantee

Sears has a nationwide policy regarding children's clothing, sizes newborn through 16. If any item wears out, upon return it will be replaced in the same size, color, and style at absolutely no additional cost. There is no time frame rule that says you must be the original owner, or that limits the number of times an item can be replaced. The only requirement is that it must be identifiable as a Sears product, so don't remove labels. This policy is known as Sears' Replacement Guarantee.

Rest and relaxation

Your clothes will last longer if you allow them to "rest" between wearings. Ideally, clothing should hang for at least 24 hours between wearings to allow the fabric to return to its original shape.

Right from left

Put a sticker inside your children's right shoes or sneakers. They will begin to learn right from left and also get their shoes on the right feet all by themselves.

Shoe odor eaters

To keep shoes and boots from developing an unpleasant odor, make your own odor eaters: Pour a few teaspoons of baking soda onto a small piece of cotton fabric. Tie the ends of the fabric together and secure them with a rubber band. Set one sachet in each shoe overnight. The sachets can be used again and again.

Shoe odors

Stuff some newspaper into your shoes and boots to remove unpleasant foot odor. The paper absorbs odors.

Shoe polish

Out of shoe polish? Spray dull, dirty-looking shoes with furniture polish, then buff lightly with a soft cloth. Self-polishing floor wax works particularly well on patent-leather shoes.

Shoe preservation

Leave your good business shoes at the office. Change into an older pair for the trip up and down steps and out to the parking lot.

Shoe rotation

You've heard of rotating your car's tires to make them last longer, but how about rotating your footwear? Research shows that your feet produce about a half-pint of water every day. If you wear a particular pair of shoes no more than once every 3 days, 3 pairs will hold up as long as 4 pairs worn more frequently. Shoes need 48 hours to rest, dry out, and resume their normal shape.

Shoes and driving

Ironically, the enemy of many good shoes is not walking, but driving. While working the gas and foot pedals, the back of the shoe is repeatedly scraped against dirty, abrasive carpet. Wear sneakers when driving, then slip into your good shoes upon arrival.

Shoe selection

When trying on shoes in the store, walk around in them on a hard surface. Standing on a carpet is deceiving. It makes the shoes feel more comfortable than they would be on hard floors or other surfaces.

Shoes in socks

Store off-season shoes inside socks to keep them scuff- and dust-free.

Shoes that slip 'n slide

When the soles of new shoes are too slippery, roughen them with a piece of sandpaper.

Shoe trees

Shoes should be stored with cedar shoe trees in them. Cedar absorbs moisture and stops moisture damage to the leather.

Shoulder pads

Fasten unused shoulder pads to the ends of hangers to cushion fragile clothing and keep thin straps from slipping off.

Sleepers

Instead of throwing out children's sleepers, which are either too small or have feet that have been worn through, cut off the part just below the elastic at the ankle. Next, get a man's adult-sized tube sock and cut all but about 3 inches of the leg part off (more or less depending on your child's size). Turn the sleeper and the tube socks inside out and sew a sock to each leg of the sleeper at the elastic (right sides together). Turn right side out.

Static cling

Annoyed by static cling? Massage a small amount of hand lotion into your hands. Then lightly rub your palms over your pantyhose, tights, or slip.

Stretching leather shoes

To stretch leather shoes that are a bit snug, pour rubbing alcohol into a fine-mist spray bottle. Spray inside the shoes, and then wear them immediately; the alcohol evaporates quickly. This technique works beautifully, but it only works on leather shoes.

Suede shoes

Rub very fine sandpaper on suede shoes to remove stubborn scuff marks.

Sweat shorts

Save the kids' sweatpants, even if they have holes in the knees. When summer rolls around, cut them off, hem them by machine, and have comfortable cheap shorts for the kids.

Swimsuits

To prolong the life of swimsuits that are exposed to harsh chlorine, buy a bottle of chlorine remover, sold in pet supply stores for removing chlorine from the water in fish tanks. Add a few drops of the liquid to a pail of cold water, pop the suits in when the kids are done swimming, and follow with a cold tap water rinse.

CLOTHING & SHOES

Tie swap

If a man in your house wears ties often and easily tires of even his favorites, find another such person who will participate in a tie swap. Twice a year the swappers should go through their tie wardrobes and get rid of the ties that have become boring or that were gifts and never liked in the first place. Make sure the items are freshly cleaned, and then do a tie-for-tie swap. Donate anything left to a local charity.

Tube socks

Buy tube socks for your kids rather than the traditional type. They last longer since the heel is not always wearing in the same spot. Get in the habit of always buying the same brand, same style, all-white tube socks, and you won't have to spend half your life matching socks into pairs.

Upgrades are optional

When buying kids' clothes and shoes, set a budget figure, and if the child wants to upgrade to a trendier brand or style, require her or him to pay the difference.

Used work clothes

You can purchase excellent used work clothes from The Working Man, P. O. Box 140204, Nashville, TN 37214, 615-758-5388. The clothing is clean and in good repair, the prices are excellent, and the service is super. Call for a free catalog.

Warm hands

To keep your hands warm and dry while playing or working in the cold weather, wear lightweight latex gloves under your gardening gloves or woolen mittens.

White sneakers

Before wearing a new pair and after each wash, spray white canvas sneakers with a fabric protector like Scotchgard. They'll be sparkling white till the day they wear out.

White sneakers

To keep white canvas shoes looking new, apply white shoe polish to them after they are washed and while they are still wet. Allow to air-dry. You won't believe the results.

Wholesale

As a general rule, don't pay full price. With so many manufacturer outlets, discount mail-order catalogs, consignment shops, thrift shops, and fabulous sales, you should never have to pay the full retail price for your clothing or shoes.

Widowed socks

Uses for widowed socks: (1) Slip one over your hand to use as a waxing, dusting, or shoe-polish mitt. (2) Put one over the top of the bathroom cleanser can to avoid spills. (3) When you travel, slide one over each shoe to keep the clothes in your suitcase clean.

Wool softening

To clean and soften new, washable winter woolens, add ½ cup of hair conditioner or creme rinse to 1 gallon of lukewarm water and soak. Rinse the woolens thoroughly with tepid water.

Zipper jams

Paint those fraying threads that constantly get caught in a zipper with clear nail polish.

Zipper tab

If the tab on your zipper is lost or broken, replace it with a safety pin or paper clip. Paint or wind fine yarn around it in a color that complements the garment.

Zipper troubles

There are several things you can do to get that stubborn, sluggish, sticking metal zipper back into tip-top shape: Run the lead of an ordinary pencil along the metal zipper teeth to lubricate them. Or, with a cotton swab, apply a bit of lubricating spray such as WD-40 to the teeth. Be careful to wipe away any excess so it won't soil the garment. Another solution: Rub the edge of a bar of soap or an old candle up and down the teeth and along both sides of the zipper.

FAMILY LIFE

Ant moats

Keep the ants away from the food on your picnic table by placing each table leg into a bowl or paper cup of water. Ants can't swim—they can't even float—so they'll leave your picnic food alone.

Casseroles to go

When you're going camping, prepare casseroles ahead and freeze them in waxed milk cartons. They will fit perfectly into the cooler and stay cold longer.

Cheap movies

Go to a movie matinee. It's always cheaper.

Cheap tickets

If you enjoy cultural events or visiting local museums and theaters, volunteer as an usher or ticket collector or to fill some other need. In exchange you will probably receive free or reduced admissions. Ask about the policy ahead of time.

Clutter no more

Keep a lost-and-found basket in a central location where family members can stash things they find lying around the house and also look for things they've lost.

Directory assistance for the visually impaired

If someone in your family has a vision impairment, apply for free unlimited telephone directory assistance. (Most telephone companies—even the local providers—charge per call for directory assistance these days.) Call your local business office.

Down with divorce

Work on your marriage. Divorce is very expensive. Just imagine how expensive it would be to support two households.

Everyone counts

Involve the whole family in vacation planning, particularly the kids. Letting them participate helps them put to use their geography and history lessons. Saving the money first and then deciding how it will be spent demonstrates to your kids the principles of economy and good money management. If everyone has a voice in making the big decisions, the result will be far less grumbling and a lot more cooperation.

Field trips

Many interesting factories offer formal and informal tours. Call the chamber of commerce in the cities you will be visiting on your next family vacation for a listing of all the factories that offer tours. While you're at it, keep a list of the ones in your own area. Typically these kinds of tours are concluded with free samples of the factory's product. I know what you're thinking. Few, if any, banks offer tours.

Free concerts

Most cities have community-sponsored entertainment during summer months. Many churches and colleges have free performances during holidays. Make it a habit to check the paper and community bulletin board for local events.

Go to college

Local colleges often show movies in a setting that's better than some small theaters and at a much lower cost. For instance, Drake University in Des Moines charges $1 for the movies it shows. What's more, live theater, student film shows, and informational speakers can often be found for free.

Ice alternative

When preparing for a family outing or vacation, fill an empty plastic water or milk jug ¾ full with water, freeze, and place in a cooler. It will keep your food items cool longer than a block of ice; as it melts it doesn't make a mess; and if you were careful to clean the jug well, you'll have fresh drinking water.

Interlibrary loans

Call your library to see if you can borrow that book you've been tempted to buy. If they don't have it on hand, ask for an interlibrary loan. Even small libraries belong to large networks of libraries, and chances are very good they'll be able to get that book for you and in less time than it would take for them to go through the channels necessary to acquire it for their own shelves.

Libraries

What a fabulous place the library is. There you and your kids will find current newspapers, magazines, children's books, adult fiction and nonfiction, videos, cassettes, CDs, and wonderful storytellers. You get to take home something new and it doesn't cost anything. If you like to shop for fun, satisfy the impulse by visiting a library.

Library fines

Avoid overdue fines at the library. Most libraries will renew books by telephone.

Mall outing

Load the kids in the car and drive to the biggest mall around. Make the rounds to the "hands-on" toy stores, such as FAO Schwartz or The Sesame Street Store. These stores where kids are always welcome have wonderful play areas.

Mealtime fun

Make eating at home fun. Rearrange your eating area. Make a new tablecloth. Use place mats. Play background music. Light some candles. Have a picnic in the family room.

Memory game

Collect 2 identical copies of each family member's photo and glue them to the lids of frozen-juice cans. On the opposite side of every game piece, glue a paper circle with the game's title such as "Reese's Memory Game." To play, lay out all pieces with photos face down. The child turns over 1 piece, names the family member, then attempts to locate its matching piece. Before long your child will recognize by face and name all family members, even those who live far away. Even a toddler can play.

Mirror notes

Leave a reminder for family members by writing notes on the bathroom mirror with a dry erase marker, available in all kinds of colors at office supply stores. It wipes right off with a tissue, and it's sure to be seen. If a note is left unerased for some time, use a bit of rubbing alcohol on that tissue to wipe it away without a trace.

Monday, no fish

The worst night to order fresh fish in a restaurant is Monday. Most restaurants don't get fish deliveries over the weekend, so Monday's fish special is Friday's delivery.

Move midweek

If you're moving, do it on a weekday. Fees can be as much as 50 percent higher on the weekend. Pack everything yourself and save at least 10 percent. Most movers provide cartons.

Negatives in safekeeping

To save precious memories in the event of a future house fire or some other horrible disaster that would destroy your family photograph collection, take some negatives from each year's pictures (not all of them because that would just be too many), and put them in your safe-deposit box. Then, heaven forbid, should you endure a disaster and lose all of your photos, you can at least get some of them reprinted.

Newsprint

Newspaper printing companies often have roll ends of newsprint available to anyone who is willing to haul them off. While there's not enough paper left for tomorrow's edition, there will be plenty for wrapping gifts, or as art paper for murals and finger painting. Make a few phone calls, and see what you can find in your area.

Our family

Write a book of your family's history. Let the kids write and illustrate their own personal chapters.

Portable toys

Use a large mesh laundry bag to carry your kids' toys to and from the beach or public pool. When you return home, hose down the bag and hang it outside or over your tub so the toys can air dry.

Quality entertainment

Check with local colleges, civic theaters, and churches. Some of the best performances you and your family will ever attend are available for a nominal fee, if any.

Rehearsals

If tickets to a special concert or local play are out of your price range, inquire if you can attend a rehearsal.

Skip first-run films

All but the biggest blockbusters are available on video 3 months (sometimes even sooner) after release. Your patience will pay off.

Stargaze

Get a book about constellations from the library and arrange a starry-night outing to identify constellations. Bring a thermos of hot chocolate and a great big, cozy blanket.

Sturdy napkins

Washcloths in lieu of paper napkins are a tidy and environmentally friendly alternative for messy young eaters.

Suite
If you need more than 1 hotel room on vacation, a suite is usually cheaper than 2 rooms. An efficiency suite will save you even more, allowing you to cook a few of your own meals while on vacation.

Surround-sound
Put a clock radio in every bedroom. Instead of the buzzer, set them all on the same station that plays lively music, and your family will get up to surround-sound each morning.

Swing grips
To keep kids from getting rope burns while playing on a swing, put foam handlebar grip pads over the rope. They can be adjusted for height.

Test photo
Taking family photos? Do some trial runs first with an instant camera. Wear different clothes and makeup colors, and see which you like best.

Video decisions
Keep a video catalog in the car so you and the kids can pick the tapes you want to see before you get to the video store. This will save some time when you get to the store and also will give the kids something to do in the car.

Wedding cake
If you are planning a wedding, contact a cake decorating class in your city. Coordinate with them to get a cake at an amazing price.

Welcome map
When you move, leave a "neighborhood guide" for the new owners. Include items such as a map of the surrounding area and names and phone numbers of the best babysitters and the block's handymen.

FITNESS & HEALTH

Aspirin miracle

Research suggests that 1 aspirin tablet, a 1-cent expenditure, taken every other day helps reduce risk of heart attack, certain kinds of strokes, cancer of the gastrointestinal tract, and possibly Alzheimer's disease, among other serious ailments. (See your doctor before beginning such an aspirin regimen.)

Bowling sub

Sign up at your local bowling alley to be a league substitute. For a nominal fee you will be able to bowl in the place of an absentee league member.

Calcium

Don't drink sodas together with calcium-rich foods or supplements. If your soft drink contains phosphoric acid (and most do), it will block absorption of calcium into the bloodstream.

Foot massage

Give your tired feet a minimassage by rolling them back and forth over an icy cold soda or juice can.

Golf

A round of golf burns 1,060 calories if you walk and pull the clubs on a wheeled cart for 18 holes. That's the equivalent of running 6 miles.

Health clubs

Try the club before you join. Most offer several free visits or short, low-cost trial memberships. Join with a group of five or so friends, and at some clubs you'll save as much as 35 percent. Pay a year's dues in advance to save up to 20 percent (make sure the club has a reasonable likelihood of still being in business a year from now). Ask about new member perquisites, such as a free session with a personal trainer. Also, if you need to take a long-term break for travel or other reasons, ask the club to freeze your membership and start it up again upon return.

Health insurance

Never be without health insurance. High deductibles with low premiums are recommended if you are and plan to remain healthy, because this type of coverage is for the big catastrophic events. One uninsured catastrophic illness or accident could wipe out everything you have saved and planned for.

Hiccups

Eating a teaspoonful of sugar gets rid of hiccups in a flash.

Hot water bottle

Fill a 2-liter soda-pop bottle about 6 inches from the top with hot tap water. Replace screw-top tightly. Wrap in terry towel and snuggle up with your very wonderful, yet cheap, hot water bottle. A smaller bottle with just warm water works well for an older child.

Ice pack alternative

Instead of paying big bucks for fancy ice packs, do this: Freeze raw rice in a freezer-weight zippered storage bag. To use, wrap it in 1 layer of paper toweling. It conforms well to most body parts like backs and sprained extremities and retains coldness for at least 45 minutes. Use gallon-sized bags for backs and legs, pint-size and snack-size for boo-boos. Double bag to discourage accidents, and don't leave packs unattended with children.

Ice packs

Make your own flexible ice packs. Pour ¾ cup water and ¼ cup rubbing alcohol into a zippered storage bag and close. Put zipped bag into another bag, seal, and freeze. You will have a slushy bag of ice whenever needed for sprains, headaches, or other ailments because alcohol cannot freeze. Label clearly.

Iron pots provide iron

Cook in cast-iron pots. Doing this boosts the iron content of food. Soup simmered for a few hours in an iron pot has almost 30 times more iron than soup cooked in another pan.

Reduce cholesterol

When making scrambled eggs, use the yolks from only half of the eggs to cut cholesterol by 50 percent without affecting taste.

Runner's secret

If the pollen count is high, warm up inside before exercising. This will minimize your exposure to allergies outside.

Ski pants

Take an old pair of jeans or canvas overalls, and turn them into cheap and comfortable ski pants. Simply spray with a good waterproof fabric protector available at fabric, sporting goods, or hardware stores.

Stop smoking

Even a smoking habit that isn't excessive will cost around $1,000 a year, to say nothing of the additional medical bills.

Take a walk

Want to beat the common cold? A brisk walk or exercise at a moderate level has been associated with strengthening the immune system. On the other hand, extremely strenuous exercise can actually lower immunity to colds and flu. So, take a walk, but take it easy.

Take vitamin C

Vitamin C works in the body as a scavenger, picking up all sorts of trash, including virus trash. It can shorten the length of a cold from 7 days to maybe 2 or 3. It has been proven to lower cholesterol, decrease arthritis pain, reduce outbreaks of canker sores, and lessen premenstrual syndrome.

Tea for fluoride

If your water lacks fluoride, drink teas. Black tea delivers more fluoride than fluorinated water.

TLC for your feet

Crush 6 aspirin tablets and mix them with a tablespoon each of water and lemon juice; work into a paste. Apply the paste to calloused spots or dry skin. Put each foot in a plastic bag and wrap with a warm towel. Sit for 10 minutes with your wrapped feet elevated. Caution: If you are diabetic or have circulatory problems, special care of your feet is essential. Get a doctor's guidance for all questions of foot health.

Walk, don't drive

Combine errands and exercise. A brisk walk to the post office, drugstore, or library will produce the same benefits as aerobics, and you'll save transportation costs in the process.

Walker caddy

Tie the handles of a plastic grocery store bag to the arms of the convalescent's walker. The bag will remain open and can be used to carry everything from eyeglasses to tissues to medication.

Winter swimsuit test

Stay motivated to stick to your exercise program during the winter months: Put on your swimsuit and stand in front of the mirror once each month.

GIFTS

Baby-shower booty

Wrap a large baby-shower present in a crib sheet or baby blanket, and secure with colorful diaper pins. Attach a rattle too.

Baby shower on ice

Here's an idea for a unique way to welcome the new baby and help the new parents in a big way. Instead of the usual baby gifts, invite the guests to bring a prepared dish, casserole, dessert, etc., completely prepared and frozen for the guest of honor's freezer. Request that each dish have the recipe attached to it, which can be put into a small photo album during the shower. You'll be able to present the expectant parent with a unique cookbook along with a freezer full of food. It's fun and inexpensive and will give your friend precious time to spend with the new baby instead of in the kitchen.

Bath salts

Kids can make bath salts as presents for a favorite teacher, grandparent, or friend. Mix 3 cups Epsom salts, 1 tablespoon glycerin (from the drugstore), a few drops of food coloring, and a bit of cologne for scent. Put the salts in a sealed container such as a small jar with a screw-type lid and paint a Valentine message on the lid.

Books

Books make great gifts. But don't limit yourself to shopping in the big bookstore chains. Secondhand bookstores are less expensive and often have out-of-print titles that can't be found in the big chains. Also these stores may sell old prints or maps that you could frame for your family members or friends.

Cards sent to hospitals

If you send get well cards to friends and family members who are in the hospital you never know for sure when the person will be going home. So instead of using your home address in the upper left-hand corner, write the patient's home address there. This way if the card must be returned to sender, your friend will still get it.

Cheer for the homebound

Brighten the life of a person who's confined indoors. Set a low, shallow pedestal birdbath near a window of his or her home. Plant a ring of flowers around the base, and change it seasonally. In winter, a wreath of holly with red berries would be like a living Christmas card. Give the new bird-watcher a wild-bird guide, notebook, and pen for recording sightings.

Create gift stationery

You can avoid spending if you get into the habit of making your own cards, stationery, postcards, gift bags, etc. You can purchase paper and envelopes in bulk then use the paper cutter at the local copy shop to cut it to the sizes you need. With a few carefully chosen rubber stamps and colored markers, anyone can make beautiful and unique cards and stationery for personal use or to give as gifts. Use postcards whenever possible. This way you'll not only save the cost of the envelope, but 12 cents in postage too.

Everything gifts

One couple we know has begun giving an "everything" present to each other for the entire year's gifts (birthday, anniversary, Christmas, etc.). One year their everything gift was a new computer; once it was a piece of home gym equipment a physical therapist had recommended. Not only does this free their time, they say they are not purchasing items they neither need nor want, just to be buying a gift. The fringe benefit they have noticed is the money they now have available at Christmastime and throughout the year to help those less fortunate than themselves.

Extraneous coupons

What to do with all the coupons you can't use? Clip neatly and categorize them with gifts in mind. For instance, for the next baby shower, make up a clever holder full of coupons for diapers, baby food, and other items for a new mom (make sure the coupons haven't expired). Provide a great coupon assortment for the newly married couple to assist them in stocking their pantry. Have a friend or relative with a pet? Enclose some good coupons for pet food or supplies in their next birthday card.

Fill-the-pantry shower

What a great idea! Give the future bride and groom a Fill-Their-Cupboards wedding shower. Each guest copies a favorite recipe or dinner menu onto a recipe card, purchases all the nonperishable ingredients to prepare the dish or meal, and wraps it up as a unique gift. Newlyweds will be thrilled to have their cupboards filled with the ingredients and specific directions for how to make favorite tried-and-tested meals.

Flowers direct

Before you call a local florist or a national floral delivery company to arrange for an out-of-area delivery, think about this: These services end up involving all kinds of middlemen, which means extra fees and surcharges for phone calls and delivery. They usually have minimums of about $40, and you're never sure what your recipient will get because you don't come close to speaking with the person who will actually create the arrangement. You can skip past all of these extra people by making one call to a florist in the neighborhood where your recipient lives. You'll get 3 times the bouquet and service for your money by dealing directly.

Food bank donations

When a local merchant has a 2-for-1 special on canned or other nonperishable food items that you intend to purchase, keep one of the items for yourself and give the free one to a food bank or charitable organization. Passing this kind of savings to someone else in need is an effective way you can give back even if you are on a limited income.

Gift bundles

One woman we know has combined her goals of giving generously, living within her means, and avoiding waste in this way: Through her wise management of manufacturer's coupons she's been able to amass dozens of toiletry items like deodorants, shampoos, lotions, razors, etc., either for free or for mere pennies. (Example: She bought one item that was on sale for $1.99. But with her $1-off coupon, and the store's double coupon day, the item was free!) When she has a good supply she bundles these items into individual kits, places them into resealable plastic bags, and delivers them for distribution to the homeless through a local rescue mission in her city.

Gift cards

Make your holiday card the gift. Include a family picture, poem, story, original song, or painting—anything of lasting significance.

Gift for seniors

What to give senior citizens who have everything and then some? Try sending a basket filled with consumable goodies such as teas, coffees, good cookies and biscuits, chocolates, and special baked and canned delicacies. Think about enclosing some ethnic snack foods unavailable at most American grocery stores. These are especially appreciated.

Gift list

Avoid returning unwanted gifts (or pretending you like them) from your spouse or immediate family members by keeping an ongoing record of the things you would like, along with the specific details. Through the year as you see items of particular interest, pick up the store's business card and on the back write the details such as: Red cardigan sweater, brass buttons, wool blend, size 8, $49.98. These cards become a practical gift list that makes gift giving a positive experience for both the giver and receiver.

Gifts of food

Personalize food gifts with your own decorated label, for example, "Marilyn's Chutney" or "Cathy's Cookies." Attach your recipe and other instructions to the gift with ribbon, raffia, or tasseled cord. Add a spoon or spreader for chutneys or flavored butters.

Gift of sight

Your used eyeglasses will put the world in focus for a person living in a developing country. Don't throw away someone's chance for a clearer tomorrow. Ship eyeglasses to: Lions Sight First Eyeglass Recycling Center, 34 W. Spain St., Sonoma, CA 95476.

Gifts of your heirlooms

Perhaps you have something that a friend or relative has long admired and enjoyed. If you're tired of dusting it, give it as a gift for a special occasion. Be careful though. Not everyone is sure to cherish your possessions the way you think they should, so be confident you have a perfect match before you wrap up that Ming vase or special possession.

Gift stash

Create a gift box in a closet or cupboard into which you can put any free samples you receive, door prizes you win, and gifts you don't like but somebody else might. Always be on the lookout for things to add to your box. When you need a present in a hurry or don't have the cash to spend, go directly to the gift box, and chances are you'll find just the right thing.

Gift tags

Use Christmas cards from previous years to make gift tags. One side has

GIFTS

the design; the other side is blank. The same idea works nicely for children's birthday gift tags, using greeting cards recycled from previous occasions.

Gift wrap for monster gifts

Don't waste time and expensive wrapping paper trying to cover an oversize package with regular-size wrapping paper. Instead, buy a colorful paper tablecloth. It works great, and you'll have enough paper to wrap a refrigerator—depending of course on the size of the refrigerator—for just a couple of bucks.

Gift wrap organization

Store rolls of tape and ribbon on a paper towel dispenser.

Glue stick

Instead of using Scotch tape to wrap gifts, keep a glue stick handy for sealing packages. Costs less, dries fast, and looks great for professional "no tape" ends and seams.

Heirloom photos

To get inexpensive copies of old photographs, take a picture of the photo with a 35-mm camera and a close-up lens. This is especially effective with antique photos and is a wonderful gesture to allow everyone in the family to have a copy.

Herb bouquet

A bunch of herbs tied together with a ribbon makes a welcome gift for any hostess. Or fill a slender bottle with cider vinegar and your favorite herbs. In a few weeks you'll have a flavored vinegar to enhance salad dressings or marinades.

IOUs

IOU gifts are often the most valuable and appreciated of all. Make up a coupon that is redeemable for something you do well, and tuck it inside a meaningful card. Examples: Shuttle service to and from an airport, babysitting the kids so Mom and Dad can have a day of fun, a day of general repair. Give what you do best, and you will have given the best gift of all.

Just like being there

Make a videotape of your kids. Grandparents, for instance, would love to see them in action, especially if they live some distance away. So instead of capturing a planned and posed session, record the everyday events—everything from bike riding to a live tooth-development demonstration, piano practice to getting ready for bed. Merry Christmas, Grandma and Grandpa.

Kids' artwork calendars

For all parents who collect hundreds of artwork papers every school year and hate to throw them out, here's an excellent gift suggestion: Start collecting large calendars for the New Year from local businesses. Next, select 12 of the most precious pieces of your child's artwork for each calendar and glue them over the printed calendar pictures. (Rubber cement will give excellent results.) This really makes a practical gift that is even more special because of its sentiment. Grandparents, godparents, aunts, and uncles are always delighted; the child is ecstatic with the gift, and the cost is minimal. Finish off the calendar by attaching the child's photograph and autograph.

Mall alternatives

You can either shop at trendy mall stores for gift items like scented soaps, bath sponges, bath beads, etc., to give as gifts (and spend a s"mall" fortune) or you can find reasonable facsimile products—often the exact same thing—at discount stores like Wal-Mart, where two bars of scented soap are $2.38 and a "squishy" or sponge is about $2.

Mother-of-the-bride or -groom shower

Gifts for this nontraditional event might include a gift certificate to have her hair done for the wedding; bubble bath and other soothing remedies; a lace handkerchief for potential tears; frames for wedding pictures; a memory book to record the details of the occasion; writing paper, stamps, and long-distance telephone certificates; new lingerie; and some new books by her favorite authors to read after the wedding.

New York Times

A great gift for a senior citizen with impaired vision is a subscription to the *New York Times* large-print edition. This edition is published weekly and provides a summary of the week's news. A 6-month subscription is $35.10, an entire year $70.20. To order call 800-631-2580 or write to the *New York Times*, Mail Subscriptions, P. O. Box 9564, Uniondale, NY 11556-9564.

Padded envelopes

Make your own padded envelopes. Start with several layers of brown paper grocery bags, cut to the size you need. Sew 3 sides on your sewing machine using a zigzag or decorative stitch. Once stitched, trim close to the stitching. Address, fill, and then sew the fourth side closed, and trim to match. You can make great-looking parcels that will please your recipient in just a few minutes, and you'll save a lot of money.

Personalized wrapping paper

Use a road map to wrap up a gift for the traveler. Wrap a woman's box in a piece of fabric or a pretty scarf. Tape together the crossword puzzles from several week's worth of newspapers for that crossword aficionado in your life. The Sunday funny papers make great wrapping, especially for kids and teenagers.

Photocopies

Before spending a lot of money for enlargements and reprints of color photographs, consider making color photocopies at your local stationery or quick-print shop. For example, an 8 x 10 color copy enlargement costs less than $2 instead of $10 or more for a color print enlargement. While the paper is not as sturdy, once a photocopy is framed or mounted it is very difficult to detect any difference. Framed photos make great gifts.

Recycled greeting cards

Greeting cards can make unique postcards. Cut off the picture side, and write your message on the back. Be sure to leave appropriate room for a stamp, address, and the postal service bar code.

Reusable gift containers

Cover gift boxes with appliqués, needlework, and quilts, or embroider the recipient's name. These kinds of containers are especially appreciated because they become part of the gift itself. Wrap the box and the lid separately, and the gift box becomes an heirloom to be cherished for years to come.

Santa sacks

Make a Santa sack for each of your kids. Using bright holiday prints make a large "sack" on the order of a pillowcase of any size you desire. Finish the top with drawstrings (optional). Now instead of wrapping each gift from Santa separately, you can load each child's gifts into his own sack, tie it up, and place it under the tree. Because the homemade fabric Santa sacks can be used year after year, it by itself becomes a tradition and an important childhood memory. Santa sacks make great gifts for another family.

Stamp collections

Your post office carries beginner stamp-collector kits for children. They are very inexpensive and geared toward the young philatelist.

Surprise in the diapers

If you need to send a fragile gift for the new baby who lives far away, pack the breakable object in a box of disposable diapers. The soft padding will keep the gift well protected, the packing material will be as usable as the gift, and you won't have to worry about finding a suitable box.

Teacher gift

Help your child create a "Teacher Feature" for a Christmas or end-of-the-year gift. Paste a drawing or a photo of the teacher on a large sheet of paper, then have the child write a lively newspaper-type action story about the teacher, complete with caption.

Videos instead of flowers

When a friend or family member is recuperating from an extensive illness, more flowers and balloons may not be the gift that will truly reflect your concern. Instead, rent several videos to cheer the patient. Just don't forget to return to retrieve them in a day or two.

Welcome map

When newcomers arrive in your neighborhood, welcome them with a useful gift: a neighborhood map. Include all the hot spots like the dry cleaner, schools, churches, grocery stores, etc. It's helpful to see the location of all of these places in relation to the others.

Wrapping paper again

Remove wrinkles and creases from wrapping paper by ironing with a warm iron on the wrong side.

KIDS

Artist smocks

Old pillowcases can be turned into inexpensive smocks for kids to use when finger painting or doing other messy stuff. Just cut 2 holes on each side for the arms and a large one at the top for the head.

Baby wipes

Make your own. Select a plastic container about the size of a roll of toilet tissue that has a tightly fitting lid. Cut one roll of high quality (such as Bounty or Brawny) paper towels in half with a sharp, serrated knife. Remove cardboard centers. You should now have two rolls similar in size and shape to toilet tissue. Mix the following in the container: Two cups water, one tablespoon baby shampoo and two tablespoons baby oil. Place one of the cut towel rolls in the liquid. Allow towels to completely absorb liquid. To use, pull center sheet from roll. Cover tightly between uses.

Bathing baby

Smear a tiny bit of petroleum jelly above your baby's eyebrows to easily channel soapy water and shampoo away from her eyes.

Big crayons

Clean out a small, flat can (a tuna can works well). Preheat oven to 250 degrees. Fill can partway full of broken and small crayon pieces that you would normally throw out (don't forget to remove any paper). Place in oven until melted, about 20 minutes. When the crayons are melted and the colors have run together (don't stir or you'll have to introduce a new Crayola color: Mud), remove and allow to cool in the refrigerator until hard. Pop the big crayon out of the can, and your kids will have a big, new rainbow crayon.

Blowing bubbles

Bubble recipe: Thoroughly mix 1 cup water, ⅓ cup Joy dishwashing liquid (must be Joy), and ⅛ cup white corn syrup. Use with a bubble blower.

Booster chair
Start with a stack of old magazines of the same size and of the desired height to properly boost your little one. Bind them together with strong tape such as duct tape. Make a simple fabric cover that can be easily removed for laundering.

Bowling pins
Empty two-liter soda bottles make great bowling pins for kids to play with. Add a little sand or some pebbles to the bottles to make them more stable, and use a lightweight playground ball as a bowling ball. Best used outdoors, in the basement, or in a clear area, such as the kitchen floor.

Card holder
Tiny hands can hold playing cards if you make a holder from two plastic lids. Use margarine lids or the plastic tops from cans of potato chips. Simply line up the lids and secure them with a brass fastener or a button sewn on with sturdy thread. The cards just slip into the hairline space between the two lids.

Cereal mugs
Serve cereal to little kids in large mugs instead of unruly cereal bowls. The handle helps them control the messies.

Chalkboard
Instead of buying an expensive chalkboard for your kids, for less than $20 you can purchase a piece of clear plywood and chalkboard paint (available at any paint store). Paint according to instructions.

Circus ticket
Every baby is eligible for a free circus ticket during the year of his or her birth to be used anytime during the child's lifetime. Send the baby's name and birthdate, plus your name and address to: Ringling Brothers Barnum and Bailey Circus, P. O. Box 5265, Clifton, NJ 07015. This makes a great gift for baby's first birthday.

Diaper rash
Rather than expensive diaper rash ointments, purchase store-brand zinc oxide from the drugstore. It works great to prevent and treat diaper rash and is very inexpensive. Always consult your pediatrician about any unusual condition that does not clear up quickly.

Doll clothes
Newborn-sized clothes from garage sales make great clothes for large baby dolls. They are better quality and a fraction of the price of new doll clothes.

Double-decked closet
In the children's closets, install a high clothes rod for seldom-worn dress clothes and a lower one for everyday items. The lower one should be positioned low enough so the child can easily reach it.

Dress up
Go to a thrift store and purchase old clothing, jewelry, shoes, hats, scarves, and purses, or ask for donations from friends and relatives. Select things that can be easily laundered and disinfected. Put everything into a special box or costume trunk. Little ones love to dress up.

Dried-up markers
Are your children's markers starting to dry out? Dip the tip of the marker in water for 5 to 10 seconds. Blot excess water, and you have just given a marker a new lease on life.

Edible finger paints
You'll need 1 envelope unflavored gelatin softened in ¼ cup warm water, 3 tablespoons granulated sugar, ½ cup cornstarch, 2 cups cold water, and food coloring. Mix sugar and cornstarch. Add water and cook over low heat, stirring constantly until thick. Remove from heat and add softened gelatin. Divide into as many portions as you choose to have colors (4 or 5 is best). Add food coloring to each portion. A pinch of detergent added to each color makes cleanup easier but eliminates the edible feature.

Edible necklaces
Tiny fingers can easily thread macaroni, Cheerios, or Fruit Loops onto a length of yarn. Tie a knot in one end, and twist a bit of tape on the other end so it is easier to handle.

Face paint
Ingredients: 1 teaspoon cornstarch, ½ teaspoon water, ½ teaspoon cold cream, and food coloring. Mix first three ingredients, and blend well. Add food coloring a drop at a time until you get the color you want. Store in small covered containers. Paint chubby little faces with a small paintbrush. Allow paint to dry. Remove with cold cream.

Fine art as placemats
Cover your kids' drawings with clear self-adhesive contact paper and use them as place mats. You can also give these great works of art to their grandparents as gifts.

Flannel board
Cover a large piece of cardboard with flannel using glue, staples, or tape.

Cut shapes from felt, such as rectangles, squares, triangles, circles, trees, letters, numbers, and so on. Kids will spend hours creating scenes and pictures by sticking the felt to the flannel.

Flashlight

If your children are fearful of the dark, send them to bed with a small flashlight. For the first few nights, they might flash it until they fall asleep, but after the novelty wears off, they will keep it nearby for emergencies.

Garden hose telephone

Insert a clean, tight-fitting funnel at each end of a garden hose. One child can speak into the "transmitter" funnel, while the other listens through the "receiver" funnel at the other end.

Goggles for shampoo

You can turn an unpleasant situation into a really fun time if you let your child wear swim goggles while you shampoo and rinse his hair.

High-chair security

Keep baby from sliding around in the high chair. Line the chair seat with a small rubber bath or sink mat. Cut to fit if necessary.

Indoor sandboxes

Here's a cheap, indoor, rainy-day activity for preschoolers. Pour coarse cornmeal into roasting pans or small boxes to make indoor "sandboxes." Provide plastic silverware, toy soldiers, cars, trucks, and small wooden blocks to use in the "sand," and you will have created hours of fun. Keep the vacuum cleaner on standby.

Indoor tennis

You'll need one leg from a clean pair of old pantyhose, a wire coat hanger, masking tape, scissors, and blown-up balloons. Bend hanger into a diamond shape. Straighten hook to form a handle. Slowly pull the hose over the hanger until the top point of the diamond fits into the foot portion. Now wrap hose tightly around the handle making sure the sharp end is well padded. Tape hose to handle. Use balloons instead of a ball to play tennis indoors. This is easy, quick, and lots of fun for little ones.

Kid's bulletin board

Need a bulletin board for a child's room? Use an old-fashioned game board—a relic from the age before electronic games took over. A no-longer-used Monopoly board is colorful and decorative for hanging on a playroom wall.

Lost mittens

If your kids keep losing their mittens, do this: Sew a button to each mitten, and teach them how to button their mittens or gloves to a buttonhole in their coat or jacket when they take it off. No buttonholes? Make two in a very secret but convenient place on the inside.

Mealtime tray

Use a muffin tin as a mealtime tray for a sick child. Paper cup liners can hold the different foods.

Paint palette

Use plastic foam trays (like the ones meat is packed in) as palettes for mixing paint colors. They won't leak, and they are especially good for kids' projects.

Paint pots

Save old muffin tins or egg cartons for kids' painting sessions.

Play-and-eat dough

Here's an alternative recipe in the event your little one is prone to wanting to eat more than play. Mix ½ cup smooth peanut butter with ¼ cup powdered sugar. Can be stored in a tightly closed container on the pantry shelf.

Play dough

In a large pot combine 3 cups flour, 1 ½ cup salt, and 6 teaspoons cream of tartar. Stir in 3 cups cool water, into which you have mixed 3 tablespoons vegetable oil and food coloring of choice. Stirring constantly, heat over medium heat. Keep stirring until the mixture coagulates and begins to pull away from the sides of the pan, or for about five minutes. Turn onto a cutting board and allow to cool slightly. Once you can touch it, knead it until it is smooth and feels like play dough. Store in an airtight container.

Playhouse

Get a big cardboard box and cut holes for a door and windows. Let the kids color the box. Help them draw flowers at the bottom, shutters on the windows, maybe curtains on the windows. The possibilities are limitless. Washer, dryer, or other large boxes are ideal.

Potty training

If your child is resistant to using the toilet, consider the "potty fort." You can "build" one out of pillows stacked up on either side of the potty with a larger pillow or sheet to complete the fort. Or you could make a more respectable fort out of a large cardboard box. Doors, windows, and peepholes can be cut for more potty fun.

Price of responsibility

Most kids go through stages when they lose every hat, scarf, and pair of gloves they own. So the next time cold-weather gear goes on sale, buy a few extras and hide them away. Whenever they can't find their winter wear, allow them to rent a substitute for, say, 50 cents. You'll make a few bucks in the beginning, but plan on business dropping off considerably as your kids quickly become responsible.

Puzzled no more

Whenever your kids get a new puzzle, number the box and each corresponding puzzle piece. This way, if the pieces are accidentally mixed in with another puzzle, the kids can return the pieces to their proper place.

Puzzles for toddlers

Glue bright-colored pictures from magazines or books onto pieces of cardboard. When dry, draw lines shaped like puzzle pieces over the picture. Cut the pieces out and teach little ones how to put puzzle pieces together. For very young tots, cut into only 2 or 3 pieces.

Rainy-day surprise

Videotape the kids in action during one fine summer day, then put the cassette away for a rainy-day surprise for the kids.

Rent it first

When your kids want a new video game, rent it first to see if it's the appropriate age and skill level for them. You'll avoid spending big bucks on a game they may never play.

Roll up the road

Make a roll-up roadway for kids to drive toy cars along. On a piece of canvas, draw or tape out highways and byways with markers or electrical tape. Draw traffic signs, buildings, trees, filling stations, parking lots, and so on. When it's time to stow the roadway, you just roll it up.

Security whistle

When going to an unfamiliar or crowded place, give small children a whistle to blow should they become separated from you.

Shaving cream finger paint

Dress the kids in an old shirt, apron, or pillowcase smock. Squirt out a small amount of shaving cream on the kitchen table. The kids can then "paint" on the table, and after rubbing for several minutes the shaving cream will disappear. Test tabletop ahead of time to rule out any adverse effect.

Sidewalk chalk

Mix 1 cup plaster of paris, 4 tablespoons water, and food coloring. Mix these ingredients to a toothpaste consistency. Pour into cookie cutters placed over waxed paper for fun shapes, or pour into toilet tissue tubes that have been covered on one end with waxed paper secured with a rubber band. Allow chalk to thoroughly dry. Remove from cutters or cardboard tubes.

Toy and game part replacements

Don't throw that game or toy away because some parts are missing. You can get a complete set of Monopoly money for $2; 32 little green houses for $1.50; a Boggle timer for $1.50; and Clue weapons or Sorry! tokens for 25 cents each from Parker Brothers. Up to 10 Scrabble tiles are free; the entire alphabet for the standard game costs $5.50. Call 413-525-6411, or write to Parker Brothers, Consumer Relations, P. O. Box 1012, Beverly, MA 01915. Fisher-Price offers a catalog of parts; call 800-432-5437 for the free *Bits and Pieces* catalog.

Toy swap

Start a toy-swapping club with other families. Trade toys your kids have outgrown or no longer play with. Plan a really special trade during the first part of December. Really young children don't care whether new toys are actually new or not.

Wading pool

To keep a child from slipping in a plastic wading pool, affix nonslip adhesive shapes for a bathtub to the bottom.

While you're away

Leave a loaded camera or camcorder with your baby-sitter so that the next time your child does something new and special, you won't have to miss it.

FAMILY

Shampoo chalk

Try new games and replace lost pieces

Don't throw that game out ... because some parts are missing ... mentos for ... 32 little green house ... for $ ... and ... Brothers ... replace ... original game.

... $ ... 90. Call 416 ... 8 ... or write to Mother Brothers' Catalog ... P. O. Box 1017, Beverly, MA 01915. Pinch Place offers a catalog ... call 800-... for the ... catalog.

...

To ... a child from ... ... bottoms.

...

MEDICAL & DENTAL

Ask questions

Seventy-five percent of all antibiotics taken each year are unnecessary. Doctors know that patients who take the time and trouble to make an office visit expect to be "rewarded" with a prescription. Doctors like to keep their patients happy too. Ask the prescribing doctor exactly what the prescription can and cannot do for you and if it is necessary for full recovery.

Baking soda bath

Dissolve ½ cup baking soda in bath-water to soothe skin irritations from sunburn, insect bites, poison ivy, hives, and itchy rashes such as chicken pox.

Baking soda for toothpaste

An inexpensive toothpaste substitute that dentists endorse is plain old baking soda. Wet the brush and dab it in the powder. The cost is a fraction of what you'll pay for toothpaste, and if you can handle the taste, or lack thereof, you'll save a lot of money. Check with your dentist.

Balloon solution

To keep a finger bandage dry and secure, pull a small balloon over it before you bathe or wash dishes.

Bee stings

To soothe bee stings, immediately wet the spot and cover with salt.

Burn

Apply cool water (not ice) to a heat burn. Flush chemical burns with water. Seek medical attention if a burn is large or blisters emerge, particularly if the burn occurs on the face or hands.

Canker sores

Prevent canker sores by adding four tablespoons of plain yogurt to your diet each day.

Canker sores

Try applying a wet, black tea bag to a nasty canker sore. The tannin acts as an astringent and will relieve the pain and promote healing.

Cash discount

Whenever undergoing a dental or medical procedure for which you will eventually pay, inquire about a cash discount. Do not be timid about expecting as much as 25 percent discount when you pay by check or cash at the time the procedure is done. Never be afraid to ask.

Dental schools

College and university dental hygiene programs are excellent places to get your teeth cleaned. Use the blue pages of the phone book to determine if your local university or community college has a dental school facility.

Emergency clinics

Find a walk-in clinic for your family's medical needs. These 24-hour clinics are popping up all over and are much cheaper than hospital emergency rooms.

Emergency rooms

Avoid emergency facilities unless you have a true medical emergency on your hands. As a rule, you should call your family doctor first in time of crisis. If that is not possible, use a 24-hour emergency clinic before considering the hospital's emergency room.

Eyeglass repair

An emergency repair for the missing screw in your eyeglasses: Insert a wooden toothpick through the hinge. Break off both ends of the toothpick, and you're all ready to go.

Generic equivalents

Ask for generic prescriptions, which cost up to 50 percent less, yet by law must have the same chemical makeup and potency. Also, buy generic nonprescription pain medication. Advil costs about $8 for 100 tablets, while ibuprofen (the active ingredient in Advil) costs about $2 for the same amount. The same goes for Tylenol. It is acetaminophen. Drug companies take advantage of the naive public and try to get them to believe that aspirin works so much better if it costs twice the price and has a brand-name. Consult the pharmacist when in doubt.

Heating pad

Here's how to make an effective, inexpensive heating pad. Take a clean sock (a man's tube sock with no holes works best). Fill halfway with about five cups of raw regular white rice. Tie a knot in the top. Warm in microwave on high at 30 second intervals until desired heat is reached. (Caution: Rice can burn, so watch it carefully.) This heating device will conform well to any body part and can be reused many times. Just make sure to keep it dry.

Hold it pencil-style

Brandish your toothbrush with a pencil-style grip rather than a racket-style grip. Foreign research shows that the pencil grip gets teeth as clean but causes less gum damage. Apparently this grip promotes a vibrating motion more than a stroking one.

Hospital admittance

Friday is the most expensive day to check into the hospital. Hospital labs usually close for the weekend, and you may waste two-and-a-half days and a lot of money just waiting for the labs to open on Monday. If you must be admitted, insist that you go in the day of the surgery. An early admittance will run up your bill and is usually for the convenience of the staff, not the patient.

Hospital bills

Carefully examine hospital bills even if you have full insurance coverage. If you go in for a knee reconstruction and are billed for infant nursery time, put up a fuss. Hospitals are notorious for making these kinds of mistakes, and a good consumer scrutinizes every charge. Report all discrepancies to the hospital, physician, and insurance company.

How to take a pill

Teach kids how to swallow pills or capsules: Give the child five M&Ms candies and a glass of water. Have him or her practice swallowing by putting one candy at a time on their tongue and downing it with water. The rest of the M&Ms in the package could be the reward for success.

Ice packs

To make an ice pack, pour 1 cup rubbing alcohol and 2 cups water into a 1-quart zippered storage bag. Double the recipe for a gallon-size bag. Squeeze out all the air before you press the bag closed. Place in freezer. Because alcohol will not freeze, the ice pack will never freeze solid. It stays slushy and perfectly conforms to any body part requiring an ice pack. May be refrozen and reused. Be sure to label the contents.

Immunizations

Keep kids' immunizations up-to-date. Look for free or cheap immunization programs through your local health department. Having sick kids sometimes means that parents must miss work or pay for expensive alternative day care. The costs really can add up.

Insect bites

Put household ammonia full strength on those chigger, mosquito, or other bug bites to stop the intensely irritating itch. Caution: Ammonia is not safe in the hands of children.

Insect bites

Make a paste of baking soda and water, and rub it on insect bites to relieve itchiness.

Kids' medications

Don't use tableware spoons when giving medicine to a child. Teaspoons and tablespoons in your silverware drawer may not hold the correct amount of liquid. A tableware spoon that's off by even one milliliter (0.0338 fluid ounce), could mean you're giving the child 20 percent more—or less—of the recommended dose of medicine. Use a proper measuring device, either one provided with the medicine or purchased separately, such as a measuring spoon, syringe, oral dropper, etc. Ask the pharmacist for a complimentary calibrated measuring device for ease in dispensing liquid medications.

Numb a splinter

Before removing a splinter from your child's finger, apply some teething gel to the area around the splinter and wait a few seconds for the skin to get numb. Gently remove the splinter with tweezers. If you don't have teething gel available put an ice cube on the splinter. It will briefly numb the area and allow the splinter, to be removed. Follow with a first-aid antibiotic ointment such as Neosporin.

Numb the taste buds

You may be able to make unpleasant-tasting medicine a bit more palatable for your children: Have them suck on a small piece of ice until their tongues are numb (this will probably occur once the ice has melted), then give the medicine. Follow with more ice. The cold dulls the taste buds just long enough to render the medication tasteless.

Oatmeal bath

If your children get chicken pox, and an oatmeal bath is in order, save a lot of money by making your own oatmeal bath product similar to Aveeno. Take old-fashioned rolled oats and a clean, old knee-high nylon. Place a handful of the oats into the stocking, tie a knot in the end, and let it sit in the bathwater. Squish it with your hand to activate it more quickly.

Orthodontic rubber bands

Anyone wearing orthodontic appliances with replaceable rubber bands should get a fresh supply of bands often, especially following an illness. When reaching into the bag of bands, the wearer will contaminate the supply, which could mean multiple recurrences of the illness.

Physician samples

Every doctor's office is flooded with all kinds of expensive prescription samples, also known as "stock bottles." When required to take a medication, be sure to ask your doctor if he or she might have samples for you to try. Asking for sufficient samples to make sure the medication is right for you is especially wise, particularly if you might be allergic to it. Don't hesitate to ask again every time you come to the office. Doctors can even write a prescription for a stock bottle to be filled at the pharmacy for patients unable to afford the prescription.

Pick your hospital

Inquire about specific hospital fees before you are admitted. Fees do vary considerably from one hospital to the next. Why pay for the availability of kidney machines and heart-transplant teams if you are having knee reconstruction? While you're in an inquiring mode, ask what rating the hospital received the last time it was examined for state accreditation.

Prevent dental problems

Finish meals and snacks by rinsing your mouth with water. It's fast, it's easy, it washes out substantial quantities of bacteria and food, and it's free.

Replace or disinfect toothbrushes

When family members have been ill with colds, flu, etc., make sure you replace toothbrushes often, or be careful to thoroughly disinfect them. Toothbrush germs can be destroyed by storing the brush, bristles down, in a glass of antiseptic mouthwash. Replace the mouthwash every few days.

Shop prescriptions

Most pharmacies will quote prices over the phone. Call around until you find the best price. You won't believe how the prices will vary.

Split those tablets

If your doctor prescribes, for example, 50 mg dosage tablets, ask about changing that to the 100 mg version so you can break the tablets in two to accomplish the 50 mg dosage. If this is possible, you will save a lot of money because the difference in price between 100 mg and 50 mg will usually be negligible. You can purchase a tablet splitter for just a few dollars at any pharmacy. Caution: Some pills' delivery systems may be affected by splitting them in half. Check with you doctor or pharmacist first.

Taming the itch

One of the most soothing topical treatments for bug bites, poison ivy rashes, and the like is your teen's over-the-counter acne medication. It will dry the infected area and reduce itching.

PETS

Anti-odor treatment
Here's an effective cleaning solution to remove odor resulting from pet accidents: Add 2 tablespoons of citronella oil (from the drugstore) and ½ cup rubbing alcohol to 1 gallon water.

Ant moat
If ants are getting into the pet food, put the dog or cat bowl into another shallow bowl that has water in it.

Baby feeder
Feed a litter of newly weaned kittens or puppies from a muffin pan. Weaker babies won't have to compete with stronger ones for food.

Bathing Fido and Frisky
When bathing a dog or cat, first lather up a ring of shampoo around the animal's neck to help keep fleas from running to its head while you are washing the body.

Burrs from dog's coat
To remove burrs from a dog's coat, soften them by applying a few drops of mineral oil or shampoo, then comb them out easily. Mineral oil is cheap and available at any drugstore.

Cat food
Feed your cat dried food instead of canned. It is cheaper, neater, and more convenient. It also lasts longer, is less likely to spoil when left in the cat's dish, and even helps clean the cat's teeth. Cats with special conditions should be fed according to a veterinarian's instructions.

Cat litter mat
Put a sisal mat or a piece of some other material that has a deep mat in front of the cat's litter box. Now litter won't get tracked all over the place. Once a week, simply shake out the mat.

Cat litter substitute
Shredded paper makes a wonderful substitute for kitty litter. You can either use the shreds from an office or shred your own newspaper. It is much better than the litter because it absorbs

waste and odors better, doesn't need to be replaced as often, and is free.

Cat scratching pads

If your cat prefers the furniture to his scratching post, try placing carpet samples throughout the house. For some unknown reason, many cats prefer them.

Cleaning cat litter box

Use hot water and liquid dishwashing detergent to clean litter box surfaces. Avoid using chlorine bleach for cleaning. Fumes can be created through a chemical reaction between the bleach and residual ammonia remaining in a litter box after it has been emptied.

Dog collar

The next time one of your leather belts wears out, don't throw it away. It will make a great collar for your pet. Just cut it down to size and punch a new hole.

Feeding cats

Always let cat food come to room temperature before serving. Cold food straight from the refrigerator can upset a cat's stomach.

Flea armor

To prevent your pet from becoming a flea magnet, rub some brewer's yeast (available at the grocery store) into his coat before you let him outside.

Fleas be gone

Purchase a ¼-ounce bottle of eucalyptus oil from your health food store. Dip a cotton swab in the oil and apply to the dog's head and collar, down the back, and on the tail. Repeat weekly. No more fleas and ticks for the entire season.

Flea treatment

When bathing your pet, add 1 cup vinegar to bathwater. Also buy a spray bottle; fill with 2 parts water and 1 part vinegar. Spray your pet daily, before his morning walk, to both prevent and eliminate fleas.

Flea treatment

For an effective flea dip, boil orange and lemon peels in water. Cool and use for pet rinse or dip. Smells nice and fresh. You can also slice citrus and rub the fruit into the dog's coat. The bugs will keel over from the smell.

Food scoop

Cut an empty plastic water or milk jug on the diagonal from top to bottom and use as a scooper for pet food or sand.

PETS

House-training puppies

Nothing makes puppies urinate more than being cold. Fix their bed in a warm spot, and they'll have fewer accidents.

Jerky trick

When you open a bag of dry dog food that your pet is not terribly fond of, put a few pieces of beef jerky in the bag and leave them. They will slowly diffuse a pleasant odor that may make the food more appetizing to your dog.

Kitten training

Discourage a kitten from scratching furniture by placing pieces of aluminum foil on upholstery and around table and chair legs. The sight and sound will frighten her off.

Litter box

Line the bottom of the kitty-litter box with ¼ inch of baking soda to prevent odors.

Low-cost spaying and neutering

An organization, Friends of Animals, offers spaying and neutering at a reduced cost. They function like an HMO. You send them a check for $25 to $59 (depending on dog or cat, male or female), and they will send you a certificate that will cover the cost of the operation, hospitalization, and suture removal. You take that certificate and your animal to one of the vets on their long list of choices in your area. Friends of Animals can be reached at 800-321-7387.

Murphy's Oil Soap

Use Murphy's Oil Soap to soothe your pet's dry, itchy, or flea-allergy skin. It is gentle and all-vegetable. Follow directions on the bottle for dilution. This is especially good for shar-peis with all of their skin problems. This product can be found in the grocery store in the furniture polish and laundry section.

Puppy repellent

Mix ¼ cup oil of cloves, 1 tablespoon paprika, and 1 teaspoon black pepper. Pour into a small container with a tight-fitting lid. Label and keep away from children. Dab this repellent on furniture legs, carpets, and other items that you want your pet to stay away from. The scent will diminish over time, so reapply until training is complete.

Remove pet hair

Remove pet hair from upholstered furniture and pillows quickly and easily by running a damp sponge over them.

Saved by the bell

Hang a bell on your doorknob. As you are about to take your pet for a walk, ring the bell. Soon, the dog will associate going for a walk with the bell and will ring the bell himself when he needs to go for a walk.

Steel-wool strainer

When bathing animals, place steel wool in the drain to keep hair from creating a clogged drain.

Stop the chewing

To cure a dog of chewing on her paws when she gets bored, paint the spot she likes to chew with oil of cloves (available at drugstores).

Tick removal

To loosen a tick attached to a dog, place a drop of vegetable or mineral oil on the tick. Then pull gently but steadily with tweezers. The point in loosening the tick first is to allow it to be removed intact. Just pulling with tweezers without first treating in this way may leave part of the tick behind.

Vaccination clinic

Instead of running to the veterinarian's office to have your pets vaccinated or treated with flea-control programs, call a local pet supply store. Many are now offering low-cost vaccination clinics. You could save at least 25 percent off the prescription costs and avoid paying an office and exam fee.

SCHOOL & EDUCATION

Assignment book

If your child is forgetful about homework and household chores, get a special notebook in which assignments can be written. This will give your youngster an incentive to keep track of homework, just like Mom and Dad jot down appointments in their special books.

Barter

Whether it's an education for your children or for yourself, you may be able to barter for the tuition. Offer to clean the music teacher's house in exchange for piano lessons or work in the preschool office. Whatever you do well may be just what the private teacher, private academy, or university needs desperately.

Become an employee

Before you enroll, find employment at a college or university. Employees are usually entitled to reduced, if not free, tuition.

Book covers

Instead of buying expensive, laminated book covers for paperbacks, children's books, or booklets, use clear contact paper. It is much cheaper and performs equally well.

Borrow if you must

But borrow against your life insurance. Borrowing money from yourself to fund education may be more advantageous than borrowing from someone else.

Cupcakes for school

Use a large, empty cereal box to transport party cupcakes to school. Lay the box on its back, and cut open the top panel on three sides to make a lid.

Discount subscriptions

If you are a teacher or have a student in your home, you are eligible to order magazines and news publications through American Educational Services. Their prices are drastically discounted. Call 800-551-1560 to request a free catalog.

Free school supplies

Keep your eyes open at the office. Instead of throwing away outdated three-ring binders, pocket folders, unprinted computer runs, and other useful supplies, bring them home for the kid's school supplies, or donate them to your local school. Company logos can be covered with popular stickers or vinyl paint designs.

High school ring

Before spending a lot on a high school ring for your student, check with local jewelry stores. Most people do not realize that local stores offer a wider variety of styles for at least two-thirds less than the on-campus company's price. Since this item commonly carries a price tag of $200 to $300, it pays to shop around.

Homework totes

Don't discard cardboard tubes from waxed paper and plastic wrap. Give them to your kids to carry homework like maps and art projects back and forth to school.

Learn another language

Borrow language tapes from the library, and practice conversational Spanish. Celebrate the fourth lesson by going to a Spanish restaurant.

Learn while you drive

If you are average, you drive about 15,000 miles each year, which expressed in time equals about a college semester. Use the time spent in the car listening to books on tape or self-improvement tapes.

Lunch ammo

If your teenager is reluctant to carry a lunch to school because bags and plastic lunch boxes are just too dorky, look at an army/navy surplus store for an ammunition box. It will be army green, very sturdy with a lid that snaps shut, and should be very cheap—less than $5. It's pretty cool, even for the girls in your family. Caution: You might wish to check with your school's principal for any possible "land mines" about this type of lunch box!

Lunch drinks

Pop-open, screw-on plastic tops that come on syrup bottles and sport water bottles fit perfectly onto one-pint plastic soda bottles. For a cheap alternative to individually packaged drinks, fill these small plastic ones with healthy fruit juice for school lunch boxes.

Map puzzles

Make inexpensive map puzzles to help your kids learn geography: Paste any map (world, country, state, or county) onto a sheet of poster board. Allow to dry. Cut into puzzle-shape pieces. For a map of the United States, cut along state borders.

Place an ad

It's crazy but has worked for many: Place a classified ad stating that you are trying to fund your education so you won't have to depend on government handouts. Invite readers to send you 5 bucks or so, and as your way of saying thank-you, send back a recipe or a joke. Don't forget to send each donor an announcement of your graduation.

Public school

Move to an area that enjoys an excellently-rated public school system, and then, instead of writing that check out every month for private elementary and secondary school tuition, use that money to get a jump on funding the kids' college funds.

Reading lessons

If your kids love to help out in the kitchen, let them read the recipe while you cook. This way, they get a reading lesson and learn how to follow directions, and you get to spend more time with them.

Ride your heritage

There must be a scholarship out there for you. Make a list of every ethnic, religious, and social organization to which you and your family belong. If you can qualify for, say, a Serbo-Croation scholarship, it might not matter what your grade point average is. The Encyclopedia of Associations at the library will list every imaginable association's address. Usually for ethnic scholarships the applicant must show a birth certificate and be at least 1/8TH of the particular nationality.

Sample a class or two

If you're not sure about a particular college or course, consider auditing a class or two. Even the most prestigious colleges and universities will allow you to take two or three courses without actually applying to the school. Inquire as to the auditing fee.

Security photo

Help youngsters eliminate first-day-of-school jitters by taping a family portrait or photo of a pet to the notebook or lunch box your child takes to school.

Send a care package

When you have all the stuff you need to qualify for a product refund or rebate, fill out the coupon with the name and address of your favorite college student. The refund check will arrive in the student's mailbox, made payable to him or her. Who doesn't love a little surprise now and again?

Seniors as freshmen

Many colleges and universities across the country offer senior citizens the opportunity to take classes and earn degrees for free or at a considerably reduced fee. Proof of age (starting at 55 to 65) and state residency is usually required. These senior discount programs are often unpublicized, so it is advisable to call the admissions department to make inquiry.

Setting a table

Teach your kids to set the table by taping a diagram to the refrigerator. While you cook, they set and learn. Teamwork in action.

Student loan forgiveness

Once you have your education, become a teacher in a shortage area, which allows you to have your student loans forgiven.

Table talk

Kids who are exposed to interesting dinner-table conversation as preschoolers do better on vocabulary and reading tests in elementary school than those who are not.

Tax-free income

Your time spent searching, researching, and applying for scholarships for yourself or your kids will be time well spent. Scholarships represent tax-free income.

Tuition reimbursement

Go to work for a company that offers tuition reimbursement to its employees. There is nothing wrong with seeking employment with companies in locations and with company policies that fall in line with your personal education goals.

Work your way through

Be a nurse or dental hygienist. By declaring one of these skills in your undergraduate program, you will have a profession that you can develop, which can also provide employment while attending medical or dental school. Becoming a nurse or dental hygienist in a shortage area or in the military also may qualify for student loan forgiveness.

Write your way through

Encourage your kids to enter as many writing and essay contests as they possibly can to raise their education funds. The harder they work, the luckier they will get.

You, Inc.

Need help funding your education? Take stock in yourself. Find people in your field of choice (if you are headed to medical school, approach doctors, for instance) who are willing to make, say, a $10 donation to your education. In exchange you promise that as you become productive you will give back by helping other fiscally challenged students to receive their educations. This technique has been tested and has worked well. Just make sure your requests are sincere, not flippant, that your gratitude is clearly evident, and that you carry through with your promise. Be sure to keep your stockholders fully informed of the current condition of their investment on a regular basis.

SPECIAL OCCASIONS

Birthday cake candleholders

Use creamy mint patties as birthday cake candleholders. Just make a hole in the center of each patty and fit the candles in. Place candle and patty on top of cake.

Birthday party favor

Take a picture of your birthday party child with each guest, holding the gift that guest brought. Have double prints made, one for your child and one to include with a thank-you note. This way, you have a record of who gave what, and each guest has a memento of the party.

Bridal shoes

Buy a pair of white sneakers and decorate them with lace, pearls, and white satin ribbon. At your wedding reception go from your high heels to these comfy shoes. Your feet will thank you.

Cake decorator

A clean, squeezable mustard bottle is great for decorating cakes. Just fill it with the color you want, screw on the pointed tip, and get to work on that cake.

Cake writing like a pro

Use a toothpick to sketch letters onto a frosted cake before you try to write "Happy Birthday" or another message with icing. If you make a mistake, smooth the top and start again. When you're happy with your lettering, simply apply icing along the sketched lines.

Cheering crowd

Make a tape recording of the cheering crowd when you attend a sporting event. Then next time a family member who's done something terrific walks through the door, play the tape to offer congratulations.

Cupcakes to school

Bake and freeze cupcakes ahead of time (make plenty if there are several occasions in the near future). On the day you need to take them to school or the club, frost the cupcakes while they're still frozen, and pack them for the trip. They will defrost just in time for the party and will have that just-baked taste.

Decorate a senior's home

Brighten an elderly neighbor's day by helping her decorate her home for an upcoming holiday.

Dress-up birthday party

Collect dress-up type clothes, old shoes, sweaters, and jewelry from friends, relatives, thrift shops, and garage sales. Launder and disinfect everything. Let the girls get all gussied up as they play dress-up. Follow with a fashion show just before refreshments. Allow the little guests to take their outfits home as party favors.

Easter baskets

Tackle boxes, backpacks, bicycle baskets, school-utility boxes, and even a bike helmet can all be used as Easter "baskets." It's a fun way to give an otherwise dull gift.

Easy pedestal display

Cakes, cookies, and other baked goods look elegant when served on a pedestal plate. If you don't have one, create your own by putting a dinner or cake plate on top of a short, wide glass or sturdy vase.

Face painting

Zinc oxide ointment (available at the drugstore) is a perfect makeup base for face painting at parties.

Family crossword puzzles

You'll have a fun game to play at your next family party when you create a crossword puzzle using unique family information. For a kiddie party, use information about the child's friends and classmates, and keep it appropriate to the age of the group.

Family video

Preserve holiday memories on a video you make every year on New Year's. Do impromptu interviews of family members about the past year, etc., with the primary goal of capturing how your kids have grown and matured in the past year. Close each video with a shot of the entire family taken in the same spot year after year.

Finger-licking good punch

Add these big, hilarious ice cubes to your party punch: Fill a new pair of surgical gloves (non-powered) with water. Close them with rubber bands and place them in the freezer. When they are completely frozen, peel back the gloves and add the frozen "hands" to the punch bowl.

SPECIAL OCCASIONS

Heart-shaped cake

No special pan is required for this cake. Using your favorite recipe or box mix, bake one round layer and one square layer, cool and remove from pans. On a large tray, platter, or foil-covered cardboard, place the square layer with corners pointing up, down, right, and left so it looks like a diamond. Slice the round layer into two equal halves. Place a half on two adjacent sides of the square layer. Frost and decorate as desired.

Holiday mantelpiece

To make a gorgeous yet cheap holiday mantelpiece, lay sprays of evergreens on the mantelpiece, thread a string of white lights on green wire through them, and nestle some of your collectibles, ornaments, or pinecones amid the greens.

Holiday soaps

Make holiday soap with heart- or other-appropriately-shaped candy molds. Melt a bar of soap in the top of a double boiler until it's soft enough to pack into the molds (about 20 to 30 minutes at medium heat). Spoon soap into molds, freeze for 20 minutes, and pop out.

Holiday supplies

After the holidays, make a list of the items you won't need to buy next year like bows, wrapping paper, ornament hooks, greeting cards, and the like, and attach it to your Christmas card list. The reminder is then easy to find the next time the holiday season rolls around.

Ice cream all ready to go

Before a child's party, scoop ice cream into paper cupcake holders, and store the treats in the freezer.

Jack-o'-lantern light

Safer than candles: Use a flashlight in the bottom of the pumpkin. Or line the bottom of the pumpkin with aluminum foil, and put a string of tiny exterior Christmas-tree lights inside. Run the cord from a hole in the back of the pumpkin.

Jack-o'-lanterns

When cutting a jack-o'-lantern, don't cut the top of the pumpkin for a lid, but instead cut the opening around the bottom. No more reaching down inside! Simply lift the pumpkin by its stem, and light the candle.

Label your film

Before parting with your rolls of film for processing (either through the mail or in a store), be sure to write your name and address on the film canister itself as well as on the envelope. Any postal employee will tell you they've seen way too many envelopes pop open and film fall out with no way to identify its owner. Imagine what the floor of the film-processing plant looks like.

Outdoor lights

Fill a kid's wagon with sand, and place candles in it for movable light at an outdoor party at night.

Pamper a teen

For a teen girl's birthday, make up a fancy coupon redeemable for her and her best friend to have an afternoon of pampering at the local beauty school. The coupon can be good for a haircut, braiding, hot oil treatment for hands, pedicure, manicure, etc. Total cost for an afternoon of pampering will be very affordable and should be paid for ahead of time.

Party absentee

When someone can't be with you to celebrate a special occasion, have everyone at the event hold up a poster that says "We miss you!" Take a picture and mail it to the absentee.

Party invitations

Make original party invitations instead of buying cards at the store. Making them as a craft project helps your child become involved in planning his or her party. And it can be as much fun to make invitations by hand as to receive them. You might be able to get scraps of heavy colored paper stock from a local printer. Call ahead and ask them to save usable scraps for you.

Patio party

An impeccably cleaned, large fish tank filled with lots of shaved ice makes a fun cooler for fruit juice decanters, cans of soda or pitchers of punch.

Personalized pumpkins

During pumpkin-growing season next summer, use a pen or other pointed tool to scratch kids' names into your pumpkins when they're about softball size or slightly larger. The name will heal over but leave scars as the pumpkins grow. Because pumpkins grow so fast, kids can watch almost daily to see their names heal right into the skin.

Place cards

When preparing place cards for your next dinner party, write the guests' names on both sides of the cards so that those across the table from each other can easily get acquainted as well.

Plain cake to customize

To get the benefits of a custom-decorated cake at a highly reduced price, ask the bakery to layer, fill, and frost the cake of your choice. You'll end up with a "blank canvas" cake you can bring home, decorate, and customize to your heart's content.

Plate decorating

To celebrate a birthday, anniversary, or other big event, use a tube of cake-decorating gel or your own icing in a clean, squeezable mustard bottle to write your message, such as "Congratulations" or "Happy Birthday," around the edge of the dessert plates. This works especially well when you don't have an entire cake to decorate, you are serving pie or ice cream, or you want to make a low-cal dessert look more festive.

Presidential greetings

Greeting cards and notes from the White House are offered to those with a serious illness, those celebrating an 80th (or beyond) birthday or a 50th (or more) wedding anniversary, and to Boy Scouts and Girl Scouts who have gone beyond the call of duty. Send the details of the greeting you are requesting to: White House, Greeting Office, Room 39, Washington, DC 20500 or call 202-456-2724.

Progressive party

Instead of everyone in your circle of friends hosting a separate holiday party, make plans to have a progressive dinner. The dinner party moves from one house to another, starting with cocktails and hors d'oeuvres at the first stop, appetizer or soup at the second, main course at the next, and dessert and coffee at the last. It's an enjoyable way to share the burden and the glory, and you get to see everyone's holiday decorations too.

Rent formal wear

Rent, don't buy, formal wear. Bridal gowns, evening gowns, and other formal wear are usually high-priced and worn once. So rent or, better yet, borrow. For men, tuxedo rental prices vary tremendously, so check around.

Santa sacks

Instead of wrapping all the Santa presents, put out a "Santa Sack" made from Christmas fabric. Use approximately 2 yards of fabric and 2 yards of 1-inch grosgrain ribbon for each sack. Santa puts the presents in the sack then ties it shut. The kids get to pull out the toys one at a time. No wasteful wrapping paper and extra time for you-know-who!

Snack shack birthday party

Set up a snack stand with hot dogs, popcorn, soda, peanuts, and candy. Give each guest play money to buy treats.

Stocking up

Be sure to take advantage of post-Christmas sales. While you're picking up deeply discounted wrapping paper and other items, look for red candies and paper goods that will work for Valentines Day, green items to help celebrate St. Patrick's Day, and red, white, and blue things for Independence Day.

Summer party

Fill an inflatable child's pool with ice to hold canned drinks for a big group of guests. Place balloons or flowers in the pool to decorate.

Teen birthday party

Take the birthday party group to the mall, armed with a camera and a roll of film. The assignment: The group sticks together, and each party guest "shops" until they find the gift they would buy for the birthday girl or boy if money were no problem. But instead of purchasing it, the group snaps a photo of the gift, the "giver," and the guest of honor. When every gift has been properly photographed, take the film to a 1-hour developing store. While waiting for the film to be developed, the group can have pizza and cokes or ice cream. The group can assemble a small photo album that can be their joint birthday gift.

Tree-trimming party

Are you feeling a little blue because your nest is empty at Christmastime? Invite a family with young children to a special tree-trimming party.

Valentine, Nebraska

Want to really impress your sweetheart? Have your valentine arrive with a postmark from Valentine, Nebraska. It's easy: Prepare your valentine, address and stamp the envelope. Put it into a larger envelope. Address it to Postmaster, Valentine, NE 69201-9998, and mail it off. Enclose a brief note asking that they postmark and send off your valentine to arrive on or before February 14.

Valentine's Day

For a Valentine centerpiece that will please the kids, invert a colander, stick red lollipops into the holes, and tie white ribbons on them.

Valentine's sachets

For small, sweet-smelling Valentine's Day gifts, sew together or hot-glue 2 pieces of heart-shaped fabric, leaving a small opening at the base. Fill with several tablespoons of talcum powder or crushed potpourri, and close the opening to make a nice sachet for linen drawers.

"We missed you" photo

Photograph your family for the friends and family members who cannot attend your special event or holiday gathering. Have your pictures developed at a place that offers a complimentary second set of prints, and send them out along with a note to tell them how much they were missed.

FOOD

BAKING

Baking location

Bake pies, tarts, and quiches in the lower third of the oven. The bottom crust will be crisp, and the rim or top crust won't overbrown.

Baking multiples

When baking more than one item at a time, make sure there's plenty of room between the pans, walls, and racks of the oven for air to circulate.

Biscuit squares

If you don't like having to reroll the scraps left over after cutting out rounds, just roll the dough into a square and cut square biscuits using a knife or large pizza wheel.

Bread dough rising

To create the perfect environment for bread rising, bring 2 cups of water to a boil in a 2-quart pot. Remove the pot from the heat, invert the pot's lid on the top of the pot, and lay a pot holder on the inverted lid. Put the dough in a mixing bowl, balance the bowl on the inverted lid, and cover with a dishtowel. The water releases its heat gradually and keeps the dough at an ideal proofing temperature.

Bread rising chamber

To create a great environment for bread to rise, turn the clothes dryer to high, and tumble a clean bath towel for 2 or 3 minutes. Turn off, and place the towel in the bottom of the dryer, then set the bowl of dough on top of the towel. Shut the dryer door to allow dough to rise. Put a sign on the door, a piece of tape across the "on" switch, or some signal in case someone decides this would be a perfect time to do a little laundry.

Brownies

For extra-fudgy brownies, add 1 tablespoon corn syrup to the batter, either a box mix or from scratch. Bake as usual. Also, don't assume it always pays to bake from scratch. Brownies, for example, are often cheaper to make from a mix.

Cake cooling

To cool a cake that has just come out of the oven, place the pan on a wet towel. The cake is less likely to stick to the pan if it's cooled this way.

Cookie dough

Juice cans, the 8-ounce size, are fine for storing excess homemade cookie dough. When you're ready to bake a new batch, push the can at the bottom and squeeze out the dough. Cut it into slices and bake, following the recipe directions. Store unwrapped dough in the freezer.

Cookies

A thin coat of nonstick vegetable spray on cookie cutters will prevent dough from sticking to the metal. This also works with your children's play dough.

Cookies

If the cookie sheet you are baking cookies on is half or less than half full of cookies, it may absorb too much heat. Place an inverted baking pan on the empty half.

Cookie sheets

If you have trouble with cookies burning in your oven, place a second cookie sheet under the first one before baking.

Cupcakes

To keep plastic wrap from sticking to cupcakes (and other homemade frosted treats), spray the plastic wrap with some nonstick cooking spray. The cupcakes will arrive at their destination with the frosting intact.

Don't peek

Don't peek into the oven when you are baking something. Each peek can cost as much as 25 degrees, will affect the baking quality, and you won't know when it's truly finished baking. Watch the timer instead.

Flour puff

Buy a powder puff to keep in your flour container. It's perfect for dusting cake pans before you pour in the batter.

Flour shaker

Put flour in an old salt shaker, and leave it in the freezer. When you need to flour a pan slightly or dust a pastry board, it will save you from wrestling with a big bag and spilling flour everywhere.

Freeze cakes

Freeze frosted cakes uncovered until solid, then wrap slightly in plastic and foil. Wrap unfrosted cakes or cheesecakes with plastic and freeze.

Thaw all cakes with the wrapping in place to minimize condensation.

Fruit pies

Always taste the fruit before making a fruit pie filling. If the fruit isn't sweet enough, slice it very thinly so there'll be more surfaces to absorb the sugar.

Grated butter

When a recipe calls for dotting the surface of a pie filling with butter, rub a cold stick of butter over the coarse side of a grater, and sprinkle the grated butter over the filling.

Icing cakes

To prevent frosting drippings and smears on the cake plate, slip several strips of waxed paper just slightly under the edge of the cake all the way around. Once the frosting is set, gently remove the paper to reveal the clean platter.

Low-fat trick

When baking, you can cut down on or omit the amount of butter or margarine used by substituting applesauce. A good rule of thumb is no more than 1 tablespoon of applesauce per 1 cup of flour.

Maple frosting

For a quick, easy, and delicious frosting, add maple syrup to confectioners' sugar, and stir until rich and thick. Spread on cakes, cookies, or buns.

Measure carefully

Too much baking powder or baking soda gives quick bread a crumbly, dry texture and a bitter aftertaste. It can also make the batter over-rise, causing the bread to fall.

Measuring cup

Dust your measuring cup with flour before measuring out molasses or honey for your next cookie recipe. The molasses or honey will pour out of the cup easily, and clean up will be a snap.

Mini hamburger buns

Use a biscuit cutter to cut the centers out of the bread ends and you have a perfect size hamburger bun for a small child. Use the scraps for bread crumbs.

Muffins

When it's too hot to crank up the oven for an hour, bake your favorite quick bread in muffin pans rather than loaves. It cuts the baking time to 15 or 20 minutes, and the muffins are great take-alongs for summertime picnics and potlucks.

Never whipped butter

Whipped butter contains more than 30 percent air, so it should *never* be used in baked goods.

No-splatter technique

When mixing batter, cookie dough, or pudding mix, place the bowl in the sink before mixing. No more splattering on the wall or window.

Peanut butter cookies

When making the traditional fork marks in peanut butter cookies, dip the tines in cinnamon, allspice, or ginger first, then press down. This is effective and tasty too.

Pie cover

Refrigerate leftover meringue or custard pies by covering them with plastic wrap that has been rubbed or sprayed with vegetable oil so it won't stick to the pie's surface.

Piecrust

Substitute icy-cold sour cream or whipping cream for water, for an extra flaky pie crust.

Piecrust

Piecrust ingredients, even the flour, should be cold to produce the very best results.

Piecrust

Body heat will melt the fat and toughen the crust, so touch the dough with your hands as little as possible.

Piecrust

Place unfilled piecrust in the free
10 minutes before baking to red
shrinkage and to hold fluted edges
place.

Piecrust

To prevent piecrust edges from o
browning, cut the bottom and s
from a disposable aluminum foil
pan, leaving the rim intact. When
crust is light golden brown and
filling isn't quite done, place the
ring on top to slow the brown
process. The foil rim can be
again and again.

Pizza

If you need a pan with sides to
your pizza, prebake the crust
pizza stone or in a perforated
and then transfer it to a deep
before filling. The crust will be s
and won't be so likely to bec
soggy.

Pumpkin pie

When making a pumpkin pie,
the filling in a 1-quart (or larger
uid measuring cup or a large pi
instead of a mixing bowl. To fi
pie shell, place the pastry-line
plate on the oven shelf, whic
been pulled out partway, and
the filling into it. Gently pus

oven shelf back into place, and bake the pie. No spills, no fuss!

Rolling pin

Chill the rolling pin in the freezer, and the dough won't stick to it. This prevents more flour from being added to the dough.

Spaghetti anchors

To keep the layers from slipping while you ice the sides of a layer cake, push 3 long sticks of dry spaghetti down through all of the layers of the cake. Frost the sides and top and pull the spaghetti out once the icing has set.

Springform pan

To easily remove a cake from the base of a springform pan, grease the base well before adding the batter or pastry. When the baked cake has cooled, place the springform pan over a hot burner for a few seconds, moving it over the burner to heat the entire bottom slightly. You may hear a pop as the cake is released. Remove pan from heat, release and remove pan sides, then slide the cake onto a serving plate.

Timing

When you put a cake, pie, or bread in the oven, write down the time. That way, if anything goes wrong with the timer, you won't be stuck guessing.

Toasted oats

To give your homemade cakes, cookies, and breads a crunchy and nutty flavor, place uncooked oats on a cookie sheet in your oven and toast them until they're golden brown; then mix the toasted oats into the cookie dough.

CULINARY TRICKS

Baby food

Puree some of the family's regular food (not highly spiced items) in the blender. Pour into ice trays, freeze, pop "food cubes" into large freezer bags, keep frozen until needed, and simply heat them in the microwave.

Bacon

Before opening a new package of bacon, roll it up like a jelly roll, then unroll. Slices won't stick to each other.

Batter

A spill-proof way to pour cupcake batter into muffin tins or pancake batter onto a griddle is to transfer it first to a clean, waxed milk carton, using a funnel. The carton's spout lets you pour with precision and provides an excellent closable container for storage in the refrigerator.

Big cubes

Save a few of those empty cups from snack-size pudding and yogurt to make large ice cubes. They're great for chilling punch bowls.

Blueberries

When making muffins, pancakes, or quick breads that call for blueberries, freeze the berries first. Folding in frozen blueberries will allow them to keep their shape, and they won't break up in the batter.

Boiling

When cooking pasta, add cut-up vegetables such as broccoli, cauliflower, green beans, or carrots to the boiling water. They can cook together even if they will not eventually be served in the same dish.

Bowls for dip

Use green peppers with the tops cut off and seeds removed as dip dishes. You'll have fewer items to wash later.

Bread

To freshen bread or rolls that have become a little bit hard, sprinkle the inside of a brown paper bag with water, add bread or rolls, fold the top over tightly, and put in the oven to heat.

Bread

Don't discard bread, rolls, bagels—even garlic bread—that have become hard. Store them in a plastic bag in the freezer, and when you need bread crumbs, simply grate a piece of your stash on a cheese grater. You'll have uniform, perfect bread crumbs.

Brown sugar

Lumpy, old brown sugar can be made usable again by running it over a cheese grater. The sugar will soften and become usable once again.

Brush

Use a bundle of thyme sprigs to brush olive oil on meat, poultry, or fish as it grills.

Burnt toast

Scrape the really dark part off with a cheese grater, and no one will have to know.

Butter wrappers

Save your leftover butter and margarine wrappers in a plastic bag in your refrigerator. They'll come in handy the next time you need to grease a pan.

Campground ice cream

Ingredients: 1 cup heavy cream, 1 cup milk, 1 egg beaten, ½ cup sugar, 1 teaspoon vanilla. Mix well and place in a clean, 1-pound coffee can. Cover and tape shut. Place in a 3-pound coffee can with 1 part rock salt and 4 parts crushed ice. Cover. Roll back and forth on a picnic table for 10 minutes. Uncover both cans and stir ice cream. Recover the small can and tape shut. Return to large coffee can with the salt and ice and roll 5 minutes more. Caution: be sure to use an egg that is not cracked and thoroughly clean the shell before cracking it open.

Cheese

Spray the cheese grater with vegetable spray to speed up grating and to avoid cheese buildup.

Cheese

To quickly shave or shred fresh Parmesan cheese, use a vegetable peeler or a zester.

Chocolate

Before melting chocolate, spray the container with nonstick vegetable spray, and the melted chocolate will slip right out.

CULINARY TRICKS

Chopping
Use a pastry blender to chop hard-cooked eggs or canned tomatoes and to slice sticks of cold butter into pats.

Clarify broth
Pour broth through a coffee filter in order to produce clarified broth that will be clear.

Coffee
A pinch of salt into the dry coffee grounds will remove any bitterness.

Coffee
Instead of making a half pot of coffee each morning, brew a whole pot every other day. Drink half and store half in a mason jar that has a screw-on lid. When you pour hot coffee into the glass jar and tighten the lid, you will find the jar actually seals as it would in the canning process. On day 2 the coffee tastes great, and you can microwave a cup whenever you want. This little ritual means using half the electricity and time in grinding and brewing, and you'll have "instant" coffee several days a week.

Crumbs
A rolling pin makes crumbs without the mess. Place dried-out bread in a large, sealed plastic bag and roll away.

Crushed ice
Freeze water in waxed milk cartons. Several strong whacks with a hammer to the four sides and bottom of the carton will produce great crushed ice for homemade ice cream and all of your other crushed ice needs.

Degrease stew
To degrease cooled meat soups and stews, put a sheet of waxed paper or plastic wrap directly on top of the liquid before refrigerating. When you're ready to reheat, peel off the waxed paper, and the fat will come with it.

Fat-free broth
To get rid of the fat from canned beef and chicken broth, store the cans in the refrigerator so the fat congeals. Don't use a can opener to open them but a beer-can opener instead. Pour the broth, and the fat will stay behind.

Fruit juice
Mix equal parts fruit juice with generic brand club soda or seltzer to cut the cost without sacrificing taste.

Fruit juice
Stretch concentrated fruit juice. Add more water than instructions recommend. You will be pleasantly surprised when you detect little difference, if any. Start by adding one

half of a can of water extra. Eventually work up to one full can of water beyond the amount recommended. This will cut your concentrated fruit juice bill by 25 percent.

Frying
When frying foods, invert a metal colander over the frying pan to prevent hard-to-clean oil splatters.

Gravy
To salvage gravy and other fat-based sauces that may separate as a result of freezing, whisk or process them briefly in a blender or food processor to emulsify.

Gravy
Serve gravy in a small thermos-type coffee decanter. It holds a lot, is easy to handle, and keeps the gravy piping hot.

Gravy
Always stir thick brown or turkey gravy with a pancake turner instead of a wooden spoon. The turner's broad, flat edge thoroughly sweeps the bottom of the pan so the gravy won't stick and scorch.

Gravy color
To make gravy brown, stir in 1 teaspoon of brewed coffee. It doesn't affect the taste, just the appearance.

Green vegetables
To keep green beans, fresh spinach, asparagus, and peas green, add a pinch of baking soda to the cooking water.

Herbs
Wrap bunches of fresh rosemary, thyme, or basil from your garden with raffia and use to garnish platters of food.

Herbs
When adding herbs to a dish you're preparing, don't hold the jar right over the saucepan while you pour out the herbs. Steam from the pan will get into the jar and be absorbed by the herbs.

Herbs
When you add an herb to something you're cooking, you should "bruise" the herb first to release the oils that give it the flavor. If it's a dried herb, crumble it into the pot. If fresh, tear or mash with the back of a spoon first.

Hot pan, cold oil
Heat the frying pan before adding oil or butter. It's guaranteed to keep food from sticking.

Hot rolls
To keep dinner rolls hot at the table, heat a ceramic tile in the oven while

the rolls are baking. Put the warm tile in a bread basket, cover it with a napkin, and lay the rolls on top. Cover the rolls with a napkin, too, and they'll stay warm for the entire meal.

Ice cream

To soften a quart of rock-hard ice cream, microwave it at 30 percent power for about 30 seconds. Hardened high-fat ice cream will soften more quickly, because the microwaves are attracted to the fat.

Ice cream

For ice cream that is too hard to scoop, and there's no microwave, peel away the carton and cut the ice cream into slices.

Ice cream cones

Fill ice cream cones as soon as you get home from the market because the ice cream is already soft and easy to scoop. Wrap them in plastic and freeze them for special treats. Your children can help themselves.

Jam

To serve jelly or jam, transfer it to a squeeze bottle like a mustard bottle. Snip the end of the tip to make a slightly larger hole. No more messy jars.

Ketchup

Ketchup flows out of a new bottle more easily if you push a soda straw to the bottom of it. This allows air to get in and break the vacuum.

Marshmallow plug

Stop leaking ice cream cones and the messes they make by dropping a marshmallow in the bottom of the cone before loading on the ice cream.

Microwaved water

Before adding anything (such as instant coffee, a tea bag, or cereal) to water you have just boiled in the microwave, stir the water to prevent the water from boiling over in your face.

Mincing

When mincing garlic, shallots, or onions, sprinkle a pinch of salt over them. This will keep the pieces from sticking to the knife and cutting board.

Natural skewers

If you have an abundant supply of strong, woody rosemary sprigs, pull off the leaves and use the stems as skewers for tiny potatoes. Just make a hole with a real skewer first, thread them onto the stem, then grill. Never use twigs or sticks from bushes or trees for skewers. Many plant materials are toxic, and you could inadvertently poison your guests.

Nuts
To toast nuts, cover bottom of microwave with wax paper. Spread with ¼ cup chopped nuts. Microwave uncovered on high for 5 minutes or until lightly browned.

Oil spray
Put cooking oil in a clean plastic spray bottle. This is much cheaper than buying oil in a spray can, and you can use the exact type of oil you want.

Orange juice
Before squeezing oranges for fresh juice, heat two oranges on high for 45 seconds to 1 minute until slightly softened and just warm to the touch. Squeezing will be easier, and you'll get twice the juice because the fibers will be broken down a bit.

Pasta
Drain pasta noodles after cooking, then add a little grated Parmesan cheese. It creates a bumpy texture for the sauce to cling to. Add noodles to sauce in the saucepan, and toss until the pasta is coated.

Pasta
To skip the step of transferring pasta from the pot to the colander to rinse, cook pasta in a pot with a removable inner basket, or use a metal colander or large strainer inside a pot of boiling water. Lift out and rinse.

Pasta shapes
Match the pasta shape to the sauce you will be serving. Serve long, thin pasta like spaghetti or vermicelli with smooth sauces that will cling to the long strands better than chunky vegetable and meat sauces. Serve long, flat pasta like fetuccini and linguini with rich sauces based on butter, cheese, or cream. Serve short pasta like fussili or rigatoni with chunky vegetable, meat, or cream sauces (good choice for baked pasta dishes). Serve fun-shaped pasta like bow ties or shells with cream, seafood, or tomato sauce.

Pasta stretch
To receive more value from prepackaged pasta dishes such as Kraft Macaroni and Cheese or Hamburger Helper, add up to a cup of extra macaroni or pasta to extend the dish without losing flavor. There is still plenty of sauce for the extra macaroni. To save on calories and fat, use skim milk and half the recommended amount of butter.

CULINARY TRICKS

Popcorn

Before putting a bag of microwave popcorn into the oven, knead it until the lumps are broken. Now all the kernels will pop.

Punch cubes

Freeze whatever drink you are serving in an ice cube tray ahead of time. If serving tea, make tea cubes; if punch, punch cubes. Drinks will stay chilled and won't get all watered down.

Quick cooking

Think of the donut shape when you need to save cooking time. Foods cook slowest in the center. By eliminating the center area, all portions of the food will receive the most energy and will cook faster and more evenly.

Quick-roasted garlic

Trim top of 1 whole head of garlic. Place in 1-cup measure with 3 tablespoons chicken broth. Cover with plastic wrap; vent. Microwave on high for about 10 minutes, until tender. Let stand 5 minutes. Spread on toasted French bread.

Rice

When cooking rice, you can substitute chicken broth or beef broth for part of the cooking water.

Rice

A teaspoon or two of lemon juice in the cooking water will make cooked rice whiter.

Salad greens

Here's how to prepare a green salad ahead of time without the greens getting soggy. Place dressing in the bottom of the bowl. Add cucumbers and other ingredients that marinate well. Then add greens. Cover with a damp towel and refrigerate. Toss just before serving.

Salad spinner

Wash salad greens thoroughly and load them into a clean, cotton pillow case. Step outdoors. Grasp the end of the case in one hand, and spin the case in a windmill-like motion next to your body. In about 30 seconds—just before your arm gets tired—the greens will be dry and the pillowcase damp. Bonus: You got some exercise, and your neighbors got some great entertainment. If you are not making a salad right away, just fold the damp pillowcase loosely, greens and all, and store them in the refrigerator.

Salad spinner

Wash fresh salad greens in a sink of cold water and transfer them into a clean lingerie laundry bag or pillow case; close the bag securely and throw it in the empty washing machine. Run on the spin cycle for 2 to 3 minutes. The case will be damp; the greens will be dry.

Salty soup

If you've added too much salt to the soup, don't panic. Just cut up a raw potato, allow it to cook in the soup for a while, and it will absorb the excess salt. Remove potato before serving.

Sauté

Sauté meat and vegetables in fruit juice or Worcestershire sauce instead of oil.

Shoe horn

Use a new, clean metal shoe horn to scrape kernels off an ear of corn. It's the perfect shape for the job.

Soda quick-chill

Chill a warm can of soda fast. Swirl the can in ice water for 5 minutes.

Soup

The general rule is that soups should be cooked in a covered pot to facilitate the retention of nutrients and flavor. However, when a very thin soup needs to reduce, the pot should be only partially covered to allow for evaporation of the water and to intensify the flavors.

Splatter guard

To prevent spatters from an electric mixer, cut a hole in the middle of a paper plate and put the beaters through it while mixing.

Squash

To remove cooked squash from its shell, use an ice cream scoop—no mess, no fuss!

Stew

If your soup or stew seems flat, don't automatically go for the salt. Add a little red wine vinegar instead.

Sticky stuff

Before using your kitchen shears to halve dates or marshmallows, coat with nonstick vegetable spray to help keep them goo-free.

Sticky stuff

It's much easier to chop candied or dried fruits if you freeze them first for one hour. Then dip the knife into hot water before cutting them.

Swizzle sticks

Use a peppermint stick to stir hot chocolate and make a minty-chocolaty drink.

CULINARY TRICKS

Swizzle sticks
Thread raspberries or strawberries on a straw or swizzle stick to dress up summer drinks quickly.

Tea
Give tea a zingy twist by adding an orange peel to the teapot a few minutes before serving.

Unsticking pasta
If cooked pasta sticks together, spritz it gently with hot running water for just a few seconds. Drain.

Vegetables
Limp vegetables like carrots and potatoes regain much of their crisp texture if soaked in ice water for at least one hour.

Vinegars
Strain fruit-flavored or herb vinegars through cheesecloth to remove the sediment. Stretch the cheesecloth over the bottle top, and secure with a rubber band before pouring.

Zest
When grating or cutting citrus peel, use fruit straight from the refrigerator. The fruit will be firmer and easier to handle.

EGGS & DAIRY

Butter
To cream butter and sugar quickly, rinse the bowl with boiling water first.

Cheese
A 1-ounce piece of cheese equals ¼ cup shredded cheese; 2 ounces equal ½ cup, etc.

Color
Don't pay extra for brown eggs. The color does not affect the nutritive value, quality, flavor, or cooking performance.

Dry milk
Use nonfat dry milk in baking or combined with whole milk for drinking (make sure it is very cold). Nonfat dry milk is cheaper than fresh milk, and having it on hand will reduce emergency trips to the store, where you will probably pick up a lot more than a gallon of milk.

Eggs
The best way to shop for eggs is to compare the prices of different sizes. When the difference in price between any two sizes is less than 7 cents a dozen, buy the larger eggs.

Egg salad
For quick egg salad, break 1 large egg into a custard cup. Puncture yolk with a knife. Cover with plastic wrap; vent. Microwave on medium (50 percent power) for 2 minutes. Chop and use in your favorite egg-salad recipe.

Egg salad
If you're making egg salad for a crowd, mash the eggs with a pastry blender or potato masher.

Eggs, easy peel
Eggs can be shelled easily if you bring them to a boil in a covered pan, then turn the heat to low and simmer for 15 minutes. Pour off the hot water, shake the eggs in the pan until they're well cracked, then add cold water. The shells will come right off.

Egg separating
Crack the eggshell and pour its contents into your clean hand, which is

held over a small bowl. Allow the white to drip between your fingers into the bowl.

Eggs, room temp

If a recipe calls for room-temperature eggs and yours are straight from the refrigerator, immerse them in very warm water for a few minutes.

Egg whites

When beating egg whites add ⅛ teaspoon acid, such as cream of tartar, lemon juice, or vinegar, per white just as they begin to become frothy during beating. This stabilizes egg whites and allows them to reach their full volume and stiffness. This is not necessary if using a copper bowl, as the natural acid on the surface achieves the same result.

Egg whites

Separate egg whites from yolks by breaking eggs, one at a time, into a narrow-necked funnel. The whites will pass through, leaving the yolk in the funnel.

Egg whites

Separate whites from yolks as soon as you remove eggs from the refrigerator. Cold yolks are firmer and less likely to break. Do not pierce yolks. One speck will keep whites from beating properly. To get the greatest volume, bring eggs to room temperature before beating. Use a small, deep bowl so beaters are immersed and mixture is thoroughly aerated.

Egg whites

Whenever you are dealing with egg whites it is important that your beating equipment be impeccably clean and free from oil or grease, which will prevent the eggs from creating the greatest volume possible. A copper or stainless steel bowl is ideal.

Fresh test

Place an egg in cool, salted water to determine if it is fresh; if it sinks, it's still fresh. If it floats, throw it out.

Frozen whipped cream

Fill a waxed milk carton with whipped cream and freeze. When you need some, cut the required amount off the top with a carving knife (carton and all). Recap the carton with plastic wrap or foil, secure with tape or a rubber band, and return to the freezer.

Half egg

To halve a recipe calling for 3 eggs, use 2 eggs and decrease the recipe's liquid by 2 to 3 tablespoons.

EGGS & DAIRY

Milk
To keep milk fresh longer add a pinch of salt when it is first opened. This will greatly increase its useful shelf life and does not affect the taste in any way.

Omelet
Add a pinch of cornstarch to beaten eggs to make a much fluffier omelet.

Poaching
Put a few drops of white vinegar in the water to help poached eggs hold their shape.

Whipping cream
Cream will whip more quickly and have greater volume if you chill the bowl and beaters in the refrigerator. The cream also should be cold. Don't try to beat cream or egg whites in a blender. It won't work because the action is different. Fold in flavorings after the cream is whipped.

FISH, MEAT, & POULTRY

FISH

Cooking time

General rule: Fish should be cooked 10 minutes per inch of thickness. Measure the thickest part of the fillet or steak; turn fish over at the halfway point. Example: Cook a 1-inch-thick fish 5 minutes per side. The fish is done when the flesh is opaque. If a fish steak is unusually thick, check the center with a knife.

Fish deboning

Tweezers are perfect for removing fine bones from cooked fish.

Freeze

Freeze cleaned fish by packing them loosely in clean waxed milk cartons and filling the cartons with water. When you defrost, save the water to use as fertilizer for your houseplants.

Grilled fish

Prepared mayonnaise generously smeared on fish fillets and fish steaks will prevent them from sticking when they are barbecued. Most of the mayonnaise will cook off, leaving the fish moist and tasty. Leave the skin on fish fillets to be grilled, and they'll retain their shape better. If desired, remove the skin after cooking.

Handling fish

Before handling fish, rinse your hands in cold water, and they won't smell as fishy later.

Pick a fish

For best quality, buy from supermarkets that display fish on ice in refrigerator cases. A fresh-caught fish has almost no odor; it will not smell "fishy." An ammonia-like smell develops when fish has been stored several days—don't buy! The eyes should look clear, not cloudy; the scales should be bright pink (not gray). The flesh should be unblemished, edges intact (not torn); when pressed with a finger, the flesh should give slightly but bounce back.

Seafood odors

Add a few drops of sesame oil to the water when boiling shrimp to eliminate the odor.

MEAT

Barbecue

For an uncomplicated, great-tasting barbecued entree, soak flank steak in soy sauce for 3 to 4 hours. Cook on very hot grill for 7 to 8 minutes on the first side, and 6 to 7 minutes on the other. Slice thinly on the bias and against the grain.

Broth for seasoning

To season meats and veggies when microwaving, add some chicken or beef broth, not salt. Cooking in broth enhances flavor, while sprinkling with salt can cause food to cook unevenly, discolor, and dry out.

Browning

Broiled meat, fish, or poultry will brown more evenly if brought to room temperature before cooking.

Cooking time

A roast with the bone in will cook faster than a boneless roast. The bone carries the heat to the inside of the roast more quickly.

Defat

To remove the fat from stews and soups without tedious spooning off of fat, place plastic wrap directly on the surface and refrigerate overnight. The next day, just lift off the plastic wrap and all the fat will come with it.

Doneness test

To check a steak for doneness, press on it: Rare will be soft, medium will give slightly, and well-done will be firm.

Ground meat

The plastic bags that come out of cereal boxes can be used for freezing ground meat. Place the meat in the bag and flatten it out as much as the bag allows. After it freezes the ground meat can be stored on end in a vertical position, taking up very little freezer space. It also thaws more quickly.

Marinade

Once the meat has been removed from a marinade, the marinade can be used for a dipping sauce or saved for future use—provided you first boil it for a full three minutes to destroy any bacteria left behind by the raw meat or poultry.

Marinade

Marinate meat in plastic food-storage bags, glass, plastic, or ceramic containers. Most marinades contain acids, which can react with metal and affect the flavor.

Marinate

For fast and easy marinating, all you need is a zippered storage bag and a straw. Mix the marinade in the bag, add the food, and zip the bag, leaving one corner open. Insert about a ½ inch of the straw into the bag, and gently inhale on the straw. As you create a vacuum, the marinade will draw up around the food. When the marinade nears the top, quickly pull out the straw and seal the bag. You'll need less marinade, use less space in your refrigerator, and have less to clean up.

Meat

Wet your hands in cold water before mixing or shaping ground meat. Meat won't stick to them.

Meatloaf

Bake meatloaf in muffin tins instead of a loaf pan or in a large free-form. It will cook faster, be easier to serve, and the cleanup will be a breeze.

Remove Grease

Use a turkey baster to remove grease from the frying pan as you're browning ground beef.

Roast

To keep rib or pot roast from sticking to the pot, place celery stalks on the bottom. This works like a rack to keep the meat up and out of the fat and the celery flavors the roast at the same time.

Salt

Salt your steaks after cooking because salt draws the juices out.

Seasoning

To check seasonings when mixing raw ground meat for meat loaf, meatballs, or burgers, cook a tiny amount of the meat mixture in the microwave. Taste and adjust seasonings if necessary.

Stew

Perk up the flavor of stew by adding a few drops of lemon juice or red wine vinegar during the last 15 minutes of cooking.

Stew

After carving jack-o'-lanterns, add cut-out pumpkin pieces, from which you've removed the shell portion, to beef and vegetable stews for a terrific fall flavor.

Stew

Here's a great way to tenderize stew meat: Add at least three wine corks to the pot. Corks release enzymes and reduce the cooking time by as much as half. Be sure to remove corks before serving!

Stew
Tea can be used as a meat tenderizer, particularly for stew meat. In a Dutch oven, sear chunks of stew meat in fat or oil until very well browned. Add 2 cups strong black tea, bring to a boil, then cover and simmer for 30 minutes. Add stock and continue to cook stew with additional ingredients as usual.

Stir-fry
It's easier to slice meat thinly for quick-cooking dishes like stir-fry if you first freeze the meat for 30 to 60 minutes.

Use before
Never purchase more meat than you can properly refrigerate and reasonably use within the following periods of time: Ground beef and beef cut into small pieces, such as stew meat, should be used within two days of purchase. Steak should be used within four days of purchase, and roasts should be used within one week. If you cannot comply, be sure to freeze as soon as possible.

POULTRY

Basting
For crisper skin on your turkey, prebaste it with margarine or butter. Avoid mess by using a plastic sandwich bag as a mitt.

Cheesecloth
A turkey, chicken, or other kind of bird will almost baste itself if you cover it with a double layer of cheesecloth that's been soaked with butter. When the cheesecloth is removed at the end of the roasting time, the bird will be moist and golden brown. For a crisp, brown skin, remove the cheesecloth 30 minutes before the bird is done.

Chicken
To keep skinless chicken moist and assure even browning during baking, spray pieces with vegetable cooking spray, then season.

Cooking time
White poultry meat cooks more quickly than dark meat, so if you're cooking pieces, add the white meat portions about 5 minutes after the rest.

Cutting poultry
It is easier to cut cooked or raw poultry with scissors; it doesn't shred the meat as much as a knife.

FISH, MEAT, & POULTRY

Ducks

Unlike turkeys, chicken, and game hens, you don't want to stuff a duck. The bread in the stuffing absorbs so much fat that it becomes inedible.

Fried chicken

Crushed cereals like corn flakes; rice, wheat, or corn Chex; etc., can be used as a coating for fried chicken instead of flour or as part of the flour mixture.

Fried chicken

For supercrispy fried chicken, use half flour and half cornstarch instead of flour only. Season as usual and add ½ teaspoon baking powder.

Game hens

When stuffing a game hen, count on about 1 cup dressing per bird.

Mayo rubdown

Rubbing mayonnaise all over the skin produces a crisp, deep golden brown roasted chicken or turkey. Low-fat or nonfat mayonnaise will not produce satisfactory results. The fat-conscious should remove skin before eating.

Skinless

To remove skin from uncooked poultry, grasp it with a paper towel and pull.

Trussing

Out of string to truss the turkey? Dental floss works well. Use unflavored because minty-fresh and turkey don't go together very well.

Turkey

For a delicious and festive roast turkey, insert sprigs of fresh herbs in a single layer between the skin and breast meat, arranging them in a decorative pattern. Then roast the turkey as usual. The herbs will flavor the meat and show through the skin in an attractive design.

Turkey

To keep turkey moist and tender after it has been sliced, drizzle turkey broth mixed with apple juice or cider over the meat.

Turkey

Cooked poultry, especially turkey, can dry out very quickly. To save your guests the ordeal of a dry meal, slice the turkey and arrange on a heat-proof platter. Prepare a sauce of half butter and half chicken broth. Pour it on the sliced bird, and let it stand in a 250 degree oven for 10 minutes to soak up the juices.

Turkey sling

Before roasting your turkey, place a 3-inch strip of folded-over cheesecloth crosswise on the rack in the roasting pan. Wash cheesecloth first, to remove sizing. Place the turkey on the cheesecloth in the pan, pulling the ends of the cloth up between the wings and the body. Roast as usual. To remove the turkey from the pan, lift it with the cloth, steadying the bird with a big spoon if necessary.

Weight

How many chickens in a cup? A 3- to 4-pound broiler-fryer will yield about 3 to 4 cups of cooked chicken, after deboning. A ¾-pound skinned, deboned chicken breast will yield about 2 cups of cooked chicken.

FRUITS & VEGETABLES

Asparagus
For perfectly tender asparagus, fold foil into a rectangular shape to form a cooking pouch and bake asparagus inside it. This will steam asparagus within the pouch.

Bananas
If you keep bananas in a closed plastic bag, they will keep at least two weeks on your counter.

Bananas
Don't throw out those really overripe bananas. They make the best banana bread.

Blanching
Serve green vegetables that are bright green and crisp: Plunge them into boiling water for 2 to 3 minutes, and immediately turn them into a bowl of ice water. Let stand in water only until cool, then drain. The veggies can be reheated quickly by returning them to boiling water right before serving.

Boiling
To cook below-the-ground vegetables (such as potatoes, carrots, and turnips), place in cold water and bring to a boil. Add above-the-ground vegetables (corn, peas, beans) to water that's already boiling.

Cabbage
When cooking cabbage, place a cup, half full of vinegar, on the stove near the cabbage, and it will absorb all offensive odors.

Cauliflower
To keep cauliflower white while cooking, add a little milk to the water.

Celery
To keep celery crisp, stand it up in a pitcher or jar of cold, salted water and refrigerate.

Citrus spray
Fill a spray bottle with lemon-lime soft drink to spray on apple and banana slices to prevent them from turning brown.

Coconut preparation

Pierce the eyes of a coconut with an ice pick and drain the liquid. Wrap the coconut in plastic wrap and microwave on high for 5 minutes or until fragrant and very hot. Let stand 15 minutes. Wrap the coconut in a kitchen towel and split with a hammer or mallet. Pry out the meat with a sturdy knife.

Cooking vegetables

Add ½ to 1 teaspoon sugar to cooked vegetables such as carrots, corn, and peas. This reduces the starchy flavors and highlights natural sweetness.

Cooking vegetables

Brighten the flavor of frozen or canned peas, carrots, green beans, broccoli, or cauliflower by dropping a piece of lemon rind into the cooking water.

Corn

Keep it cool. Don't pack fresh corn on the cob in a hot trunk after you leave the store. Be sure to put it in the refrigerator immediately when you get home. To get the silk off the corn quickly, put on a pair of rubber gloves and rub the cob. The silk will come off easily. When boiling corn, add sugar to the water instead of salt. Salt will toughen the corn.

Fruit bowls

Garnish fruit bowls with fresh basil, which repels fruit flies.

Fruit juice

Use the leftover juice from canned fruits to sweeten your iced tea or lemonade. This gives both the tea and the lemonade an excellent tropical flavor, and you won't waste that juice.

Greens

If you buy root vegetables like beets and carrots with their leaves attached, remove them as soon as you get home or ask that they be removed at the checkout. These greens leach the moisture from the vegetables.

Lemon juice

Store lemon juice in a shaker for quick seasoning. Keep in refrigerator.

Lemon juice

Get more juice out of a lemon. Roll it around on the countertop with the palm of your hand to break up the fibers inside, or put it in the microwave for 30 seconds to a minute before cutting.

Lemons

For seedless lemon juice, wrap half a lemon in a piece of cheesecloth before squeezing.

FRUITS & VEGETABLES

Lemons
If you have an overabundance of lemons you can squeeze the juice into ice cube trays, freeze, and then keep cubes in a plastic bag for future use.

Lettuce
To restore wilted lettuce, quickly dip in hot water, then rinse in ice water to which you've added some salt. Shake and then refrigerate for an hour.

Onion peeling
Peel onions under cold running water, then freeze them for 5 minutes before chopping or slicing them. This will keep you from crying while working with them.

Onions
Chop enough onions to fill two skillets, then sauté them in margarine until they're translucent and slightly browned. After letting them cool, wrap portions in plastic wrap and freeze them in a large plastic bag. When you need them, just add or thaw in the microwave.

Onions
Boiled onions that have become too soft can be firmed up again by dipping them briefly in ice water.

Onions
To freeze onions, chop, then spread out in one layer on a cookie sheet. Place quickly in the coldest place in the freezer. When frozen, transfer to a bag or container and seal.

Onions
While sautéing onions, sprinkle with a bit of sugar if you notice they are browning unevenly. They should begin to cook evenly thereafter.

Onions
Before chopping onions, sprinkle a little vinegar on the cutting board. It will keep your eyes from tearing.

Potatoes
Place potato slices in a cup of cold water containing two vitamin C tablets. They'll keep for 24 hours without turning brown.

Potatoes
When you have to wash a lot of potatoes for a church supper, picnic, or family reunion, just put them in your dishwasher and don't add soap! Set it on a short wash cycle. The clean potatoes can go right into the oven or pot.

Potatoes
A teaspoon or two of lemon juice in the cooking water will keep potatoes white after cooking.

Potatoes
Potatoes soaked in salt water for 20 minutes before baking will bake more rapidly.

Potatoes, baked
Use a curved grapefruit knife to scoop out baked-potato halves when making twice-baked potatoes or preparing a halved eggplant for stuffing.

Potatoes for salad
Cut potatoes for potato salad quickly with a hard-cooked egg slicer.

Potatoes, mashed
Make mashed potatoes with buttermilk or skim milk and butter-flavored seasoning instead of using butter and whole milk.

Potatoes, mashed
Make mashed potatoes ahead of time by spooning preprepared whipped potatoes into a buttered casserole dish. Dot with pats of butter and cover with plastic wrap and refrigerate. Before serving, bake in 350 degree oven for about 25 minutes, or until a knife inserted in the center comes out hot. Or cook in microwave until hot.

Potatoes, mashed
Add a good quality mayonnaise along with the butter, salt, and pepper to your mashed potatoes. Prepare as you would for whipped potatoes.

Potato salad
For more flavorful potato salads, add a vinaigrette dressing while drained potatoes are still hot so they'll absorb some of the dressing.

Ripening
Tomatoes, avocados, peaches, and nectarines ripen faster when enclosed in a brown paper bag and kept at room temperature in a dark place for 2 to 3 days.

Steaming vegetables
Put fresh vegetables in a resealable plastic bag, add a bit of water, and seal the bag, but leave a small opening for the steam to escape. Place in the microwave and cook for about 2 to 3 minutes or until tender.

Tomatoes
Slice tomatoes from top (bud end) to bottom. They'll lose less juice, and sandwiches won't get so wet and soggy.

Tomatoes
When fresh tomatoes are high-priced or poor quality, use canned tomatoes for salads. Drain well and save the liquid to dilute condensed soup.

Tomato puree

Purchase a huge can of tomato puree from your local grocery warehouse club. Divide it into small amounts by filling small zippered storage bags and placing them in the freezer until needed. After one is thawed, add water to make it the consistency of tomato sauce, add salt and spices for flavor. Tomato puree contains no additives or preservatives.

GROCERY SHOPPING

Bagging groceries

Bag your own groceries so you can group items together to match the way your kitchen, pantry, refrigerator, and freezer are arranged. You'll save a lot of time putting things away. You'll also know exactly what and how much has been added.

Bargains

Search for bargains in the day-old baked goods, dented can, and meat-that-is-about-to-expire bins. You have to be careful, but as long as the cans are not bulging or leaking and the appearance and dates meet your approval, go for it. Also look for generic and off-brands for additional savings.

Cash

Grocery shop with cash only. You will be a much more careful shopper knowing you cannot go over your limit because you do not have a checkbook or credit card to fall back on. (This is particularly helpful for the compulsive shopper, who would rather stick toothpicks under her fingernails than go through the checkout only to find out she doesn't have enough money.)

Cereal add-ins

Buy plain cereals and then add your own extras like raisins, sliced almonds, honey, and dried fruit and save a lot.

Cooler

Keep a cooler in the trunk of your car. You can stop for groceries without having to go straight home.

Coupons

Ask your newspaper delivery person if you can pick up any leftover sets of coupons that remain once the Sunday newspapers are stuffed and put together. Most will gladly comply because there's that much less to dispose of.

Coupons

Find a market that will double the coupon's value. This practice varies throughout the country, but if you do have good coupons, make sure you find a way to double them. Some stores even triple them on certain days.

Coupons

If you have a qualified coupon, you'll usually save a higher percentage of the purchase price by buying the smallest size.

Coupons

Use coupons only for items you would normally buy even if you didn't have the coupon and only if it is truly a savings. Check other brands that might be on sale or are already cheaper. Manufacturers often offer coupons as incentives on new products. But you're not saving anything if you buy something that was not on your list.

Discontinued products

Today's grocery stores will only carry those items that move well in order to maintain their profit margin. Watch for product shelf labels with either a line drawn through the price code numbers or the letters "DC" or "Discontinued" written on them. By purchasing these "unadvertised" specials, you will often find savings of at least 20 percent or more on your register tape.

Ethnic groceries

Purchasing certain items at ethnic markets can often result in remarkable savings. Purchase 25 pounds of rice for $9.25 and 22 ounces of soy sauce for $1.20 at an Asian grocery store for instance. It's best to go into any new store with a good idea of what a comparable product would cost elsewhere. Just because the Asian market offers spices, water chestnuts, bean sprouts, and bamboo shoots, for example, doesn't necessarily mean they'll also be such a bargain as compared to your discount grocery.

Eye level

When grocery shopping, look high and low: Usually you'll find the less expensive store and generic brands at the bottom and top of the shelves. The higher-priced name brands are conveniently located at eye level—yours and your children's.

Generic

Some generic grocery items are exactly the same as the more expensive brand-name version. By law, certain items, such as aspirin, baking soda, cornstarch, honey, molasses, peanuts, pecans, salt, sugar, unbleached flour, and walnuts must be exactly the same content and composition, regardless of packaging or quantity gimmicks. Always buy the lower-cost generic brands when buying these items.

Grocery list coupon holder

Save business reply envelopes from your junk mail and use the back for grocery lists. Your coupons will fit nicely inside the envelope, and you won't have to worry about losing them.

Hungry

Never shop when hungry. You will be compelled to buy everything in sight, regardless of what's on your list.

Impulse control

When you pick up an item that is not on your grocery list, place it in the child's seat of the shopping cart. Then just before checking out, reevaluate the budget-breaking items, and make yourself put all of them back except for one item. That's your reward for carefully controlling your impulses in the grocery aisles.

List

Arrange your shopping list according to the general layout of your supermarket. You'll save steps as well as unwanted exposure to impulse items.

Meat

The marked-down price of meat that will expire soon can be dramatic. The meat is still good, but if you cannot use it on or before the expiration date, make sure to freeze it immediately and then use within three months.

Meat

When you purchase meat that you intend to freeze, slip it into one of the free plastic bags from the produce department before you put it into a freezer-quality zip lock bag. This way you can reuse the expensive zippered storage bag again and again without having to wash it out or worry about bacteria contamination. There is no need to label the bag, since you'll be able to see the label through the plastic.

Meat

When buying meat, bear in mind that an expensive lean cut may be more economical than one that requires you to throw away excessive bone, gristle, or fat.

Milk runs

When you need to make milk and produce runs between your regular major shopping trips, but you are tempted to turn the trip into an excuse to stock up on impulse items, make a precise list and engage the services of an errand runner, such as a responsible child.

Perimeter

Concentrate on the perimeter of the grocery store rather than the center aisles. Around the outside is where you'll find healthier food with the least packaging and processing: produce, meats, fish, and dairy.

Perishables

When shopping for perishable foods, buy only amounts that can be used while they are still good. Buying in larger quantities just because you get a low price is no bargain if you end up throwing part of it away.

Price book

Keep a price book that lists the prices of regularly purchased items at a variety of grocery stores in your area. Refer to it when you see specials or ads to determine whether or not it's really a bargain.

Price by volume

When you buy iced-tea, lemonade, or fruit-punch mix, figure cost not by weight but by the per-quart yield the whole container will make. Packaging on these types of items can be very deceiving.

Produce

Buy produce in a bag for the best value. Watch out: Often the bruised and spoiled fruit will find its way into the bottom of a bag. So pick out the best bag and the heaviest one. Weigh a few before you decide.

Produce

Find a farmer's market. You can typically buy locally grown fruit and vegetables at great prices. Some cities hold these markets only in the warm months; in other areas they're held year-round.

Rain checks

When the supermarket sells out of the loss-leader items, always ask for a rain check so you can still buy that item at rock-bottom prices when supplies are replenished.

Sale ads

Design your week's menus around the weekly grocery store sale ads. Take full advantage of the store's loss-leaders, those items the store has priced below their cost in order to get you into the store.

Shelf life

Become a shelf-life expert. Buying in bulk will do you no good if you end up throwing most of it away due to spoilage. Some things last indefinitely, while others spoil, even if frozen, after a certain period of time. (See Shelf-Life Secrets chapter.)

Shop less often
See how long you can go between grocery shopping trips. Start by doubling the time between trips. If you go to the market every day, stretch it to every other day. Once a week? Shop for two weeks next time. You'll waste less, use less, and spend proportionately less.

Shopping list
Make your grocery shopping list at home when you are hungry. You will be more creative and thorough.

Shopping partner
If you are single and want to take advantage of bulk buying, find a shopping partner—someone with your same situation—and pool your shopping needs. Examples: No one should eat more than 2 to 3 eggs per week, so splitting a money-saving flat of eggs with a partner lets both persons reap the savings but doesn't create an egg glut. Two-for-one is a real waste if the second item goes stale before it can be used. But with a partner, each gets one for half price.

Spices
When purchasing spices and herbs, first check your health food store. Many carry spices and herbs in bulk quantities, and you can measure out and purchase as much or as little as you like. Don't buy more than you know you will reasonably use in the next 6 months.

Timing
Avoid shopping on the first day or two of the month. Some stores have been known to raise their prices during the time that welfare and Social Security checks come out.

Timing
Shop midweek and during off hours. Typically, store sales and double-, even triple-, coupon savings occur midweek. Also, there's less distracting hustle and bustle early or late in the day or at mealtime, which allows you to do a more efficient job of shopping.

Timing
Plan ahead and know what you're going to buy so your grocery shopping trips will be short and sweet—under 30 minutes if at all possible. If you linger longer, it will cost you. Market surveys indicate that shoppers spend an extra 50 cents each

minute for every minute over 30 spent in a supermarket.

Vacuum seal

If you buy large quantities of staple items, consider investing in a vacuum-sealing machine. But don't buy one unless you're sure you'll use it.

Weigh produce

Prepackaged produce must have a minimum weight as printed on the packaging. However, not all potatoes are created equal, so a 10-pound bag may weigh 11 pounds, and a 1-pound bag of carrots may weigh 1.5 pounds.

MAKE YOUR OWN

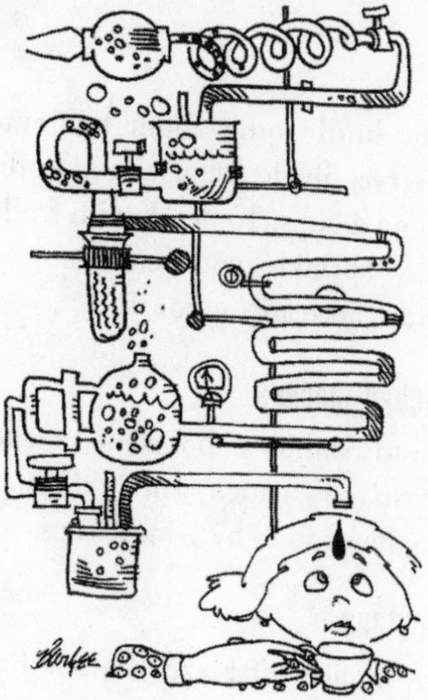

Breadmaker mix

Combine 13 cups bread flour, 2 tablespoons salt, ½ cup sugar, and a ½ cup instant, nonfat dry milk. Label and package in six 2¼-cup containers if using a 1-pound loaf breadmaker, or in four 3⅓-cup containers for larger capacity breadmakers. Store in a cool, dry place. Use within 6 months. To make a small loaf: 1½ teaspoons active dry yeast, 2¼ cups breadmaker mix, 1 tablespoon butter or vegetable oil, and ¾ cup warm water. To make a large loaf: 2 teaspoons active dry yeast, 3⅓ cups breadmaker mix, 1½ tablespoons butter or vegetable oil, and 1¼ cups warm water.

Brown sugar

If you use brown sugar so infrequently that it turns rock-hard between uses, stop buying the stuff, and make your own as needed. Measure out granulated sugar in the amount of brown sugar required. Stir in enough molasses to make either light or dark brown sugar. Color is the key.

Butter spread

To make your own butter spread, combine 1 pound softened margarine with 1 cup buttermilk, ½ cup vegetable oil, and 1 teaspoon butter flavoring. Mix well, store in the refrigerator in a container with a tightly fitting lid. Tastes just like butter and stays soft.

Café mocha

Company's coming, and you're nearly out of coffee. Make this café mocha, and you can serve 6 people with just 2 cups of coffee. Add ⅓ cup cocoa and 3 cups warmed milk to 2 cups of coffee. Sweeten to taste, or add about ¼ cup sugar.

Cappuccino

To make four cappuccinos, place 2 cups of milk in a glass measuring cup. Microwave on high until hot, about 2 minutes and 20 seconds. Place hot milk and 1 tablespoon of sugar in a blender. Cover with a vented lid and blend until frothy, about 1 minute. To serve, divide 2 cups strong coffee among 4 cups. Top each with frothy milk. Sprinkle with cinnamon or grated chocolate (optional).

Chicken tenders

Pound skinless, boneless chicken breasts to ¼-inch thick, then cut lengthwise in 2- by 1-inch strips.

Croutons

Cut 4 slices of bread (stale is fine) into ¼-inch cubes. Toss the cubes with 2 tablespoons Parmesan cheese, 1 teaspoon Italian seasoning, ¼ teaspoon garlic salt, and 2 tablespoons canola oil. Bake at 300 degrees for about 20 minutes, or sauté in hot olive oil.

Crystal light

Make your own product like Crystal Light with these ingredients: 1 cup lemon or lime juice, 5 cups cold water, and 5 packets sweetener (Sweet n' Low or Equal). Mix in pitcher, serve over ice, and enjoy!

European coffee

To make European-style "light" coffee, purchase coffee beans—half decaf and half regular—and have them poured into the same container. To use, set the grinder at the finest setting, which produces European-style ground coffee. Use a much smaller amount of grinds than you are accustomed to because of the fine grind. Store ground coffee and coffee beans in the freezer to keep them fresher longer.

Gourmet coffee

Break up a cinnamon stick or sprinkle ground cinnamon into coffee grounds before brewing. Or add a drop of vanilla to the coffee once it has been brewed.

Mousse

For a quick, cheap, and low-fat chocolate mousse: Mix cocoa powder into Cool Whip. Add as little or as much cocoa powder as your palate dictates. Stir well and serve. Also can be used to frost cakes.

Orange Julius

Ingredients: 2 cups orange juice, ½ cup powdered coffee creamer, ½ teaspoon vanilla, 2 tablespoons sugar, 5 large ice cubes. Place ingredients in blender, add ice cubes one at a time. Blend until frothy. Yield: 1 to 2 servings.

Pancake syrup

Mix 1½ tablespoons cornstarch into 1 cup cold fruit juice. Heat to boiling, stirring constantly. Or stir a cup of corn syrup and four tablespoons of your favorite jam or preserves in a saucepan over low heat.

Salad dressing

Ingredients: 1 teaspoon celery salt, ½ cup sugar, 1 teaspoon dry mustard, 1 teaspoon paprika, ¼ cup vinegar, ½ tablespoon grated onion. Mix all ingredients, add 1 cup vegetable oil slowly while beating with an electric mixer. Let stand in refrigerator for 24 hours before using.

Shake and bake

Ingredients: 1 cup bread crumbs, 2 teaspoons celery salt, 1 teaspoon garlic powder, ½ teaspoon salt, ½ cup flour, 2 teaspoons poultry seasoning, 1 teaspoon paprika, ½ teaspoon pepper, 5 teaspoons onion powder, and ½ teaspoon cayenne pepper. Mix all together, and store in a tightly closed container. Will keep for up to 4 months in the pantry. To use: Dip chicken pieces in mixture of ½ cup milk and 1 beaten egg. Pour 1 cup coating mix into bag, drop in chicken one piece at a time, and shake. Bake at 375° for 1 hour or until juices run clear.

Soft cream cheese

Make your own soft cream cheese. Combine one room-temperature, 8-ounce package regular cream cheese with 2 tablespoons milk, or one 3-ounce package regular cream cheese and 1½ teaspoons milk. Store in the refrigerator.

Sweetened condensed milk

To make your own, combine 2 cups instant, nonfat dry milk, 1½ cups sugar, ⅔ cup boiling water, and 6 tablespoons butter, melted and slightly cooled. Mix dry ingredients and slowly add to boiling water. Stir in melted butter. Whip in blender or by hand until smooth. Store in refrigerator for 1 week or freeze for up to 6 months. Yield: 20 ounces.

FOOD

SHELF-LIFE SECRETS

Asparagus

Asparagus will stay fresh all week long if you set the spears upright in a container in the refrigerator with the cut ends sitting in an inch of water.

Berries

Berries keep well for several days if stored unwashed in a colander in the refrigerator. Wash as eaten.

Bread

Loaves freeze better than slices; small amounts of bread and smaller breads such as rolls freeze best. Freeze bread uncovered until solid, then store in plastic bags. Thaw in the bag.

Celery

Tired of throwing out celery that's lost its crunch? Cut the bottom stem off and separate the stalks. Fill a pan that is deep enough to cover the celery with cold water, and stir in ¾ cup granulated sugar. Let the celery soak for 4 or 5 hours. Drain well and refrigerate.

Cheese

To keep cheese fresh and mold-free, place two sugar cookies in a plastic bag with a zipper lock, then add the cheese.

Chicken

Freeze skinless, boneless chicken breasts uncovered in a single layer, then wrap them individually and stack in plastic bags. Thaw in the refrigerator, or if you're in a hurry, submerge them in the airtight bag in a bowl of cold water.

Cookie dough

Most unbaked cookie dough can be refrigerated for at least a week, and frozen for up to a year if it has been wrapped airtight in freezer-weight plastic bags or foil.

Cookies

Put a slice of bread in the cookie jar to absorb the moisture that causes cookies to become stale.

Cream
Heavy cream can be frozen if you intend to use it for cooking, but it won't whip once it has thawed. Whipped cream can be frozen in dollops on a flat sheet. Once the dollops are solid, store them in zippered freezer bags.

Cucumbers
To extend the life of a cucumber once it has been cut open, wrap it in a paper towel. The cucumber will not get soggy for up to 2 weeks.

Dairy
The date on dairy products is the date when retailers must pull unsold products from the shelf. Properly stored, the product will be good for at least 7 days past the printed date. Unsalted butter has a shorter shelf life than salted. Whichever kind you buy, extra sticks are best stored in the freezer. Milk, cream, cottage cheese, and similar products should be stored in their original containers.

Dessert thaw
Thaw bread, desserts, and baked goods at room temperature in their original wrapping to avoid moisture loss.

Dry staples
To extend the useful life of dry staples such as flour, meal, grits, pastas, and rice, pop in a couple of bay leaves. This won't affect the taste, but it will prevent pesky bugs from ruining these products before they can be consumed.

Eggs
Eggs will stay fresh all month in the refrigerator if you keep them on the shelf in their original cartons instead of putting them in the egg holder on the refrigerator door. The movement of the door and temperature variations from opening and closing cause eggs to spoil more quickly.

Eggs
If you have more eggs than you can use in the near future, crack them open and place individually in an ice cube tray. When they're completely frozen, unmold them and keep frozen in a sealed freezer bag for future use. Frozen eggs should always be thawed in the refrigerator and used in recipes in which they will be thoroughly cooked.

Eggs
Always store eggs large end up. This keeps them fresher and helps keep the yolk centered. Never store eggs near pungent foods like onions because they easily absorb odors right through their shells.

Egg test

When you hard-cook eggs that you plan to save for a few days, put a tea bag in the water. The shells will turn beige, and you'll be able to distinguish them from uncooked eggs.

Fish freeze

Fish with a relatively high fat content, like salmon and trout, freeze best. Thaw, without unwrapping, at room temperature in a bowl of cold water or in the refrigerator. Before you freeze a fish it should be cleaned, gutted, rinsed, and dried.

Freezing

Label and date new items for the freezer and place them in the back. Rotate items from the back to the front as a way of reminding what's in there, and so things that are older will be used soonest.

Herbs

Place stems of fresh herbs like basil and parsley in a small container of water, cover with a plastic bag, and refrigerate to store and keep fresh before using.

Herbs

Clean and pat dry fresh basil leaves, then layer with coarse (kosher) salt in a wide-mouthed glass jar.

Herbs

Place fresh herbs in tightly sealed plastic bags and freeze. The color will fade slightly, but the flavor will remain true. Another method is to mince the herbs, place into ice-cube trays, and add water to freeze the herbs in cubes.

Herbs

Even though it seems convenient, don't store herbs and spices right over the stove. Heat is bad for them, as is direct sunlight. The best storage place for dried herbs and spices is in a cool, dark cupboard.

Herbs

If you have an overabundance of fresh herbs, try storing them by making herb butters, which can be frozen and used during winter months on homemade bread, melted over vegetables, or swirled in a simple sauce to provide a great burst of summer flavor. To make herb butters, chop a cup or more of fresh herbs and combine with a stick of softened butter; blend until smooth. Add a few drops of lemon juice.

Ice cream

If large quantities of ice cream disappear too quickly in your house, divide it into individual portions ahead of time. Put single servings into empty yogurt containers and freeze. Or line a baking pan with graham crackers, then a layer of softened ice cream, followed by a top layer of crackers. Freeze, cut into individual squares, wrap, and refreeze.

Ice cream

Store ice cream in the freezer compartment, not in the freezer door. This keeps ice cream fresher because it isn't exposed to sudden changes of temperature from the door's opening.

Lettuce

Remove the core from the lettuce head with a nonmetal utensil, fill the cavity with cold water, and drain well. Wrap head in a clean damp towel and refrigerate. As long as the towel is kept damp, you will be able to enjoy salads without concern that the lettuce will turn color or become dehydrated.

Liquid freeze

Allow at least a ½-inch space for expansion when freezing liquids.

Meat

Don't season or marinate uncooked meats before freezing.

Mint

Freeze washed mint leaves or edible flowers in ice cubes to be used for special occasions. They look pretty and add a subtle hint of flavor.

Nuts

Buy walnuts, almonds, pecans, and other nuts after the holidays at sale prices. Shell, then store the nuts in individual plastic bags in the freezer. The nuts won't stick together, so it's easy to remove only what you need for each recipe.

Nuts

Keep nuts in the freezer to retard spoilage. Nuts left in the pantry will become rancid.

Onions, potatoes

Cut off a leg of an old, clean pair of pantyhose, drop potatoes or onions into it, and hang it in a cool, dark place. The hose lets air circulate, which helps keep the onions and potatoes longer. However, because of the interaction of their natural gases, storing potatoes and onions together can cause the potatoes to rot more quickly.

Pasta

Fresh pasta can be wrapped airtight in a plastic bag and refrigerated for up to five days or double wrapped and frozen for up to four months.

SHELF-LIFE SECRETS

Popcorn

Keep popcorn kernels in the freezer. They will stay fresh much longer, and freezing will encourage every kernel to pop.

Raisins

Raisins stay fresh longer when stored in an airtight container in the refrigerator. If they become hard, pour very hot water over them. Drain immediately, and spread on a paper towel to dry.

Rice

Store white rice in an airtight container in a cool, dark place for up to 1 year; store brown rice for up to 6 months. In warm climates, or for longer storage, refrigerate or freeze rice.

Salt

Add a few rice kernels to a salt shaker in humid weather to keep the salt fresh.

Single portions

To freeze single-size portions if you don't have lots of small containers or you have limited freezer space, spoon a single serving of food, such as chili or stew into a large container, freeze it briefly until firm, cover with two pieces of waxed paper, then add another serving. Repeat layers with remaining food. When ready to use, just grab the edges of the waxed paper, lift out what you need, and return the rest to the freezer.

Snacks

Keep marshmallows, potato chips, pretzels, and crackers in the freezer. They are best if frozen in their original unopened containers.

Soup

Freeze soup or casseroles in a loaf pan. When they are solid, remove, wrap, label, and return them to the freezer. You'll have use of your pan again immediately, and the product will easily stack in the freezer.

Soup

Store cans of condensed soup upside down in the refrigerator for a while. The excess fat will rise and then stick in the bottom of the can when it is turned upright and opened. It's an easy way to get some of the fat out.

Soups

Don't freeze soups containing milk, cream, or coconut milk, which can separate or curdle.

Spices

If the summer heat and high humidity play havoc with your powdered spices and seasonings, store the closed bottles in the door of the freezer compartment or your refrigerator. They'll be handy and fresh when you need to use them.

Stock pot

Keep a container in the freezer specifically for the collection of fresh scraps, juices, and bones that might otherwise land in the garbage. When the supply becomes sufficient, make the stock. If not needed immediately, freeze for future use.

Sugar

Freezing brown and powdered sugars will prevent lumps.

Vegetables

Blanch vegetables before freezing. They contain enzymes that, if their action is not stopped, will cause the vegetables to become coarse and flavorless. Before freezing, drop fresh vegetables into boiling water and transfer them immediately into ice water. Work with small batches.

SUBSTITUTES

Brown sugar

One cup of granulated sugar is an adequate substitute for 1 cup of packed brown sugar.

Buttermilk

Add 1 tablespoon of lemon juice to enough milk to equal 1 cup. Let stand 5 minutes before using.

Cornstarch

Use 2 tablespoons of flour for every tablespoon of cornstarch called for.

Corn syrup

To make, mix 1 cup sugar and ¼ cup water.

Cracker crumbs

One cup fine, dry bread crumbs can substitute for ¼ cup fine cracker crumbs.

Eggs

Use 2 tablespoons of mayonnaise for each egg required in your recipe.

Garlic

A ⅛ teaspoon of garlic powder can be used in place of a clove of garlic.

Herbs

It takes three times as many fresh herbs to give the same flavoring of one measure of dried herbs.

Honey

One cup of honey can be replaced with 1¼ cups sugar and an additional ¼ cup of whatever liquid is used in the recipe.

Mustard

One tablespoon prepared mustard is equal to 1 teaspoon of dry mustard.

One pound equivalents

The following amounts are equal to one pound: 2 cups butter; 2⅓ cups white granulated sugar; 2 cups packed brown sugar; 3¾ cups confectioners' sugar; 3½ cups all-purpose flour; 4 cups cake flour; 3¾ cups whole-wheat flour; 4 cups cocoa; 3 cups loosely packed raisins; 2¾ cups sliced apples; 2 cups fresh pitted cherries; 5 cups sliced, fresh mushrooms; 3 cups sliced white potatoes; 4½ cups coarsely sliced cabbage.

Onions

Out of onions for gravy or stock? A few teaspoons of dried onion soup mix makes a tasty substitute.

Stock

One cup of beef or chicken stock can be replaced with one cup boiling water plus one bouillon cube or one envelope instant broth granules.

Vinegar

Use 2 teaspoons lemon juice for every teaspoon of vinegar needed.

HOME

APPLIANCES

Air conditioner location

If you have an option, install window air conditioners in north- and east-facing windows. South- and west-facing windows receive more sun and will make the unit work harder.

Appliance refinish

If you have a home appliance that runs well but is simply the wrong color, have it repainted at an auto body shop. This type of finish looks great, holds up well, and isn't terribly expensive.

Cheapest clothes dryer

Gas dryers are so much cheaper to operate than electric ones that under typical circumstances you will recoup the higher purchase cost of about $100 in a year. Electric dryers perform slightly better than gas, but the lower cost of gas more than compensates for these minor differences. If you get a gas dryer, buy one with an electronic ignition. A dryer with a pilot light uses 30 percent more gas and will increase your fuel bill by about $25 a year.

Chest freezer

Think twice about buying a separate home freezer. It can be convenient, but it takes a lot of savvy food management to make it really pay for itself. If a freezer makes economic sense for you, a chest style costs less to run than an upright model.

Coffeemaker with timer

Rather than purchase an expensive automatic coffeemaker with a built-in timer, buy a model without the timing device. Pick up an appliance timer at the home improvement center (the kind used to turn lamps on and off) for about $10, plug your coffee maker into it, set the time, and you'll have a quality, timed coffeemaker for a lot less money than the built-in variety, and it will work equally well.

EER tags

Buy energy efficient. When selecting a new appliance, look for the yellow

EER tag, which indicates energy efficiency. The higher the number, the less wasteful of energy and more efficient it will be.

Freezer

Be sure to keep your freezer packed full to consume the least amount of energy. As your store of food is depleted, fill the gaps with plastic jugs filled with water. You'll accomplish a keep-it-full technique and have a good supply of fresh water in the event of a power failure.

Refrigerators

Manual defrost refrigerators typically use about half as much electricity as automatic defrost models, but if you don't keep up with the defrosting, the refrigerator's efficiency will drop. Side-by-side refrigerator/freezers typically use 35 percent more energy than models with the freezer on top.

Warranty book

Save receipts, warranties, and owner's manuals. Often these are all you will need to have an appliance repaired at no charge. Find a 3-ring binder fitted with plastic pocket protectors to keep everything neat and orderly.

Wash, dry, and wax

To preserve the finish of your washer and dryer and other appliances, wax them with car wax twice a year.

White appliance touch-up

The nasty black chip on any white home appliance, porcelain sink, ceramic tile, or even your white car can be quickly repaired with a liquid correction fluid like Wite-Out or Liquid Paper, available at office supply stores. Carefully paint the chip, and it will dry in just a few minutes.

BATHROOM

Bathroom cleaner

Dissolve 4 tablespoons baking soda in 1 quart of warm water for a basic bathroom cleaner. Use dry baking soda on a damp sponge for tough areas. Baking soda will clean and deodorize all kitchen and bathroom surfaces.

Bathtub ring

To remove that really gross bathtub ring, apply a paste of hydrogen peroxide mixed with cream of tartar to stained porcelain surfaces. Scrub lightly, let dry, then rinse with warm water. Repeat if necessary.

Between cleanings

Cut some old rags into small squares and stuff them into a jar. Add water and a bit of pine-scented cleaner. Keep these handy for between-cleaning bathroom touchups. When finished, simply wash to be used again.

Cabinet liner

Use an old bath rug to line the cabinet under your bathroom sink. It will soak up spills and leaks, and is easy to clean. Just toss it in the laundry.

Coal in the bathroom

Learn a plumber's trade secret and hide a few pieces of coal in your bathroom to absorb moisture and odor.

Decal removal

To remove stubborn decals or residual adhesive, soak a rag in mineral spirits or Soilove laundry stain pretreatment (see p. 347 for ordering information) and lay it over the area. After 10 minutes or so, scrape away decal or adhesive with a plastic scraper or an old credit card. Wash as usual.

Drying racks

Create a convenient drying rack in your bathroom. Install a towel bar or two on the ceiling over the center of the tub. Drips will go down the drain instead of all over the floor.

Eliminate odors

You can buy all kinds of room deodorizers and pretty-smelling things for the bathroom that do nothing more than cover up bathroom odors. Or you can simply light a match and blow it out immediately to completely eliminate the odor.

Empty the toilet bowl for cleaning

Make toilet cleaning easier by quickly dumping a pail of water into the toilet (without flushing) so the bowl will be almost empty as you work on it. Don't ask why this works. It must be physics.

Eucalyptus

Available at a reasonable cost from many florist shops, eucalyptus makes a unique bathroom air freshener. Simply place fragrant eucalyptus stems in a vase and add enough water to cover about 2 inches of the stem bases.

Extra storage space

Hang a shoe bag on the back of the bathroom door. The pockets are perfect for washcloths and toiletries and other small items that cause such a clutter problem in the bathroom.

Fiberglass showers, tubs

Clean fiberglass showers and tubs with baking soda sprinkled on a damp sponge. Scrub clean and wipe dry.

Flip the hooks

To prevent shower curtains from slipping off the hooks, alternate the direction each hook faces.

Garden watering can

Use a garden watering can to pour clean rinse water on tub or shower walls. The water will go where you'd like it to go because you'll have more control.

Glass shower doors

Mineral oil will remove stubborn scum from the inside of glass shower doors. Give the tiles, faucets, and outside of the shower door a final once-over with glass cleaner to make them really shine.

Hair spray on no-wax floor

To remove hairspray from a no-wax floor: Mix ¼ cup ammonia with a gallon of warm water. If you are not sure about the durability of the floor's finish, test this mixture on an inconspicuous part of the floor.

Impossible toilet stains

If you have stains in your toilet that will not budge with any other method, here's the severe, last-ditch, toilet-stain-removal secret. Pick up some wet/dry sandpaper at the hardware or automotive supply store. This is very fine sandpaper that, when used with water, will not scratch the porcelain but should remove the offending stain. Use the method on page 132 to remove as much water as possible from the bowl and go to work on the stains.

Magnet corral

If you often misplace tweezers, manicure scissors, and nail files, try this trick: Attach these items to a large magnet placed on the inside of your metal medicine cabinet.

Mildew

Here's a way to get rid of mildew buildup in your shower stall without using harsh, household bleach: Fill an empty spray bottle with vinegar and a cup of salt. Spray the stall, allow the solution to sit for at least a half hour, and then rinse thoroughly. Tougher jobs may require a second application.

Mildew

To remove mildew from tile, wet surface with water then spray with a solution of 1 cup liquid chlorine bleach mixed with 1 quart water. Let the solution remain on the tile about 15 minutes, then rinse. Caution: Never mix chlorine bleach with other cleaning products that might contain ammonia. A potentially fatal gas may result.

Mildew

Get rid of mildew in caulking between the walls and tub by saturating paper towels with undiluted chlorine bleach. Allow wet towels to sit for a few hours or until all traces of mildew have vanished.

Mildew in corners

To remove mildew from the corner of the tub or other hard-to-scrub places, dip a cotton ball into bleach and let it sit on the mildew for an hour or two. Rinse with warm water, and repeat if necessary.

Mop that tub

Mops offer an easy-on-the-back-and-knees alternative for cleaning the bathtub. Sprinkle tub with cleanser and swish away grime.

No more slimy soap puddles

Avoid buildup in the soap dish by placing a sponge or washcloth underneath the soap. Cleanup is simply a matter of wringing out the sponge and drying the dish.

Not down the toilet

Do not throw dental floss or colored toilet paper or colored tissues down the toilet. Since the insides of sewer pipes are very rough, dental floss has a tendency to stick to the pipe and accumulate over time. Colored toilet tissue might look good, but it doesn't break down as readily as white toilet paper and could cause problems down the line.

Odor absorbent

Keep an open, shallow dish of baking soda behind your toilet to absorb odors.

Office supply store

Check out those acrylic desk organizers you see in office supply or art stores. They're ideal for cosmetics, brushes, and nail polish and are much cheaper than the same thing sold for cosmetic organization.

Oven cleaner on water spots

Remove severe mineral deposits on bathroom tile with oven cleaner. Apply and allow it to set overnight before rinsing. Repeat as necessary for heavily affected areas.

Prevent a lock-in

Toss a towel over the top of a bathroom door so it won't close completely. This way, little ones are less likely to lock themselves in.

Reduce water consumption

Fill a plastic bottle (1-liter is a good size) with water. Place it in your toilet tank on the side opposite the flushing mechanism. This will reduce the amount of water required to flush the toilet and will decrease your total water consumption.

Shower curtain

If mildew and soap scum are only at the bottom of the shower curtain, fill the tub with enough water to cover the spots, add a little bleach, and let soak. Rinse the curtain and the tub well to remove the bleach.

Shower curtain with mildew

To clean mildew and soap scum from a shower curtain, place the curtain in the washing machine along with two or three white towels. Fill with warm water; add detergent and ½ cup baking soda. Add one cup white vinegar to the rinse water to prevent further mold from forming. Hang on the shower rod to dry.

Shower curtain with water marks

Having trouble getting those filmy water spots off your shower curtain? Fill your washing machine with warm water, liquid detergent as you would for any load, and one capful of liquid fabric softener at the beginning of the wash cycle. Add fabric softener again in the rinse cycle. Your shower curtain will come out sparkling and not a water spot in sight.

BATHROOM

Shower door tracks

To clean the shower door tracks, fill them with white vinegar and allow them to soak a few hours. Scrub with an old toothbrush. Flush with water to rinse away the gunk.

Showerhead

Looking for a quick and easy way to clean a dirty, clogged-up showerhead? Pour a cup of vinegar into a large plastic bag and twist-tie the bag to the shower head so that it is fully immersed in the vinegar. Let stand for an hour or two, or overnight for a very challenging situation, then rinse.

Showerhead declogger

A showerhead that is really mired in sediment that cannot be completely removed with vinegar needs a heavy-duty treatment. Dissolve a denture-cleaning tablet in the plastic bag of water. Tie the bag over the shower-head so that it is completely immersed in the liquid. Attach with a rubber band or twist tie. Allow to sit for several hours. Remove and turn on shower to clear all traces of sediment.

Soap scum away

Remove soap scum from faucets with an old toothbrush dipped into a 50/50 ammonia and water solution.

Soap slivers

Here's a solution for those irritating soap-sliver remnants: Make them go piggyback. Soften the remnant in warm water for a few seconds and then mold it onto the back of the new bar before leaving the shower. Once dry, it will be melded to the new bar.

Toilet cleaner

If your toilet bowl has really stubborn stains, drop one or two denture-cleaning tablets into the bowl and allow to sit overnight. Brush and flush.

Toilet cleaning

Using a plunger, plunge the water in the toilet until the bowl is nearly empty. Sprinkle baking soda onto the sides of the toilet bowl, then drizzle with vinegar and scour with a toilet brush. This both cleans and deodorizes. Flush to rinse and refill bowl.

Back up

Backing up your computer's hard drive regularly will save you much time and distress on that fateful day when your home computer's hard drive crashes. It will crash, and all the information on it will be lost, so plan on it. That way you won't freak out when it happens. And if it never crashes, consider that a bonus beyond expectation. Even if you do not have a sophisticated backup system, you can easily copy important documents and files to a floppy disk, which you should then keep in a safe place.

Children on-line

To be sure your kids are safe while on-line and to protect your budget, don't allow them to log on unless an adult is present to supervise. Get to know their on-line friends by reading the messages they send and receive, and don't hide the fact that you are watching. Set time limits for on-line use, and cancel the service immediately if you get a large bill or see things on the screen that you don't like.

Disks in the mail

Computer disks received in the mail or from other unsolicited sources can be cleaned off and used as new disks. However, rather than simply deleting the information you see on the disk, perform the full reformat function. Now you have a disk that can be used to back up your critical files and documents.

Dryer sheets

Save the dryer sheets from your laundry after they've softened a load of wash. They make great dusting and cleaning cloths for television and computer screens. Not only will they clean the screens, the antistatic properties will treat the screens to repel rather than attract dust.

Dust deflector

Dust sucked in through the front of your floppy drive will unnecessarily add to the drive's wear and tear. If your drive lacks a dust cover, fashion a flap from masking tape that shields the entrance slot when the drive is out of use.

E-mail off-line

If your on-line service charges by the hour after a flat number of hours each month, conserve that on-line time by composing E-mail messages off-line. Once your message meets your satisfaction, perform your dial-up procedure and hit "send." This should take only seconds rather than many minutes if you were to dial up and compose while the on-line meter is running. If you do not know how to accomplish off-line composition, call your E-mail provider for help.

Internet access

If you are interested in checking out the Internet but don't want to pay a monthly access fee, turn to your area college. Many have a local dial-up number that will allow you to explore their library catalog. From there they may offer a window to the World Wide Web that allows further free exploration of computers around the world.

Keyboard maintenance

A new paintbrush is great for dusting hard-to-get-at crevices in computer keyboards and monitors. Unplug the keyboard and vacuum it regularly, using the soft brush attachment. To dislodge particles of dirt and dust, turn the keyboard upside down and hit it several times with the flat of your hand. Periodically, clean the keys with a lint-free cloth that has been dipped in rubbing alcohol.

Leave it on

Computers don't like being turned on. The chance of failure during that time is high enough that many businesses never turn off their machines. If you step away from the computer and intend to return within three or four hours, leave it on. However, if you do not have a screen saver, turn the monitor off to avoid burning images into the display. Every monitor has its own on-off switch.

Preloaded software

When shopping for a computer, don't let yourself be seduced by a lot of preloaded software. If the deal you're considering without taking the preloaded software into account is mediocre compared to other stores you've checked, pass. Most people never use most of that preloaded software they thought was so valuable to the deal.

COMPUTERS

Printer ribbons

If you are not using your computer printer on a daily basis, remove the printer cartridge between uses and store it in a zippered storage bag. This limits the exposure to air, which tends to dry the ribbon before the ink is fully used.

Printer trash

If you generate a lot of computer printout, sort through what would normally be headed for the trash, use what you can for notepaper or donate usable paper to your local schools. Even computer run that is blank on one side can be very useful and highly appreciated by a school that is trying to operate on a limited budget. Check twice about any printed information that's leaving your office. As for the tear-off strips, save them in a plastic trash bag to use as packing material when you're mailing breakables. Computer-paper boxes are the perfect size for many gifts and storage.

Ribbon trick

Some computer ribbon cartridges can be renewed to produce many more pages of printing. Simply spray the faded ribbon that is otherwise in good condition with WD-40. This will take some experimentation on your part, but the effort will be well rewarded.

Screen cleaning

Spraying glass cleaner directly onto the monitor screen can cause damage. Instead spray a mild cleaner or rubbing alcohol onto a soft lint-free rag, then wipe the screen.

Surge protector

Voltage spikes and surges through the power lines can fry the electronics of your computer and printer. A good surge protector is far better insurance for your machines than an extended-warranty policy. This item into which you plug your computer is quite inexpensive and available at any computer or hardware store.

DECORATING

Art gallery

If you enjoy decorating your home or apartment with framed art prints, discover a wonderful resource offered by many public libraries. Some carry hundreds of framed art prints that library patrons may check out free of charge for a specified time period of two, even three months. Designate a particular wall in your home as your "revolving art gallery," where you enjoy a broad range of artistic styles at no cost to you.

Base for artificial flowers

To hold artificial flowers in place, pour salt in the container, add a little cold water, and arrange the flowers. As it dries, the salt will solidify and hold the flowers.

Bed coverlet

Cutwork and lace bed coverlets can be expensive. Use a lace tablecloth instead. A 70-by-90-inch oblong cloth will fit a full-size bed.

Bedsheets

Buy flat bedsheets instead of yardage. Buying sheets on sale gives you extra-wide yardage at a fraction of the cost of yard goods. They're perfect for making curtains, tablecloths, napkins, pillows, nightclothes, and crafts.

Black

A touch of black adds punch to any decor. But use a light hand: a lamp shade, needlepoint pillow, or area rug is all it takes.

Bulletin board

Need a bulletin board for a recreation or child's room? Use an old-fashioned game board. You know, from the days before electronic games took over. A no-longer-used Monopoly board is colorful and decorative for hanging on a playroom wall.

Candleholders

Coat the inside of a candleholder with a tiny amount of petroleum jelly to ensure easy removal.

Centerpiece
Create an impromptu centerpiece by arranging different fruits and vegetables in a big bowl or on a platter.

Curtain rod
Instead of the typical drapery rod, hang curtains from a copper pipe or a sturdy tree branch set on brackets.

Custom-blend paint
If you have miscellaneous quantities of leftover paint sitting around, you can pour it all into one container for your own custom blend. As long as you are careful to only mix latex with latex or oil-base with oil-base, it won't matter if you mix flat, glossy, and semigloss. If your garage is a typical one, it won't be hard to come up with a full gallon that easily paints an averaged-sized bedroom. You'll achieve the best results if you mix colors that are similar. Store tightly sealed paint cans upside down to extend usable life.

Cut flowers
Hold cut flowers under lukewarm water as you trim the stems. It gives them a surge of water they don't get if you cut first, then put them in water. Put heavy and tall stems in the vase first, and use lighter ones to fill out the arrangement.

Decorator album
Fill a purse-size photo album with paint, fabric, and wallpaper samples organized by room. Take the album when you go shopping or to garage sales, and you'll take the guesswork out of finding coordinating accessories for your home.

Doorstop
If you would like a nice-looking and functional doorstop but don't want to spend a small fortune, fill a tin box that has a lid (the kind that holds cookies or candies at holiday time) with dried beans. You can choose a size and style to coordinate with your room's decor for a fraction of the cost of a ready-made doorstop. What a simple way to add a unique and functional decorator item to any room in the house.

Dripless candles
To make new candles dripless, soak in a strong saltwater solution for a few hours, then dry well.

Dye to change your look
When redecorating, remember Rit dye. Light-colored curtains, bedspreads, and throw rugs can be dyed a darker shade of another color and will give a room an entirely new look. Remember to wash these items sepa-

rately in cold water. Drying in the dryer or direct sun will fade the colors quickly, so remember to allow time for air-drying indoors or in a shady place.

Fabric paint

A touch of washable fabric paint, available at craft and fabric stores, can customize plain-Jane napkins, place mats, or tablecloths into fabulous accessories that coordinate with your dishes, floors, or wall coverings.

Family posters

Enlarge family photos to poster-size and frame them. Modern color photocopiers do a marvelous job of enlarging. Check enlargement prices at a quick print company like Kinko's. Or have the negative enlarged to an actual poster-sized photograph.

Flower frog

Wad up a mesh produce bag and stuff it in a vase. It will act as a "frog" to hold fresh or artificial flower arrangements.

Foam cushions

To replace a foam cushion that has been removed from a zippered cover, place the cushion in a plastic garbage bag and insert the bag open-end first into the cover. The cushion will easily slide right in. Once in place all you have to do is pull the bag out, leaving the foam perfectly in place.

Fresh bouquet alternative

If you forget to pick up flowers for the table, set a houseplant in a basket and add a pretty ribbon.

Fresh flowers

Here's a remarkable method for greatly increasing the useful life of freshly cut flowers. Add ¼ teaspoon of bleach to the vase water. Recut flower stems at an angle to encourage absorption and arrange them in the bleach water. Place in a cool, dark place for several hours, then put out on display. Flowers should be angle-cut and refreshed daily. The bleach retards the growth of bacteria in the water, which causes flowers to wilt much more quickly.

Full to queen

You don't need all new bedding if you replace your old double bed with a queen-size one. Lay a full-size flat sheet on your new queen-size mattress. Fold a hospital corner (this has a pleated rather than gathered look) at all four corners and pin them in place. Stitch elastic completely around the pleated corners. You will have a queen-size fitted sheet. Buy coordinating flat queen-size sheets when you see them on sale. Make extra pillowcases from the full-size fitted sheets.

Furniture moving

When moving heavy furniture across the room, protect the floor by first placing a soft-sole slipper, thick sock, or empty milk carton under each leg of the furniture. The piece will slide across the floor easily without scratching or damaging the floor.

Hang a picture

This is the formula that professional picture hangers use: (1) Measure up 60 inches from the floor. (2) To this, add half the height of the framed picture. (3) Subtract the height of the wire (the height of the triangle that the wire would form if the frames were actually hanging in place). This magic number is the distance from the floor at which you should nail the picture hook regardless of the height of the ceiling or even your height.

Headboard

Use a length of picket fence as a headboard. Cut it to size, stain or paint it to coordinate with your room, and bolt it to the wall or bed frame.

Inside window boxes

To show off your plants, hang a window box under the window, inside the room.

Lampshade pizzazz

Brighten up a boring lamp shade: Sponge or stencil designs on the shade with fabric paint.

Nails in place

If you can't hammer a nail without hammering your fingers in the process, use the tines of an old fork instead of your fingers to hold the nail in place.

Paint goofs

Most home improvement centers, paint stores, and hardware stores have bins of "goofs"—gallons and quarts of high-quality paint in custom colors that have been mistinted. Typically these items are available at near-giveaway prices, such as gallons for $3 and quarts as low as 50 cents each. A gallon of paint is plenty for the typical-sized kid's room or bathroom. There's nothing wrong with the paint or the colors—it's just that for some reason the color didn't exactly match someone else's expectations.

Paneling

If you want to give a room with dark wood paneling a new look but a complete remodel is not in the budget right now, consider painting the paneling. First treat the walls with a paint deglosser. This will remove all grease, dirt, and the high gloss. Next apply a coat of white primer and follow with regular wall paint. This is a very inexpensive way to redecorate a room. Check with the paint professional at your home improvement center regarding the kind of products that would be best for this job.

Picture marks

Put masking tape on the backside of the corners of a picture to keep them from marking the wall.

Pillowcases

Pillowcases are very expensive these days—one pair can be as much as the price of a sheet—which is the reason you might want to consider making your own. When buying new sheets, pick up a fitted sheet and two flat sheets, making sure the second flat is queen-size, regardless of the size of the bed you will be outfitting. Out of the queen-size flat sheet you will be able to make three sets of pillowcases. By analyzing a commercially made pillowcase, it is easy to measure, create a pattern, and see how it is put together.

Pillowcases

To turn an extra printed pillowcase into 2 that match, open up the side seams and cut across the bottom fold so you end up with 2 single pieces the size of a pillowcase. Now do the same with another solid-colored pillowcase. With right sides together, sew each print half to a solid half, turn, and display them on the bed with the print side showing.

Pillows

To save money on decorative pillows that match your room's decor, you can stitch them yourself from elegant cloth napkins.

Pot holders

Paint small terra-cotta flowerpots pastel colors and place on a small tray in the bathroom to hold makeup, soaps, and other small items.

Queens for kings

Buy queen-size top sheets for king-size beds. King-size top sheets are usually way too big and require a lot of tucking in. Queen-size flats work great on most king-size beds and are a lot cheaper. Note: All sheets vary in size, and it seems the better the quality, the more generous the amount of fabric.

Quilt tablecloth

A baby-size quilt draped over a plain table rather than being hidden in a drawer can give a room an instant "face-lift."

Reupholster

If you have a lovely old couch you don't want to part with, consider having it redone at an upholstery school for a fraction of a professional upholsterer's price. There is a fee, and advanced students typically charge $100. You'll be expected to purchase fabric through the school. Plan on students taking a little longer to complete the job, whose work is done under the supervision of teachers. Look under "Upholstery Schools" in your Yellow Pages or call the industrial arts divisions of high schools and colleges.

Shelf lining

Put adhesive-backed shelf paper in the freezer for about an hour before using. The frozen paper will be less limp and easier to put down. Smooth it out with a blackboard eraser or dry squeegee.

Shower curtain

Give your current shower curtain a brand-new look. Remove the rings, slip pieces of ribbon through the holes, and tie the curtain to the rod with big bows.

Table pedestal storage

Top a new trash or garbage can with a piece of plywood and cover with a floor-length fabric to turn it into a lamp table. The receptacle provides a fairly large storage space for Christmas decorations or other items used on a limited basis.

Table runner

Use a pretty muffler or scarf as a unique table runner.

Wallpaper over wallpaper

It is best to not apply wallpaper over wallpaper. Proper adhesion of the new paper to the old can present a problem, and even if you can finally get it to stick, years later, the layers will be very difficult to remove.

Wallpaper removal

To remove wallpaper, mix equal parts white vinegar and hot water. Dip a paint roller into the solution, and apply until the paper is wet thoroughly. After two applications, most paper will peel off in sheets. Patience is the secret.

Wide curtain rods

Current home decorating styles often include window valances that are hung on 2 ½-inch rods rather than the typical skinny ones. If you don't want to spend money to get the wider ones, you can update your skinny rods. Cut 2½-inch strips of wood from an old piece of paneling and use a hot gluegun to attach the strips to the skinny rod. Attach to the existing hardware, which should still be in place on the wall. New valances can be slipped right over the rod.

Winter candle arrangement

Set white votive candles in a clear, glass bowl filled with coarse salt to make an inexpensive "candles in the snow" centerpiece.

Wood paneling

If you're tired of your wood paneling but can't spring the time or cash to remove it and start over, wallpaper over it. You'll need wallpaper, paste, sealer, and wallpaper liner, all available at a home supply or wallpaper store. Apply the liner horizontally with a good wallpaper paste to cover wood irregularities and grooves. Next apply sealer just as you would to bare walls. Now you're ready to paper the room in the usual way. Many home improvement centers have how-to videos you can borrow if you need a brushup or beginner's lessons on wallpapering.

GARAGE SALES

Ambience

Take time to create the right sale ambience. Play upbeat music on a tape recorder. You want to make an inviting atmosphere. Make sure your best and biggest items can be easily seen by drivers who drive by to do a quick curbside survey.

Appraisers

If you suspect you have true collectibles, consult a professional appraiser before declaring them to be garage sale merchandise. Call an antique or collectibles store owner to get a feel for the value of the item in question. Contact the Appraisers Association of America at 212-889-5404 for a referral to someone in your area. An appraiser can be costly (from $75 to $300 per hour), but you'll be glad you hired one if you were planning to put a $4 tag on an item worth $400.

At noon, go for broke

At noon, or a time you feel appropriate, significantly increase the prices on the items you wouldn't mind keeping, then put up a sign announcing: "Everything Now Half Off!"

Curbing consumerism

While having garage sales is marvelous for freeing up closets and generating cash, there is another tremendous benefit—one that is often overlooked. Garage sales help to curb consumerism. After haggling over whether an article—for which you paid more than you care to admit—was worth $1 or not, you will probably think long and hard before mindlessly purchasing things in the future.

Display

Create an inviting display. Your knickknacks should not look cluttered. Put them against a dark background and arrange the tables so the sale goods can be easily viewed without customers' movement becoming restricted. Hang clothing items to make them visible.

Early birds

Avoid negotiating with early birds. If a buyer is hot for an item at 6 A.M., chances are you'll get your asking price before the day is over. Be nice but firm. Offer to take their phone number. If the item hasn't sold by day's end, do not hesitate to call.

Exchange instead of sell

Instead of selling at a garage sale and not ending up with enough money to replace a desired item in a larger size, don't offer big-ticket items like old rollerblades, party shoes, and bicycles the kids have outgrown. Instead, organize a neighborhood exchange. You'll be surprised to find out how many of your neighbors are in the same boat.

Garage sale map

Before checking out other garage sales, make a special garage-sale map: Start with a map of your local community and cover it with clear contact paper. Using a grease pencil, mark the locations of the garage sales you want to visit this weekend. Now you can design a logical route to make the best use of your weekend time. Erase the marks after you attend each of the sales.

General guidelines

Be ready to begin your sale an hour before your advertised start time. Keep the doors of your home locked while you are having your sale. You'll get the best prices if your merchandise is clean and well displayed. Have batteries available so shoppers can confirm that items like toys and radios work.

Giveaways

When advertising your garage sale, mention you'll have "giveaways." This conveys a spirit of generosity on the part of the seller.

Keep it clean

When holding a garage sale, it is important that both your sale area and merchandise be inviting. The object is to attract shoppers to your sale—not repel them. Most people will not even bother to stop at a sale that appears to be junk. The prices you get for your merchandise will be better if each item is clean and displayed as attractively as possible.

Kid care

When holding a garage sale, hire a baby-sitter for the very young kids. You'll be more focused if you're not watching kids.

GARAGE SALES

Make coffee
People will stay longer, be in a better mood, and—who knows—you may even sell the coffeepot.

Permit
Check with your city hall to see if you need a permit to hold a garage sale. The last thing you'll need is the police showing up to shut you down just when things are picking up.

Pick the perfect day
Saturday with a good weather forecast still proves to be the best day for a garage sale. Sundays pose a conflict for churchgoers, and many people travel on holiday weekends.

Popular items
If two potential customers have checked out an item thoroughly, but do not buy it, do this: Tell the next customer who comes along that several people have been interested in that piece, but if she takes it now, you'll reduce the price by 20 percent.

Price things in advance
Price all items that you put aside for a future garage sale before you store them away. Doing the pricing ahead of time will make preparing for the actual sale a breeze.

Pricing
For fairly new items in good condition charge ¼ of what you originally paid for them.

Scheduling
Check your local newspaper to make sure there's no big community event scheduled for the day you've chosen for your garage sale. It will draw away your customers.

Seasonal
Seasonal merchandise sells best. If it's spring, haul out that old lawn mower, gardening tools, etc. People buy what they can use now, not what they're going to have to store in their own garage.

Signs
Post signs directing customers to your sale. And be sure to remove those signs as soon as the sale is over.

Sold
Make sure you mark "Sold" on any garage sale items buyers will be picking up later in order to avoid accidentally selling the same item twice. It's embarrassing to watch your neighbors fight over your junk.

Take a photo
Does this sound familiar? You've made a commitment to dejunk your

life, and now it's garage sale season. Suddenly you and your family get hit with the sentimental bug. Instead of hanging on to all that stuff, why not take a photograph of the special item? A photo of the giant stuffed animal that was your daughter's favorite when she was three will take up a lot less room in the photo album than in the attic. You'll find the picture will call up the same memories as the item itself, and you'll be freed emotionally to get rid of the things that are cluttering your life.

Thrift store instead

If your garage sale merchandise is mainly old clothes in not-so-great condition, consider a trip to the thrift shop instead of a garage sale. At a tax benefit of $10 or more per bag of clothes, this tactic may possibly be more lucrative in the long run.

Twenty-percent tactic

Decide on the price of each item and then mark it up 20 percent. This allows room to negotiate with a customer, and you'll find most yard-salers love to bargain.

GARDEN & LANDSCAPING

Acid lovers

For beautiful azaleas, gardenias, and other acid-loving plants, add 2 tablespoons of white vinegar to a quart of water and use to water, occasionally.

Aerate lawn

Wear golf shoes or other spiked athletic shoes while mowing the lawn. You will aerate the grass roots with each step, and that allows much needed oxygen and water to nourish the lawn.

Ants

Follow the ants' trail to their point of entry into the house and seal it with caulk. Then find their nest (at the other end of their trail) and destroy it by pouring several gallons of boiling water into the entrance, stir it up, and pour more boiling water.

Ashes

Ashes from a wood-burning stove or fireplace make wonderful fertilizer for rose bushes and other prizes in your yard and garden. Collect the ashes, and scatter them around shrubs and bushes. Ashes enrich the soil's texture and will produce a greener garden. Fireplace ashes act like lime in the garden, making your soil more alkaline. If your soil is already alkaline, you don't need to use them. A gallon of dry ashes equals about 3 pounds and if used as a soil additive, apply at the rate of 5 pounds per 100 square feet.

Baking soda dusting

Here's a safe way to bust pests that bother your cabbage and broccoli plants! Dust the plants in late afternoon with baking soda. The mixture of morning dew settling on the soda will form an antiworm enzyme that won't harm humans. It will wash off easily with a little water.

Basil et al

Don't allow fresh basil to flower. As buds form, pick them off to keep that basil sweet. When it comes to any type of herbs—use them. The more you pick them, the more vigorously they will grow. Some herbs flourish in cool weather. Dill, cilantro, and parsley all prefer cool temperatures. Plan to enjoy them during spring and early fall.

Birdbath

Now that you have a beautiful yard and garden, invite songbirds to splish-splash and entertain you. Pick up a large 12-inch diameter drip tray—the kind used under a potted plant. Don't spend over $2, and try to find a green one. Put the tray on the ground in a sheltered part of the garden, positioning rocks or small logs around the perimeter. Put a large rock in the middle of the bath to act as an island. Fill with water and wait for the action. Flush and replace water every two or three days.

Bird feeder

A waxed milk carton makes a good bird feeder. Cut out large windows on all four sides, leaving 2 inches at the top and bottom. Poke holes through the top of the carton, run a string through the holes, and hang the carton on a tree branch. Fill the bottom with bird food. Try decorating the feeder with adhesive-backed paper.

Bird treat

Smear a pinecone with peanut butter, and hang it from a tree in your garden for a bird treat.

Bountiful ferns

For beautiful ferns, poke a few holes in the surrounding soil and then pour a ½ teaspoonful of castor oil into each hole.

Brightly colored tools

Paint your garden tool handles bright red so they can be spotted easily in the grass or garden. If your neighbor has taken notice of this terrific tip, you might want to select a color opposite of the one he chose.

Bug detector

If you are concerned about bringing in bugs along with your just-picked produce, rinse garden-fresh vegetables well, then let soak in mixture of 1 gallon water and 1 cup vinegar for about 5 minutes. Insects will be easier to pick off, and your produce's flavor will not be affected.

Bug spray

To make a terrific bug spray for your garden, mix 2 tablespoons flea and tick powder, 1 tablespoon Wesson oil, and 1 gallon water. Spray on plants.

Bulb markers

When you're planting bulbs in your garden and can't finish the project on that same day or weekend, stick wooden clothespins in the ground to indicate the exact location of each bulb. This way you'll know exactly where to continue planting when you're ready to finish the job.

Carpet the garden

If you want to set out tomato plants or some other plants but are overwhelmed by the immensity of the project because your only suitable spot is covered with weeds, try this unorthodox tactic, which has been reported to work very well: Take a large piece of old carpet and lay it over the garden patch. Make X cuts with a utility knife at the location where each plant should grow. Lift up the cut carpet flaps, dig a hole beneath, and sink the seedling. Water as usual and watch your plants grow. You won't have to worry about weeds because they won't be able to penetrate the carpeting. It might look a little goofy, but the carpeted vegetable garden makes a lot of sense.

Cheap sod

If you have more time than money and need a new lawn, visit your local sod farm and purchase their "scraps," which are the odd-sized roll ends. You will have to patch it together, which takes time, but you can pick up these odd pieces at a tremendous savings.

Club soda

Don't throw away your fizzless club soda. It has just the right chemicals to add vigor and beautiful color to most house plants. Use it as you would water to hydrate the plant.

Compost bin

To make a compost bin, all you need are four wooden pallets (free, or a dollar or so from stores or warehouses). Stand the pallets on their sides and wire them together into a square. When you need to remove compost, open one side like a door.

Cut early

The best time to cut flowers is in the early morning while they retain some moisture from the cool night air and the early-morning dew.

Cutworm shield

Cut the bottom out of an empty tuna can and sink this "ring" into the soil around a young seedling. This will keep the cutworms and other predators away from the plant.

Dill repels worms

Worms won't bother your tomatoes if you plant a few sprigs of dill nearby.

Dog-spots in the lawn

To prevent those yellow dog-spots in your lawn, feed your male dog a couple of tablespoons of tomato juice each day. This works with female dogs, but not quite as well.

Drainage pellets

Use Styrofoam packing peanuts in place of rocks as drainage for potted plants.

Dryer sheets

A sheet of fabric softener rubbed over the skin or pinned to the hair will keep insects away as you work in the garden.

Easy spacing

Mark the handles of your gardening tools with 1-inch increments. You will no longer need a ruler when planting or spacing plants, shrubs, or flowers.

Fake flagstones

Instead of using expensive flagstones for garden paths, used salvaged pieces of cement, which you can find at apartment complexes or city streets where sidewalks are being replaced. They create the same rustic effect when randomly placed and edged with thyme or other greenery.

Fall tilling

The reason you should plow or till your garden in the fall is to expose both hibernating insects and weed seeds, which in most climates will then perish in the winter.

Fertilizer: One cent a gallon

Here's a great way to brew up your own plant fertilizer at a cost of about 1 cent per gallon: Add 2 teaspoons of plain household ammonia to 1 gallon of water. Allow to sit for a full 24 hours. Use on plants instead of using costly commercial fertilizer. Caution: If you use more than a capful to 1 gallon of water it will be too strong, and you will burn your plants. In this case more is definitely not better.

Filtered foliage

Drop a coffee filter in the bottom of a pot before repotting a plant. The water will drain from the pot, but the soil won't wash out with it.

Florist prepared plants

When you receive live floral plants in those beautifully wrapped containers, the wrapping material may become deadly to the plant. The pot in which the plant is planted has holes at the bottom, but the foil or plastic wrapping prevents drainage. To eliminate this problem hold the container high, punch a hole in the center, tear outward, and with scissors carefully cut all around to within an inch or so of the edge. The overall appearance is left undisturbed and the plant can drain properly and will be able to thrive.

Flowers with long life

To extend the life of cut flowers, fill a vase with warm water and add about ¼ teaspoon household liquid bleach. Remove all leaves that will be below the waterline. Holding the stems under water, cut them at an angle and plunge into the vase water immediately. This procedure should be done as soon as possible after the flowers have been picked from the garden. Keep the vase out of direct sunlight, heat sources, and drafts. Change the water daily, and repeat bleach process.

Fruit flies away

After you pick fruit, put it in a pail and cover with water. When you bring fruit into the house, no fruit flies will follow. Pots of basil outside the front door or on the porch will also repel fruit flies.

Garden cart

Use a child's plastic snow sled as an off-season garden cart. It glides easily over the grass for cleanup chores and is especially handy when it's time to lift and divide clumps of perennials.

Gardener hands

Two ways to remove garden soil from your hands and from beneath your fingernails: (1) Soak your hands in water in which one of those fizzy denture-cleaning tablets has dissolved. An added bonus: soft cuticles. (2) After a day of gardening, wash your hands with soap and water and a teaspoon of regular table sugar. The rough granules will scour your hands clean.

Garden gear hut

Get a large weatherproof mailbox, roomy enough to hold small garden tools and gear. Stake it in the ground in a convenient spot under a tree or near a hedge.

Garden snakes

To keep garden snakes from getting under or into the house, spray hairspray along the foundation of the house and the bottoms of doors, then sprinkle the area with black or cayenne pepper.

Garden tools

Keep a bucket of sand sprinkled lightly with mineral oil in the shed or garage where you store your garden tools. When you're done using the tools, scour them with a bit of the sand to keep them clean and rust-free.

The oil will leave a light protective coating on the blades to prevent rust.

Garlic harvests

Every time you use a head of garlic, take the last three or four little cloves from the center plus any that have started to show green and plant them between other plants and shrubs in your flower beds. Plant each clove about ½ inch deep, flat end down, pointed end up. They will grow about 18 inches tall, and then they will start to dry out. This is the sign it's time to pull out a fresh garlic head. It takes about five months to get your first harvest. If you're always planting, you will have plenty of garlic for yourself and others. At $3 a pound, that's a fairly lucrative hobby.

Germination test

Test old seeds to see if they're worth planting: Place 10 seeds on a dampened paper towel. Cover with plastic to keep them moist. Check seeds after the germination time listed on the package has passed. If some but not all seeds germinate, you can still use the packet, just be sure to sow the seeds more heavily than usual.

Get those suckers

To get rid of ivy rooting in cracks and mortar of bricks, cut the vine away, wait for the suckers that cling to the brick to dry out, then simply brush them away.

Gophers and deer

Dog hair, available from a dog groomer, will repel gophers and other annoying furry pests. Human hair (get clippings from the local beauty salon) will repel deer, rabbits, and other garden invaders.

Grass clippings

Place grass clippings around plants to repel weeds. The clippings also retain moisture and are a good source of nutrients.

Grow lights

You don't need to buy an expensive grow light for your vegetable and flower seedlings. Regular fluorescent lights are just as effective, cost less, and last longer than fancy grow lights. If you combine one "cool white" with one "warm white" fluorescent tube in a standard shop fixture, your plants will thrive.

Hose holder

Use an old leather belt to store the garden hose. Wind up the hose, slip the belt through the loops, buckle it, and hang it from a nail in the garage or basement.

Hosiery in the garden

Save old pantyhose, nylons, and tights for your garden. Cut them into long strips and use them to tie tomato plants to stakes or tomato cages. They are also great for tying other vegetables like string beans, cucumbers, and viney plants to fences. Nylons are better than string because they "give" and don't cut off the plants' circulation the way string, wire, or twist-ties do.

Insecticide

Add two drops of liquid dish soap to a quart of water. Pour into a spray bottle and spray plants periodically. This is especially effective on rose-loving aphids.

Keep cats out

If the cat is digging in the window box, put pinecones or horticultural charcoal around the plants. If the window box contains seedlings, staple screening over the top of the box until the plants mature a bit.

Lace and strawberries

Save dirty, yellowed, or torn lace curtains to cover your strawberry patch or raspberry bushes to keep birds off.

Lawn fertilizer

If you buy commercial lawn fertilizer and lawn weed-control products, purchase a single product that contains both a fertilizer product and weed control. It is cheaper than buying the products separately.

Lawn mower care

If you will not be using your mower for several months in the winter, drain the gas and disconnect the spark plug. If you cannot drain the gas, add a gas conditioner to the mower tank and to your gas can to prevent the fuel from going bad.

Lawn snack

Try this on your lawn every three weeks during the summer: You will need 1 can of beer, 1 cup baby shampoo, and household ammonia. Pour beer and shampoo into a 20-gallon, hose-end sprayer jar; fill the jar with ammonia and apply according to the hose-end sprayer instructions. Every third snack, add ½ cup clear corn syrup or molasses to the mixture. You're going to have very happy grass.

Lettuce carriers

Protect flowers and vegetables from slugs, snails, cutworms, and grubs by scattering lettuce leaves or citrus rinds around them. The pests will attach themselves to the food, which should be removed daily and replaced.

Lubricate the garden hose

To prevent the hose end from becoming attached to the spigot so tightly that you cannot easily remove it without the aid of tools, rub a light coating of petroleum jelly on the garden-hose nozzle and the spigot to keep them from sticking.

Luscious and slow-growing lawn

Most commercial lawn fertilizers are loaded with nitrogen because lawns love it. But the more nitrogen you feed your grass, the faster it grows, and the more often you have to cut it. The following mixture uses half the normal amount of lawn food and gives you deep green grass, thick blades, and increased root structure, but the growth will slow down to give you a break: 4 pounds magnesium sulfate (Epsom salts) and 1 bag of lawn food that covers 2,500 square feet. To cover 5,000 square feet, mix ingredients together, then feed your lawn only half the amount recommended.

Marigolds to the rescue

It's true, marigolds really do discourage insects. No scary chemicals involved. Just plant these beautiful flowers among your vegetables for natural pest control.

Master gardener

Most states offer gardening programs through their county extension offices. Gardening experts teach enrollees all aspects of gardening. Typically there are no fees; however, "students" are required to donate time to the community in trade for the education. Call your local directory assistance for the office nearest you.

Melon pedestals

Set baby melons and cantaloupes on top of tin cans in your garden. The melons will ripen faster and be sweeter.

No cats allowed

To keep cats out of the garden, put fir boughs around shrubs or spray the area with a weak dilution of vinegar and water.

No-drip watering

To keep hanging plants from dripping water, place a few ice cubes on top of the soil instead of watering with water. The cubes will melt slowly, releasing only the amount of water that the soil can easily absorb. By the time it melts, it will be warm enough to not shock the plant. This method is not acceptable for tropical or tender-leaf variety plants like African violets and orchids.

Pests and diseases

Here is a preventive pest and disease formula for your garden so you won't have to resort to chemicals: Mix the following in the bottle of a 20-gallon hose-end fertilizer dispenser: 1 cup antiseptic mouthwash, 1 cup flea-and-tick shampoo containing pyrethrum, 1 cup chewing-tobacco juice. (No, you don't have to chew the tobacco. Just tie 4 fingers of chewing tobacco in a nylon stocking, and steep, uncovered, in 1 quart boiling water until the water turns dark brown.) Fill the balance of the jar with water. Apply to plants, following directions on the hose-end dispenser. This is very effective to keep everything bug-free in your yard and garden: flowers, shrubs, trees, evergreens, vegetables, fruits.

Photograph your hard work

Use up the last few frames on a roll of film to photograph your garden in bloom. This is a great way to keep a record of what grew well and what plantings you particularly enjoyed.

Pickle juice

Work leftover pickle juice into the soil around an azalea or gardenia bush or around any other plant that needs acidic soil.

Plant nutrition

Don't throw out the water in which you've boiled eggs or pasta. The calcium and starches are great for watering houseplants.

Plant saucers

Substitute black oil-changing pans for saucers under large plants. These are available in the automotive section of discount stores.

Plant with purpose

Plant deciduous trees (the type that lose their leaves in winter) on the south side of your house. They will provide summer shade without blocking winter sun. Plant evergreens on the north to shield your home from cold winter winds.

Portable plants

To transport a large plant or shrub, roll it onto a snow shovel. You can drag the shovel across the lawn quickly without hurting your back.

Rabbits away

Sprinkle red pepper or talcum powder around the base of plants to keep rabbits away.

Rapid bulb planting

Here's a quick way to plant 100 bulbs in less than 45 minutes. Instead of digging lots of holes for lots of bulbs, dig out the area you wish to plant to a depth of 7 inches. Spread the bulbs out evenly with their tips facing up. Add compost to the excavated soil; then shovel the soil lightly over the bulbs. Don't worry if some of the bulbs tip over; they'll develop normally.

Root rehydration

Before planting bareroot plants like roses and grapevines, make sure the roots haven't dried out. Unwrap the roots, remove any packing material, and soak the roots in tepid water for 6 to 12 hours.

Roses fresh longer

To keep cut roses looking beautiful longer: Every day remove the roses from the vase, and refill the vase with fresh warm water and one crushed aspirin. Angle cut a tiny bit from the bottom of each stem and quickly plunge it into the vase. This makes the roses open more slowly.

Rusty garden tools

Rub the rust spots with a new steel wool pad soaked with soap, then dipped in turpentine. Finish by rubbing with a crumpled piece of aluminum foil.

Sawdust and seed

When seeding grass by hand, how can you tell if you've missed any spots? Mix fine sawdust with your seed; you'll be able to see the sawdust and the missed spots easily, and the sawdust will not adversely affect the new lawn.

Scare a bird

To keep birds from nesting on an air conditioner or dryer vent, where the hot-air exhaust can kill the babies, place a big-eyed stuffed animal in the window or near the vent.

Seat belt those gates

While you're at the junkyard, pick up a few seat belts from discarded cars. The straps make great gate latches. Just nail one to your wooden gate post, and the other to your gate. If it is metal, attach both strips to the post, then pass one buckle end around the upright member on the gate and back to the other. Seat belts are weatherproof, easily installed, don't cost much, and never get out of alignment the way most conventional latches do eventually.

Seed life

If you have seeds leftover after planting your garden for the year, don't throw them out. They'll still be good next year if you keep them in an airtight container in the refrigerator. Here's a general guideline for the shelf life of seeds: corn, lettuce, and parsley—1 to 2 years; asparagus, beans, carrots, radishes, and spinach—3 to 5 years; beets, cucumbers, and tomatoes—more than 5 years. Exception: onion seeds must be purchased fresh each year.

Seedling hothouses

Those clear plastic containers with the lids attached that you get from a grocery store salad bar or corner deli make great mini "greenhouses" for seeds you start indoors. Fill the container with potting soil and add seeds and water. Keep the lid down, and place it on a windowsill in direct sunlight until seedlings shoot through the soil.

Seedling incubators

Save plastic scoops from laundry detergent boxes for planting seedling starters.

Shiny plant leaves

Apply a thin coat of petroleum jelly to the top surface of smooth houseplant leaves for instant shine. Do not do this to the underside of the leaf because it breathes through the underside. You don't want to smother your plants.

Slippery slope

Ants can't climb up to a hummingbird feeder if you cover the pole or cord with petroleum jelly or baby oil, reapplying every two weeks or when it rains. To keep them out of the house, seal the point of entry with toothpaste, caulk, or masking tape.

Soap in a rope

Put a bar of soap in the toe of a pantyhose leg, tie a knot over it, and tie the other end to an outdoor spigot. Gardeners can easily wash up after working.

Soapy hands

If you don't wear garden gloves when gardening, coat your hands lightly with a mild liquid soap. The dirt washes off easily.

Square-foot system

Plant a garden; reduce grocery bills. Consider the popular square-foot gardening method, which requires very little time, space, and trouble. Check with your librarian for a how-to book.

Squirrels
If your bird feeders are being pillaged by furry marauders, divert their attention with this simple ploy: Hang dried ears of corn, a favorite food of squirrels everywhere, from a tree some distance away from your bird offerings.

Tired hose
Keep your garden hose rolled in an old tire. It will stay clean, dry, and ready to use.

Tool grips
Put a pair of kids' bicycle handlebar grips on the handles of your gardening tools to give yourself a firmer, more comfortable grip when doing yard work.

Tools
To keep garden tools from developing rust, rinse and dry the tools, then coat the metal parts with a thin layer of petroleum jelly.

Tool wax
Prevent rust from garden tools by cleaning and rubbing with car wax.

Trellis
Tie plastic loops from soda cans together, attach to a fence or pole, and use in the garden as a support for climbing plants.

Trial garden
Make a temporary garden out of a plastic kiddie pool. It's just the right size for beginners and children because it can be placed in the best light and can be disassembled and put away for the winter.

Wagon recycle
Baby's first wagon can be recycled as a hothouse for seedlings. Fill with dirt, cover with a piece of glass or Plexiglas, and move into the sun.

Warm shelter
Cut off the bottom of an empty plastic water or milk jug and place over young plants to protect them from freezing.

Water
Gardens need an inch of water a week. But how do you know how long to water to achieve that goal? Place a can, pot, or glass under your sprinkler and see how long it takes for the container to collect an inch of water. Once you have this information, install automatic timers on your watering systems. Watering less often for a longer period of time allows deep penetration and reduces

the total amount of water consumed.

Weed killer

Here's a great weed killer you can make for less than $2 a gallon. Dissolve 1 pound table salt in 1 gallon white vinegar (5 percent acidity is ideal). Add 8 drops of liquid dishwashing detergent (helps plant material absorb the liquid). Label and keep out of reach of children. Use in an ordinary spray bottle. This nontoxic formulation acts as a temporary soil sterilizer, so don't spray near roots of trees, shrubs, or plants you'd like to keep. I find it especially effective on my gravel driveway.

Wick while away

If you must leave small potted plants unattended while on vacation, push a needle threaded with wool yarn into the soil, and put the other end in a jar of water. The plants will stay moist through this wicking system.

Wilted roses

Don't throw away wilting roses; dry them instead. They can almost always be salvaged by hanging them upside down, stems and all, and putting them in a dark, dry place. It takes one to two weeks, but when they're good and dry, they are absolutely gorgeous. Just spray them carefully with shellac or craft glaze and use them in wreaths, vases, or give them as gifts. Dried roses cost up to $12 per half dozen in craft stores.

Worms and bugs

To keep bugs and worms away from outdoor plants and houseplants, add a clove of garlic to the soil.

[illegible] the right amount of water con-[illegible]

Weed killer

[illegible] weed killer you can make for less than $2 a gallon. Dissolve 1 pound table salt in 1 gallon white vinegar (5 percent acid). [illegible] dead. Add 8 drops of liquid dish-washing detergent [illegible] Use in an ordinary spray bottle. This non-selective [illegible] so don't spray near [illegible] plants you [illegible] to keep [illegible] especially [illegible] growing [illegible]

[illegible] while away

If [illegible] have small potted plants [illegible] while on vacation, push a needle threaded with wool yarn [illegible] the soil and put the other end in a [illegible] of water. The plants will stay moist through this wicking system.

Wilted roses

Don't throw away wilting roses [illegible] them instead. They can almost always be salvaged by hanging them upside down, stems and all, and putting them in a dark, dry place. It takes one to two weeks, but when they're good and dry, they are absolutely gorgeous. Just spray them carefully with shellac or hair spray and use them in a vase, or give them as gifts. Dried roses cost up to $12 per half dozen in craft stores.

[illegible] and bugs

[illegible] outdoor pots and houseplants, add a clove of garlic to the soil.

HOME IMPROVEMENT & REPAIR

Aluminum like new

Make aluminum doors or window casings look new by scrubbing a ball of aluminum foil back and forth across the pitting.

Balcony solution

If your home or vacation spot has widely spaced posts on an outdoor balcony, get a roll of plastic webbing for repairing lawn chairs and weave it between the posts to protect anyone or anything from falling through.

Battery changes in smoke detectors

Fire safety officials remind us to change the batteries in our smoke detectors and home security systems every 6 months. Get into the habit of changing batteries whenever the time changes in the spring and again in the fall. But don't throw away the old batteries. They still have lots of life remaining and can be used in radios, toys, pagers, etc.

Bleached-out rug spots

Color in the bleached-out spot in your carpeting (often occurs near a bathroom where bleaching products have splashed or dripped) with a nontoxic marking pen in a shade as close as you can find to that of the rug. This is exactly what a carpet professional would do if you called for repair.

Bookcases

If you don't have a free wall for a bookcase, try squeezing a compact library around a doorway. Find a home for cookbooks in the same way by encircling a kitchen window with shelves.

Bucket stilts

If you need to do some work on the ceiling, 5-gallon buckets make good, stable stilts. Remove or tape down the wire handle on each bucket, turn the bucket upside down, make a foot stirrup out of duct tape, and off you go. You don't want the tape to stick to your shoes, so double it, sticky side to sticky side, on the part that your foot slides under.

Built-in shelves

You'll gain shelves without sacrificing floor space if you break into the wall and install built-in shelves between the studs (vertical structural supports).

Carpet bargain

If you are not in a big hurry and are fairly flexible as to color and quality, let the carpet stores in your area that offer "Complete Satisfaction Guaranteed" know that you would be interested in purchasing the carpeting someone else rejected. Many times when new carpet is installed, the homeowner for one reason or another is not completely satisfied with some aspect of the carpet and takes advantage of the carpet supplier's satisfaction guarantee. You should be able to make a real bargain on the like-new goods, including installation.

Caulking

For the smoothest finish, run an ice cube over fresh caulking to shape it and get rid of lumps.

Circuit breakers

Never turn circuit breakers on in pairs or more. Turn them on one at a time, and pause slightly after each to prevent a power surge.

Citronella in the paint

A few drops of oil of citronella added to a bucket of paint will keep mosquitoes and other flying insects away from a fresh paint job.

Clean a saw

Oven cleaner will remove gummy deposits on the teeth of a saw.

Clogged drain

If a drain is completely stopped up, don't try to clear it with chemical drain cleaners. They may bubble back up into the sink or tub and cause permanent damage to the finish of the fixture. If there's only a moderate clog, pour boiling water with a few teaspoons of ammonia down the drain, wait a few minutes, then plunge.

Clogged drain

Pour ½ cup washing soda (not baking soda) directly down the drain, then slowly and carefully add 2 quarts boiling water. This weekly preventive maintenance will ensure that clogs will never be a problem.

Coffee solution

Make your own inexpensive cover-up for furniture scratches: Mix instant coffee and water into a thick paste and apply it to hide nicks and scratches on dark wood furniture.

Control the paint mess

When you're painting or doing other messy jobs around the house, keep a couple of plastic sandwich bags nearby. If you have to answer the door or the telephone, just slip your hand in a bag and avoid spreading the mess.

Cracked window

If you suffer a broken window, protect yourself and the sash frame until you can replace the glass by taping the crack with packing or weather-stripping tape. Don't count on this temporary fix to hold for very long.

Cubbies

Here's an uplifting idea: Don't forget to look up for extra storage. A row of cubbies (storage boxes) attached to the wall over coat hooks is one example of found space. Other logical locations are above a washer or dryer, chest of drawers, medicine cabinet, or window.

Doors that slam

To cushion the bang of a door that has a habit of slamming shut, glue ⅛-inch-thick pieces of foam rubber along the stop.

Doors that stick

Use carbon paper to find where a door is sticking. Place the carbon paper between the door and the jamb with the dirty side facing the door. Close. Open and the high spot on the door should be covered with the carbon.

Drain maintenance

To clear a sluggish drain, pour 1 cup baking soda into the drain followed by 1 cup white vinegar. Allow to sit overnight. In the morning flush with a kettle full of boiling water. Plunge the drain a few times with a plunger. This is an excellent maintenance tactic to keep drains running well.

Drill a water leak

If you notice water leaking through the ceiling, drill a hole immediately to allow the water to drain out before it damages the plaster or drywall. Later, after the leak is repaired, all you'll need to cover the emergency repair is a dab of Spackle and touch-up paint.

Drips into the sponge

Push a paintbrush handle through a slit in a sponge. It'll stop the drips from running onto your hand.

Exact measurements

Mark pint, quart, and gallon measurements on a bucket with red fingernail polish to make sure you never have to guess on the measurements.

Finishing wood

Soft woods like pine, poplar, and fir may absorb stain unevenly. To test for firmness, press your thumbnail into the wood. If it leaves an indentation, it's a soft wood. Seal all soft woods before staining by coating with a wood conditioner.

Fix leaky faucets

A faucet leaking 60 drops a minute wastes 113 gallons of water a month. That's 1,356 gallons a year down the drain.

Freeze rollers and brushes

When tackling a painting job you may not be able to complete in one day, don't waste the paint in the rollers and brushes by cleaning them. Simply wrap tightly in plastic wrap and store in the freezer. Remove them from the freezer a little while before you start painting again, and you can pick up right where you left off.

Frozen pipes

First open the faucet to release pressure from thawing water. Then apply heat with a hair dryer, heat gun, or heat lamp, starting at the faucet side of the frozen area.

Frozen pipes prevention

If a particular pipe in your home freezes regularly, allow the corresponding faucet to drip ever so slightly when subfreezing weather is predicted.

Furnace filter restoration

Instead of replacing your furnace filter each month or as recommended by the manufacturer, vacuum it, and spray the cleaned filter with Endust. This will restore the dust-catching ability of the recycled filter, allowing it to continue working effectively for three additional periods before it should be replaced.

Glued-on glue caps

If your glue cap keeps getting stuck to the tube, coat the inside with petroleum jelly, and it will open easily.

Glue it up

Almost anything can be attached to a wall with a hot-glue gun. When you want to move it or simply reposition, a few seconds from your hair dryer will reheat the glue, soften it, and then you can move it easily. The best part? No more unsightly nail holes. (Test this first inside a closet, and use common sense in determining how much weight to hang with this method.)

Grease marks on wallpaper

Remove a grease spot from wallpaper by rubbing baby powder into it. This serves as an absorbent.

Hair dryer revival

If your once-trusty hair dryer sounds like it's gasping for its last breath or turns itself off midsession, check the intake vent before you toss it out. When those air holes are clogged with hair or dust, the unit overheats, and its built-in safety mechanism turns off the motor. To clear the air holes, run a vacuum over the clogged holes.

Hanging on papered wall

To hang pictures on wallpaper: Cut a notch in the paper, bend it back gently, then drive the nail into the wall. If you remove the nail later, you can simply glue the paper flap over the hole, and there won't be an ugly blemish on the paper.

Hinges that squeak

Lubricate the pin on a squeaky hinge with petroleum jelly instead of oil. You won't need to worry about drips on the floor.

Hold nail with a comb

The best way to hammer a very small nail into the wall is to place the nail between the teeth of a tiny comb, hold the comb to the wall, and hammer away.

How much paint is left

Mark the level of paint on the outside of the can so you can tell how much paint is left without reopening.

Identify clear finish

To identify the type of clear finish on wood so you can refinish it, touch the finish with a cotton ball dampened with nail polish remover. If the cotton ball sticks or the finish softens, it's varnish, lacquer, or shellac. If there's no effect, it's polyurethane. The best tool for removing old finish from carvings and other hard-to-reach areas is a natural bristle paintbrush with the edges trimmed to a stubby length.

Insulate

Many utility companies give rebates for this type of home improvement because it conserves so much energy. As a bonus, you'll save a lot of money on heating and cooling costs.

Keyholes glow in the dark

Brush keyholes with luminous paint, and you won't fumble for the lock in the dark.

HOME

Ladder socks

Place a pair of athletic socks on the top of an extension ladder to protect aluminum siding from the ladder's sharp edges.

Leaking toilet

Find the water leaks. Give your home this test: Turn off all running water in the house. Find your water meter and take a look. Is it still moving? Chances are you have a water leak, and chances are even better it's your toilet. Put a few drops of food coloring into the toilet's tank. If without flushing, the color shows up in the bowl, it's leaking all right. Get a toilet repair kit at the home repair center. This is a very simple do-it-yourself repair.

Miniblinds

Instead of replacing worn metal miniblinds, paint them. Wash them with soap and water in the bathtub, rinse thoroughly, and dry completely. Carefully spray paint them. Selecting the same or similar shade will make the job easier.

Nails, screws, and heat

To keep the wall or plaster from splitting or cracking when hammering in a nail, drop the nail into a pot of hot water for 15 seconds, then carefully hammer it in. To remove a stubborn screw, pass a lighted match over the end of the screwdriver; the hot tip will then twist out the screw.

No doors painted shut

Fold a couple of sheets of newspaper over the top of doors. You won't be able to paint the door shut—no matter how hard you try.

Nonslip paint

When painting outside steps, add a bit of fine sand to the paint to create a nonslip surface.

Nursery security viewer

So that you can check on your sleeping infant without making noise or waking her up, install a security door viewer in the nursery door.

Overbuilding the neighborhood

Be very cautious if you're tempted to overbuild the neighborhood. Usually, the most expensive house in the neighborhood appreciates the least.

Paint barrier

Cover hands and face with a very thin film of petroleum jelly before you start painting. Paint splashes will simply wash off.

Paintbrushes

Soften hard paintbrushes in hot vinegar for a few minutes. Then wash paintbrush in soap and warm water and set out to dry.

Paint can drips

Glue a paper plate to the bottom of a paint can to catch drips. Before you open the can, apply several dots of glue from a glue gun to a plate. Position the can on the dots and let sit 5 minutes. (Or place a small amount of paint on the paper plate) It's much more convenient than newspaper because when you pick up the can, the plate goes along.

Painter's trick of the trade

Before you begin painting window frames, cut strips of newspaper, dip them in water, and press them onto the glass close to the frame. When the paint dries, moisten the newspaper with a damp sponge and peel it right off. Presto! No messy window panes to scrape clean after the painting is done, and no sticky tape to remove.

Painting around door hardware

Before painting a door, coat the knobs, locks, and hinges with petroleum jelly. Afterward, use a cloth to wipe off the jelly and any paint that may have been spilled. Use this method on window edges as well.

Painting stairs

If you need to paint the stairs while living in the house, do this: Paint every other step. Let those dry thoroughly, mark them with a piece of masking tape and then paint the rest. Taking the steps two at a time during this renovation should give the family some great exercise.

Paint scraper and remover

An old, metal kitchen spatula is perfect for scraping up softened paint remover and paint. Regular paint scrapers have sharp corners that make it all too easy to scratch or gouge the wood.

Paint storage

Store partially full cans of paint upside down. The paint will form an airtight seal, extending its useful life.

Paint strainer

If the paint appears lumpy or contains debris, stretch a pair of pantyhose over the top of a clean bucket and strain the paint by pouring it through the hose into the bucket.

Papering around outlets

When wallpapering over outlets, first insert childproof electrical outlet plugs. When you cut through the paper, you won't get a shock.

Penetrating oil substitute

If you don't have penetrating oil and need to loosen a nut, screw, or bolt, use vinegar, lemon juice, or hot pepper sauce instead. All of these products contain acid that attacks minerals and rust.

Picture grouping

To hang a group of pictures, try arranging them on a big piece of butcher paper first. When you have a grouping you like, trace around each frame with a pen and mark where to put the nails. Tape the paper to the wall and nail through the marks; remove tape and paper.

Picture marker

Replace picture hooks with thumbtacks before you paint a wall. Paint over the tack, then remove it once the wall is dry. Now you can rehang pictures in exactly the same spot, using the same hole for the hook.

Quick funnel

Cut off the bottom of an empty, plastic, quart soda bottle and use the top as a funnel.

Reference information

When you finish refurbishing a room in your home, write down this important information on a piece of paper and tape it to the back of the switch plate: the brand and color of the paint, how much it took to paint the room, how many rolls of wallpaper were required, and the circuit breaker number that serves this room. You'll be happy to find the information the next time.

Refinish ceramic tile

If your kitchen or bathroom is suffering from outdated avocado green or some other 1970s colored ceramic tile, and you don't choose to replace it at this time, do this: Purchase a product like Fleckstone (manufactured by Plasti-kote), available at home improvement centers. It is a multihue, textured spray paint sold together with a clear acrylic topcoat that, when applied as directed, produces "new" tile that can be cleaned with a damp sponge. Even if it takes five kits to do the job, you'll spend around $50, and that sure beats remodeling.

Relaxing wallpaper

If vinyl wallpaper is too tightly curled, you can relax it with a hair dryer set on warm. Hold the dryer 6 to 8 inches away, and wave it back and forth over the paper.

Remove transparent tape

Remove transparent tape from walls by warming it slightly with a hair dryer.

Remove wallpaper

To strip stubborn wallpaper before painting or repapering, saturate the paper with equal parts vinegar and hot water or 1 part fabric softener to 3 parts water. Use a tracing wheel (a sewing notion) to puncture holes in the paper and stripping will be even easier. The holes permit the vinegar or fabric softener solution to get behind the paper and soften the old paste quickly. Work in small sections at a time. Peel after 10 minutes.

Rolling painter

Borrow your kid's skateboard when painting baseboards. Sit on it and roll along as you work.

Roof repair

If you have a loose or missing roof shingle, slip a piece of sheet metal or builder's felt (tar paper) over the damaged area and under the shingle above. Hold it in place with dabs of roofing cement.

Rubber mallet

Cut an X in an old tennis ball and put it on the head of a hammer to make a rubber mallet.

Rust-free nails

Prevent nails from rusting by placing them in airtight jars with a little WD-40 or oil.

Safe, not sorry

Before you take something apart to fix it, take an instant photo so you can see how it fits back together. To help you remember how to reassemble it, place each part in the correct sequence onto the sticky side of a piece of duct tape.

Sagging clothesrod repair

To fix a sagging wooden closet rod, buy a length of ½-inch galvanized pipe and a length of ¾-inch thin-wall PVC (plastic polyvinyl chloride) piping, both the same length as your rod. You can get these at your local home improvement center. Slip the pipe inside the PVC and slide them into the existing rod brackets. If you are bothered by the printing on the PVC, clean it off with rubbing alcohol.

Sanding block

To sand irregular edges of tabletops or chair legs, use a deck of playing cards as a sanding block.

Sanding dust
Dampen a rag with rubbing alcohol, and clean sanded surfaces prior to applying stain or finish.

Sanding tiny spaces
Use an emery board to sand small or hard-to-reach areas like shutter slats or drawer runners.

Sandpaper
To make sandpaper or emery paper last longer, back it with masking tape. The tape helps keep the paper from tearing or creasing while you are working and increases its longevity by 2 to 3 times.

Sandpaper cases
Use old 45-rpm record sleeves to store sandpaper. The covers keep the sandpaper sorted, with the holes in the covers showing the grade and grit of each paper. Find these sleeves at garage sales and thrift stores.

Save the caulk
Keep a caulk-gun tip covered with a ballpoint-pen top to prevent it from drying out.

Scraping paint from windows
To quickly scrape the dried paint from windows, use a single-edged razor blade that you dip into a solution of liquid soap and water. The blade will glide along and the job will take little time and effort.

Screw anchor
Here's how to anchor a screw in a plaster wall: First make the hole by driving a nail into the plaster. Plug the hole with fine steel wool. The screw will go in firmly—and stay.

Screw hole
If a screw hole in wood furniture becomes too large to hold the screw, try this: Remove the screw and pack the hole with toothpicks and wood glue. Wait for the glue to dry, then trim the toothpicks even with the surface. Redrill the hole, and replace the screw.

Sharpen scissors
Sharpen scissors by cutting several times into 220 grit sandpaper. Turn scissors over and repeat to sharpen bottom blade too.

Showing your house
If you're looking for a buyer, be sure to present your home at its very best when a potential buyer looks at it. Get rid of knickknacks, extra furniture, and anything that makes the house look cluttered. Too much clutter distracts from the house's good

points. Draw the curtains back, open the doors, and turn on the lights. Bright light makes your rooms look larger and more spacious.

Shuttered screen

To hide an under-the-window radiator or air conditioner when not in use, hinge together three 30-inch-high shutters to form a folding screen.

Slide that drawer

To remedy a sticky drawer, rub the sides with a candle.

Small parts

When repairing appliances, line up small parts on masking tape to keep them in order and to prevent their mysterious disappearance.

Smoke detectors

To keep detectors operating properly, carefully vacuum them annually.

Soft paintbrushes

Keep paintbrushes soft by giving them a final rinse in water into which you've added a bit of liquid fabric softener.

Spray cans

Hold a spray can of anything upside down to clear the nozzle between uses. While completely inverted, spray a few times to clear the passage.

Spring-clean windowsills

Instead of trying to scrub windowsills clean each spring, just paint them. It's faster, and the results are much better.

Squeaky stair step and floors

Both squeaky stairs and floorboards can often be silenced temporarily with talcum powder. Work the powder into the cracks and wipe away excess. Repeat as necessary.

Squirt gun as wallpaper tool

Keep a child's squirt gun handy when wallpapering. It is perfect for dampening corners that have dried out or didn't get quite wet enough the first time around.

Sticking screen door

Sliding screen door lost its smooth gliding action? Rub an old candle along the bottom metal track of the door's frame. It will work like new again without a drippy, oily mess.

Storing wood stain

Store leftover water-based stain in a thoroughly cleaned-out ketchup bottle with a flip-top lid. You'll be able to dispense exactly the amount you want with no mess. Be sure to label the bottle with the exact contents.

Storm windows, screens

To keep track of where storm windows and screens go, draw a diagram of the house, and number each window frame. Use a permanent marker to write the same number on the corner of the appropriate storm window or screen. Attach the diagram to the garage or basement wall, and you'll never have to guess which window or screen goes where.

Stubborn clothesrod

If hangers don't glide along the clothesrod, rub it with waxed paper or a candle.

Stud finding

Studs are the vertical wooden supports behind your walls. They're handy for hanging pictures and such because a nail or screw is more likely to stay in place when it's been driven into a stud (as opposed to just the drywall). Locate studs behind a wall by finding the electrical outlet (which is attached to one side of a stud), and measure 16 inches in either direction to find the next stud. Note: Some new homes have studs 24-inches on center.

Take a freezer break

If you want to take a break from painting for a couple of hours—or a couple of days—store the brush in a zippered storage bag. If you won't get back to the job until tomorrow, wrap the brushes and rollers tightly in plastic wrap and place in the freezer.

Temporary fix

If your roof leaks, control that leak by tacking a string into the roof sheathing where the water comes through. Place a bucket under it. The water will run down the string into the bucket rather than your ceiling.

Toilet replacement

Before forking out the big bucks to purchase a toilet or sink, check with a local plumbing contractor. Many times they have used items that are in perfect condition because they were removed from new homes when the homeowner wanted to upgrade or change the color.

Uneven furniture legs

If a furniture leg is uneven, try buttons of different sizes under the leg until you find one that makes it even. Hot glue around the button edge and position in place.

Unstick a painted-shut window

Don't try to pry open with a screwdriver a window that has been painted shut. Instead, move a pizza cutter back and forth in the stubborn groove.

Unstick the stuck

Items stuck together with a glue gun can often be pried apart if heated with a hair dryer. You may also heat a thin-bladed knife from a hobby or art supply store, then carefully work it between the two items.

Use a potato

If an electric bulb breaks off in the socket, follow this simple procedure: Turn off power to the fixture by either unplugging the fixture or turning off power at the main service panel. Cut a potato in half, and push one of the halves into the broken bulb piece. Turn the potato, and the broken piece will come right out.

Vinyl tile removal

To remove a vinyl floor tile, aim a hair dryer set on medium at the tile's corners and center. Heat will cause the adhesive on the underside of the tile to become moist and sticky. Slowly work a putty knife between the tile and the floor to pry loose.

Wallpaper bubbles

Remove bubbles and blisters from wallpaper by cutting an X with a very sharp razor blade and regluing.

Wallpapering tricks

If you're using prepasted paper, use a plant mister to moisten it. A hand-held squeegee is a great tool for smoothing prepasted wallpaper quickly and evenly.

Wallpaper preparation

Two days before you plan to wallpaper, reroll the roll of paper the opposite way. The paper will be flat, and the job will go faster.

Wallpaper removal

To remove wallpaper, start by cutting several crisscrosses in each panel of paper with a utility knife so the wallpaper remover or steam can seep into the cuts and help loosen the paper.

Water heaters

Periodically drain off some hot water to keep sediment from accumulating at the bottom of the tank. In areas with hard water, draining is best done every month.

White glue rescue

To soften white glue in a plastic bottle, place the bottle in boiling water for a few seconds until the glue softens. If it's in a glass bottle, run hot tap water over the bottle for a minute or two, then place in simmering water. Or simply add a bit of white vinegar and stir with a skewer.

White grout

Use white shoe polish, the kind with an applicator top, to clean, whiten, and brighten stained tile grout. Simply apply the polish, wipe the tiles with a damp cloth, allow to dry, and buff.

Window screen patch

To repair a small tear in a window screen, cut a square patch a little larger than the damaged area. (You can buy screening at the hardware store.) Unravel and remove a few strands of wire from all four sides. Bend the wire ends over till you can slip them through the screen. Then bend them farther to hold the patch in place.

Air conditioner filter

To clean an air conditioner or humidifier filter, take the foam filter out of the grill and soak it in a solution of equal parts white vinegar and warm water. If you clean the filter regularly, an hour of soaking will be plenty. Just squeeze the filter dry when it's clean, and place it back in the air conditioner.

Air freshener alternative

Instead of using highly perfumed and expensive room refreshers, you can easily get rid of unpleasant odors simply by lighting a match.

Area rugs

Instead of buying finished area rugs, purchase a remnant from a carpet store, have it bound, and save a bundle. The carpet store can either bind it for you or refer you to someone who can.

Art display

To display posters, maps, or children's artwork on the wall without marring the art or the wall, put a dab of toothpaste at each corner and press on the wall. Sounds goofy, but it works really well, and you end up with an undamaged, minty-fresh wall.

Ashes

Wood ashes can be used as a degreaser. Sprinkle 4 tablespoons of ashes on a greasy pot or grill, then scrub with a sponge or brush dipped in warm, soapy water.

Baking soda

Baking soda is a nonabrasive cleanser. Use it without worry on fine china, porcelain appliances, the inside of the refrigerator, stainless steel, aluminum, and cast iron. You can use it either in its powdered form or mix it with water to make a paste. Baking soda is a wonderful cleaner for everything from countertops to rolling pins to gold-trimmed dishes. If you want to remove an offensive odor, think baking soda.

Baking soda dispenser

Keep baking soda handy by pouring some into a dispenser with a sprinkle top. An old salt or pepper shaker or parmesan cheese dispenser that is refillable works well. Use it for microwave oven cleanup and to rid the counter of coffee stains.

Ball-point ink

Really cheap hairspray removes ball-point ink from plastic because it has a high amount of acetone.

Black heel marks

To remove black scuff marks from any hard surface floor, rub them with a paste of soda and water and a plastic scrubber. Use as little water as possible to ensure best results.

Blocked vacuum hose

To dislodge a vacuum hose clog, turn the vacuum off and unplug. Unwind a metal hanger and, leaving a slight hook on the end, slide hook into hose to remove blockage.

Blot it out

After you clean a spot on the carpet, don't rub it dry. Instead, place a clean, white towel on top, and weight it down with a book or heavy jar. Leave it overnight and it will act as a blotter to transfer all traces of the stain and whatever you used to treat the stain to the towel.

Bottle brush

Remove hair from a drain with a bottle brush.

Brass

Polish outdoor brass with lemon and salt. Cut a lemon in half, dip the cut side into salt, and use as an applicator. Do not use this on brass that has a permanent protective coating.

Brass cleaner

Rub the surface of brass with a slice of fresh lemon sprinkled with baking soda. Rinse well; wipe dry.

Brass, copper, bronze

Small brass, copper, or bronze objects can be cleaned and gleamed with a little toothpaste. Be sure to remove all traces of toothpaste with a soft brush, soap, and water. Any that is left will dry as hard as cement.

Buying or selling a home

Take photographs both inside and outside of the house, and make them part of the contract along with a list of what stays with the property after the sale. This eliminates debate at the closing as to whether the dining room fixture was a crystal chandelier or a bare bulb.

HOMEKEEPING

Candleholders
Remove wax from candleholders by placing them in the freezer until the wax freezes and snaps off.

Candleholders
Clean wax drips from candleholders by putting them on a cookie sheet lined with a paper towel in a warm oven. The towel will catch the wax as it drips.

Candles
Clean dusty, dingy candles by wiping them with rubbing alcohol.

Candles
Fit a candle into a really tight holder by holding the bottom end of the candle under hot running water. It should soften just enough so that you can firmly place it in the holder.

Carpet barrier
Use a small plastic basket in which berries are sold to cover a place on the carpet you've just spot-shampooed. Upside down, the basket permits air to circulate, yet keeps family members, even pets, off the spot until it dries.

Carpet cleaning
Plan your departure time wisely enough so you can shampoo your carpets right before you're ready to walk out the door for a weekend trip or vacation. The carpet can dry without foot traffic for several days while you're gone.

Carpet maintenance
Two high quality, $40 doormats, one outside the back door and one outside the front, can save your $1000 carpet. Buy them large enough so that everyone has to take at least two steps on them to reach the door.

Carpet scrubber
The best tool for scrubbing a carpet spot is another piece of carpeting.

Carpet stains
Rubbing alcohol is an easy and inexpensive spot remover for carpets. Lightly rub a drop or two of alcohol into the stain, then blot the spot dry with a clean, white cloth.

Carpet stains
Here's a highly effective and economical way to remove stains from carpeting: Mix together one part Tide powder, two parts white vinegar, and two parts warm water. Scrub soiled area, then rinse with clear, warm water. From oil to mud to wine stains, they'll all disappear.

Cedar chips vs. moths
Here's an easy and inexpensive way to make moth repellent. Purchase a bag of cedar chips from a pet supply shop where a large bag is only a few dollars. Put one or two cupfuls into resealable bags and poke small holes in them. Hang the bags in your closets and drawers. The lovely, fresh scent repels moths.

Ceiling fan
An umbrella hung upside down from a ceiling fan catches dirt and drips when you're cleaning the fixture.

Ceramic tile floors
Mop ceramic tile floors with a solution of 1 gallon hot water and 1 cup vinegar—no soap. The floor will shine and sparkle like new—no rinsing required. While hot water might work to remove dirt, it will have a dulling affect because of the minerals in the water that are left behind. Vinegar cuts and removes those minerals, getting rid of that cloudy film.

Chandelier
Hang an umbrella upside down from the chandelier to catch the drips while you're cleaning it. Pour 2 parts isopropyl rubbing alcohol and 1 part warm water into a spray bottle. Spray chandelier liberally, and allow the fixture to drip dry.

Charcoal in a bag
Fill a net vegetable bag with charcoal and hang in the musty basement or damp garage to absorb odors.

Chrome
A quick and easy cleaner for chrome is baby oil sprinkled on a damp cloth.

Chrome
To clean chrome, wipe with a soft cloth dipped in undiluted white or cider vinegar.

Chrome
Nail polish remover gives chrome a nice sparkle. Be careful. It's strong stuff and could remove the color from anything it touches around the chrome.

Chrome fixtures
Clean chrome fixtures with a damp cloth sprinkled with baking soda.

Cinnamon in vacuum
Place a cinnamon stick in the vacuum bag before vacuuming to naturally deodorize your home.

Cleaning cloths
Handi-Wipes (disposable dishcloths) purchased at the supermarket are sold

to be disposable but are actually very reusable. Rather than discard them when you've completed your cleaning, just toss them in the washing machine along with your regular laundry.

Cleaning deadlines

Invite company over at least once a month so you'll be forced to clean up. Keep the bathtub clean so you can hide clutter in it at a moment's notice.

Cleaning house

Get an apron with lots of pockets. Put the supplies you need for each room in the pockets so you have everything you need at your fingertips. Use one of the pockets to hold a soapy sponge (in a plastic bag) for touch-up work around light switches, doorjambs, etc.

Cleaning rags

To save yourself from rummaging for cleaning rags every time you clean, use a rubber band to attach a cloth to each cleaning product that requires one. When you're finished, just tuck the rag back under the rubber band. Wash or replace cloths periodically.

Cleaning skinny spaces

How do you clean that little bit of floor between the refrigerator and the wall? Tie a nylon net scrubbie over the end of a yardstick or broom handle, securing it tightly with string or twine. Use it first to pull out any debris and dust, then wet it with a detergent-water solution and scrub away.

Clean wallpaper stains

First, blot with talcum powder to absorb the stain. Then wash delicate wallpaper with warm, soapy water. Add white vinegar to the water to clean grease stains.

Closet fragrance

Keep the linen closet smelling fresh: Spray cotton balls with your favorite fragrance. Once dry, stash them into closet corners and shelves.

Cloth napkins

Rather than buying paper napkins, keep a decorative wooden basket on the kitchen table filled with cloth napkins you've made from new cotton sheets. You can make 16 to 24 napkins from 1 twin sheet. You can either serge the edges or hem them on a regular sewing machine. Throw them into your regular laundry, and in no time you'll get into the habit of fresh, soft, cloth napkins. They also make nice gifts that even an amateur seamstress can make.

Copper
For tarnished copper, fill a spray bottle with hot white vinegar and 3 tablespoons salt. Spray liberally, let sit briefly, then rinse with warm, soapy water and wipe clean. Don't use on lacquered items.

Copper, brass
To clean copper and brass that does not have a factory-applied protective coating, dissolve 1 teaspoon salt in ½ cup white vinegar. Add enough flour to make a paste. Apply the paste and let sit for 15 minutes to 1 hour. Rinse with clean, warm water, and polish dry.

Cord hiders
Put self-stick plastic hooks on the wall or window frame next to drapes and blinds. Keep any loose cords looped around the hook.

Crayon marks on chalkboard
An oil-based lubricating spray like WD-40 or a prewash treatment like Soilove should easily remove the crayon marks without damaging the chalkboard. Test first, then spray the stains and allow to penetrate for a few minutes; wipe off with a clean, dry cloth. Add a few drops of liquid dishwashing detergent to warm water, and with a clean sponge wipe down the board to remove all oily residue. Rinse well with warm water and dry with a clean cloth.

Crayon marks on floors and walls
Get rid of crayon marks from a linoleum floor by rubbing lightly with a dab of silver polish. To remove your child's crayon marks from painted walls, dip a damp cloth into baking soda and rub the spot gently.

Crayon marks on slate
To remove crayon marks on a slate fireplace hearth: Use an art-gum eraser available at an art supply or stationery store. Just knead it until it's pliable, then press it against the crayon marks, and "pull" them off. Continue kneading and pressing until all the marks are removed.

Creaseless cloth napkins
To store cloth napkins without creases, wrap and store them around a cardboard tube.

Crystal
Clean crystal vases, glasses, chandelier crystals, or any kind of bottle that's been clouded by a calcium coating: Fill a large container with soapy water and add a good shot of white vinegar. Allow items to sit in the solution for 2 to 3 hours.

Curling iron

To clean the buildup of scorched hairspray and other products from a curling iron, scrub the iron with a soft cloth that has been soaked with undiluted rubbing alcohol.

Curtain key weights

Place old keys in the hems of curtains to keep them hanging straight. If necessary, put a stitch or two through the holes in the top of the keys to keep them in place.

Cushions

To keep your sofa cushions from slipping and sliding, place a bath mat or square of foam rubber under each cushion.

Daffodils

Place daffodils in a separate vase of water for half a day before combining them in a bouquet with other flowers. They excrete a sap that clogs the stems of other flowers.

Dejunk your home

If you are like most people, you have about twice as much stuff as you really like, use, or need. Here's a new rule to live by: Have nothing in your home that you do not know to be useful or believe to be beautiful. If something doesn't fit into one of those two categories, get rid of it.

Diaper pail

To clean a foul smelling diaper pail, begin by filling the empty pail with a solution of 1 cup liquid chlorine bleach to each gallon of hot water, and allow to soak overnight. Empty the pail into the toilet or bathtub, rinse it out, and rub the inside with a paste of baking soda and water; let stand overnight. In the morning, rinse the pail, and it will be ready to use. To prevent odors from returning, change water often and sprinkle the pail with baking soda.

Dog hair from carpet

Try this trick to remove unsightly dog and cat hair from your carpet: Spray a mixture of 1 part fabric softener to 3 parts water on your rug, wait a minute or two and then vacuum. No more animal hair.

Drawer liners

Place mats, because they're washable, make excellent drawer liners.

Drip, drip, drip

If a leaky faucet is keeping you up nights, try this trick until you can get it fixed: Tie a piece of fabric, long enough to touch the drain, around the faucet. The water will run down the fabric, thus eliminating that annoying drip.

Dust cloths
Make your own dust cloths by dipping cheesecloth into a mixture of 2 cups water and ¼ cup lemon oil. Do not rinse, and allow to dry thoroughly before using. When dirty, wash and repeat.

Dusting delicately
New paintbrushes are terrific for dusting something delicate that needs a light touch, such as a lamp shade or silk flowers.

Dusting those tight places
Wear cotton gloves sprayed with furniture polish to dust hard-to-reach places.

Dust mop
To clean a dust mop indoors, pull an oversized plastic bag over the head of the mop, tie the top, and shake the mop vigorously so the dust falls into the bag.

Dustpan
Spray your dustpan with furniture polish, and the dust will slip right off.

Dusty curtains
Don't dry-clean curtains that are simply dusty. Toss them in the dryer with a couple of dry sheets on "air-dry." This will fluff them up and loosen and release the dust.

Dusty curtains, pillows
Put dusty pillows, curtains, and slipcovers in the dryer. Set it on cool, and toss in a fabric softener sheet for fragrance.

Earring down the drain
If you drop an earring or pin down the drain, attach a small magnet to a stiff piece of twine or wire, and use it to grab the item and pull it out.

Extension-handled duster
Stick a fluffy feather duster into the hollow end of a cane fishing pole, sold at import stores for about $1. Now you have an extension handle that will allow you to remove cobwebs that form on your high-vaulted ceilings and ceiling fans.

Faucets
Lime deposits around faucets can be softened for easy removal by covering the deposits with vinegar-soaked paper towels. Leave paper towels on for about one hour before cleaning. Leaves chrome clean and shiny.

Fireplace bellows
Empty, squeezable plastic bottles can serve as bellows; use them to fan a wood or charcoal fire.

Fireplace doors

To clean those dirty, glass fireplace doors, mix some of the wood ashes with a little water. Apply this paste with a sponge in a circular motion and rinse off.

Fireplace odor

Remove ashes often for optimum fireplace performance. Each time you remove the ashes, place a shallow pan of baking soda in the fireplace and leave it overnight to attract and absorb unpleasant fireplace odors.

Fireplace starter

For a fireplace log starter, stuff the cups of a paper egg carton with lint from the dryer. Melt paraffin or an old candle, and pour the wax over the lint and allow to harden. Cut into sections. To use, place one of these neat fire-starters under the logs. Light it and it will burn for about 20 minutes.

Firewood

A full cord of firewood is a stack that equals 128 cu. ft. Although usually defined as 4' x 4' x 8', obviously it can be an equal dimension, such as 2' x 4' x 16'. A face cord is a stack of firewood where the "face" is the traditional 4' x 8' but the depth is not the 4' measurement. (It may be any number of feet deep.) This can occur when the wood has been cut in an odd length so that it stacks up to an odd depth (such as two rows deep of 18" wood adds up to 3' deep.) When you purchase firewood, make sure you are getting a full cord.

Firewood in the bag

When gathering kindling or pieces of wood from outdoors for the fireplace, carry them into the house in a brown grocery bag. Place the entire bag and contents into the fireplace and light the bag. This prevents that inevitable trail of wood dirt and debris that always follows the person carrying wood into the house, and it's a tidy way to start a fire.

Floor maintenance between waxings

For a quick shine between floor waxings, dust-mop all the dirt off the floor, then put a piece of waxed paper under the mop and buff the floor lightly.

Floor scratches

Get rid of light scratches in resilient flooring by rubbing with a soft cloth moistened with a small amount of paste floor wax.

Floor wax removal

Mix isopropyl rubbing alcohol 3 to 1 with water for an excellent floor wax remover.

Flower bouquet care

Cut flower stems on a slant with a knife. Angled cuts permit drinking even when the stem rests on the bottom of the container. To aid water intake, scrape stem ends for about an inch; split woody stems with a knife or mash with a hammer. Plunge stems in water immediately after cutting. Remove excess and damaged foliage as well as foliage below water level. Fill the container with clean water; refresh as often as possible by holding the vase under the faucet and flushing with tepid water until the old water is forced out.

Flower extenders

To give stemmed flowers more length for an arrangement, slide them into soda straws before putting them into an opaque vase. If you need to shorten any stems afterward, just snip off the bottom of the straws.

Flowers

Put cut flowers in the refrigerator when you're at work, asleep, or otherwise unable to enjoy them. This will extend their indoor life.

Fragrant home

Here are several ideas for a home, sweet, home: (1) To make your house smell sweet, sprinkle cinnamon on a pan and warm it on the stove. (2) To fill your home with the smell of citrus, throw a handful of orange peels in a pot of boiling water. (3) Each time you clean a room, place a few drops of a fragrant oil on a light bulb, or spray the room with a fresh potpourri scent to give the house a nice smell and to leave a subtle sign that this room is clean! (4) To make your own carpet and room deodorizer, mix 1 cup Epsom salts with a few drops of perfumed oil. Spread the mixture on waxed paper to dry. Store in an airtight container. To use, sprinkle the grains on the carpet, allow to stand for a few minutes, and vacuum as usual. (5) Put a cinnamon stick in the vacuum bag before vacuuming to add a natural deodorizer to your home. (6) Don't throw away lemon rinds or old spices. They make fabulous room deodorizers. Simply place them in a pot of water and bring to a low boil. The scent is better than any potpourri you can buy.

Framed art

When you wash the glass that covers framed art, spray the cleaner on your cloth, not the glass. Otherwise the liquid may work its way inside the glass, damaging the mat or the artwork itself.

Freezer paper
White freezer or butcher paper is perfect for lining kitchen and bathroom cabinets because it is sturdy, extra wide, and quite inexpensive. Place the coated side up to make for easy cleanups, and use thumbtacks to hold down the corners.

Furniture socks
Slip socks over the legs of furniture you're moving to make heavy pieces slide easily and to prevent scratching the floor.

Garbage can odors
To inhibit the growth of odor-producing molds and bacteria, sprinkle ½ cup Borax in the bottom of the garbage can.

Glass thermos
To clean the inside of a glass thermos bottle, place a denture-cleaning tablet in it, fill with warm water, and allow to sit overnight. Rinse thoroughly.

Glass-top tables
Glass-top tables will repel lint if you wash them with a solution of 1 quart warm water and 1 capful liquid fabric softener.

Glycerin attracts dust
Dampen vacuum brushes with a solution of several drops of glycerin to ½ cup water. It attracts dust and hair like a magnet. You can find glycerin in the drugstore.

Green air cleaners
The world's best home air fresheners are green plants. Houseplants help filter the air of indoor pollutants like formaldehyde and benzene. The best of these green air cleaners are spider plants, philodendron, and aloe vera. Work plants into your home's environment whenever you can. One plant for about every 100 square feet can remove up to 87 percent of toxic organic pollutants. And their gift to the home? They produce oxygen.

Grout
Whiten grout between tiles with bleach dabbed on a cotton swab.

Grout
Scrub grout using an old toothbrush with denture-cleaning paste or cleanser.

Grout
Use lengths of cotton stripping (the kind you'd use to protect your hairline during a dye job) that have been soaked in undiluted bleach. Push the

wet cotton against the grout and leave it there. After half an hour, pull away the cotton. This same method works well to clean mildew that forms along the caulking between wall and bathtub.

Grout

Make a paste made of automatic dishwashing detergent and water. Apply to grout using an old toothbrush. When it's dry, rub it off with a terry washcloth.

Grout refinish

If the white grout on your tile has become gray and grimy, that's a fairly good sign the grout was not sealed, in which case there is no way to make it completely white again. But you can paint it white, using an oil-base paint. Ask at your local paint or home improvement store about which type to use. Do this only if the tiles are glazed (sealed); any paint that gets on them can be wiped off with a dry cloth. If paint gets on unglazed tiles it will be absorbed, leaving the tiles looking even more unsightly.

Gum

Raw egg whites will remove chewing gum from anything, including hair, without leaving a trace.

Hairspray on mirrors

To remove hairspray spots from the mirror, dampen a soft cotton cloth with rubbing alcohol and, using a circular motion, wipe them away.

Hanging plants

Here's a way to water a hanging basket indoors without excess water dripping on the floor. Put a few ice cubes on top of the soil, but not against the plant. As the cubes melt, the water will reach the roots slowly enough to be absorbed. By then, it will be warm enough, too.

Hanging sheer curtains

To hang sheers and curtains quickly and easily, insert a table knife—blade-first—into the open end of the curtain rod. It will act as a guide and sheers will glide onto the rod without snagging.

Hard-water marks

Clean hard-water marks from chrome with white vinegar or club soda. Allow to sit a few minutes to dissolve mineral deposits. Polish to a shine with a dry cloth. For stubborn buildup, soak a paper towel in white vinegar and lay it right on the chrome; leave overnight.

Herbal fragrance

For a subtly sweet-smelling table setting, put cinnamon, raspberry, orange, or lemon herbal tea bags in the drawers where you store your table linens.

Hose on hose

Attach panty hose with a rubber band over the end of your vacuum hose when cleaning drawers or searching for a tiny lost object like a contact lens or earring back. The small items cannot be sucked into the nozzle, but you'll find what you've been looking for because it will stick to the hosiery.

Household radiator cleaning

Tape slightly damp newspaper to the wall behind the radiator, and aim a hair dryer set on low right at the dirty, dusty radiator. Hidden dust will blow off and stick onto the damp paper behind.

House-hunting

Take along an instant camera and snap pictures of each house you're interested in. Attach the photos to corresponding notes and information, and at the end of the day, rather than being confused, you'll have a clear record of exactly what you saw.

Iron

You can clean the scorched starch from the bottom of an iron by making a paste of baking soda and a little water, rubbing it on the iron with a soft cloth, and wiping it off with a clean cloth.

Iron cleanup

To remove burned-on starch from your iron, sprinkle salt on a sheet of waxed paper and slide the iron across it several times. Then rub the iron lightly with silver polish until the stain is removed.

Ivory

To clean anything ivory, like piano keys or carved objects, wipe with a solution of 1 tablespoon hydrogen peroxide and 1 cup water. No need to rinse.

Jewelry cleaner

Here's the fine jewelry cleaner professional stores use: Mix equal amounts of household ammonia and water. Drop jewelry into a small container of this cleaner. Allow to sit for a few minutes and brush with an old toothbrush. Rinse well in clear water. It's cheap and it works. Caution: Never use this solution on opals, pearls, or other soft stones.

Jewelry cleaner

Dissolve a denture tablet in a cup of water. Add diamond rings, earrings, and other jewelry. Let them sit an hour. Do not use this with opals, pearls, or other soft stones.

Knives and scissors

To remove rust from knives or scissors, soak them in a mild solution of water and ammonia for 10 minutes. Scrub off rust with a steel-wool soap pad. Rinse and dry.

Labels on wood furniture

If your kids decide to decorate the fine wood furniture with stick-on labels, remove them with lemon oil (the labels, not the kids). Using a paper towel or cloth, dab oil on the labels and allow to soak in for only a few minutes. The oil will penetrate into the glue and act as a solvent to soften it. Rub the labels off with a nylon-net scrubbie, being sure to rub in the direction of the wood grain.

Laminate surfaces

Plastic laminate countertops like Formica that have become dull with age can be brightened by applying a coat of a good automobile wax; allow to dry slightly and buff off. This will also make the surface stain- and scratch-resistant. None of the wax will remain except the shine, so it's perfectly safe to put food on the counter afterward.

Lemon shine

Rub a glass decanter with a lemon or lemon juice to renew shine. Dry with a lint-free cloth.

Light bulbs

Don't dust light bulbs when they're turned on. They might pop in your hand. Switch them off and allow to cool first.

Light globes

Clean the glass globes of your light fixtures in the dishwasher.

Linen storage

For quick and easy bed-making, keep linen sets together. For each set, fold and wrap a top and bottom sheet and one pillowcase together. Then stick them all in the matching pillowcase and store in a drawer right next to the bed.

Locks

Dab a little petroleum jelly on your keys and move them in and out of your car and house locks to keep them working smoothly during the winter months. Petroleum jelly doesn't freeze.

Long duster

Slip a pillowcase over a broom's bristles, tie it on with a twist tie or piece of twine, spray lightly with furniture polish or water, and you'll be able to easily dust high spots and ceilings.

Louvered doors

To clean, dampen a disposable foam paintbrush and wipe between the slats.

Mesh bag

Stuff a mesh produce bag into a drain to catch food particles, hair, and other debris. Be sure to wash it in hot water or in the dishwasher to get rid of bacteria.

Messy pot

Coffee burned on the bottom of your glass pot? Try this old restaurant trick: Fill it with a handful of ice cubes, add two teaspoons of salt, and swirl the pot around for a few minutes to remove coffee stains.

Metal furniture

To clean aluminum, steel, or wrought-iron furniture, wash with a mild liquid detergent and water, then rinse and dry thoroughly. Once a season, apply a coat of automobile wax. If a scratch occurs on wrought iron or steel, apply matching exterior paint with a small artist's brush.

Microwave

Steam clean the interior of your microwave: Stir 2 tablespoons baking soda into a cup of water. Set in the microwave and allow to boil for at least 5 minutes. Remove the bowl and wipe down the inside with a sponge. Once the microwave is clean, place a sheet of wax paper on the bottom to catch future crumbs and spills. When the paper's dirty, replace with a fresh piece. This will not interfere with the microwave oven's operation.

Miniblinds

Use a dampened fabric softener sheet to quick-clean miniblinds and reduce the static cling that attracts dust.

Miniblinds

Clean metal or vinyl miniblinds the fast and easy way: Simply lay the miniblinds in your driveway and spray them with an all-purpose liquid or foaming bathroom cleaner. Rinse with the garden hose, then hang the blinds on a clothesline to dry.

Miniblinds

Put on a rubber glove and an old sock over it. Douse the sock in straight rubbing alcohol and clean away while blinds are in place.

Mirrors

Clean mirrors with cold tea. They'll really shine.

More than dishes
Use the dishwasher to clean brushes, dustpans, and even the dish drainer.

Moving to a new home
If you have a wall arrangement you are particularly fond of or a furniture arrangement that works particularly well, photograph it to use as a reference when you rehang and resettle everything in your new home.

New life for sheers
If your sheer draperies are looking a little limp and tired, wash them and dip them into a sinkful of warm water in which you've dissolved a cup of Epsom salts. Do not rinse. Hang to dry.

Newspaper logs
Make homemade fire logs for the fireplace: Stack some folded newspaper, alternating the folded sides, until the stack is about 1 inch high. Don't use colored comics or advertisements. Roll the stack as tightly as you can. Hold it together with wire or by slipping over each end a small tuna fish (or similar size) can from which you've removed both the top and bottom. Don't use string because it will burn off, and the paper will fly all over the place. When rolled and secured, thoroughly soak the "logs" in water and set them outside to dry completely. Burn with can rings in place.

No-wax floors
To clean a no-wax linoleum floor quickly, mist with a foaming bathroom spray and let stand 5 minutes. Damp-mop the floor to remove the cleaner.

Oatmeal pot
Love hot cereal but hate the mess? Coat the pot with a nonstick cooking spray first. Cleanup will be a breeze.

Odors in upholstery
To get rid of the unpleasant smell of smoke on chairs and sofas, sprinkle baking soda on the fabric and allow it to sit there for a few hours; vacuum.

Oil stains
To remove oil stains from your driveway, sprinkle kitty litter on the stain and "scrub" with a brick in a circular motion. Repeat for stubborn stains.

Old wooden cabinets
To improve the look of wooden surfaces that have become dark or cloudy with age, make your own fantastic furniture restorative by combining 1 part each boiled linseed oil, turpentine, and vinegar. Shake well.

Apply with a soft cloth and wipe completely dry. With a second clean cloth, wipe again. Incidentally, don't boil linseed oil. Buy it already boiled at a hardware or paint store and use as is. Caution: Work in a well-ventilated room and wear rubber gloves. *Never* store rags that have been soaked in turpentine or linseed oil.

One bite at a time
Set aside 15 minutes each day to clean one area of your house. By the weekend, you won't have much more cleaning to do.

Onion odor
Remove onion odor from your hands by rubbing a stainless-steel spoon between them while they're under running water. Or rub hands with the end of a celery stalk to remove the odor.

Oven
Sprinkle water, then a layer of baking soda on oven surfaces. Rub gently with very fine steel wool for tough spots.

Oven
To clean a really dirty electric oven, make sure the oven is off. Heat 2 quarts of water to a rolling boil in a large pot. Keeping the water at arm's length, pour in 1 cup ammonia and place in the oven. Close the door and let it sit overnight. The next morning wipe the oven clean. You may have to scrub the really heavily soiled areas. For a gas oven you must turn off the gas at the source and extinguish the pilot light before proceeding.

Oven cleaner
Commercial oven cleaner removes grunge from iron skillets, encrusted food from glass cookware, and overly stubborn hard-water marks from windows and shower doors.

Oven door
To clean away baked-on "glaze" on your oven door window, wipe with ammonia, wait a few minutes, then remove the goop with a plastic ice scraper; wipe clean.

Oven racks
Put dirty oven racks into a large, black garbage bag along with 1 cup of household ammonia and close tightly. Sit outdoors in direct sunlight and leave overnight, tightly closed. Any debris will simply wash away.

Oven racks
To clean grease buildup from oven racks, bathe them. Put enough hot water in the bathtub to cover the

racks, add ¼ cup dishwasher detergent and ¼ cup white vinegar. Stir to dissolve detergent. Wait for an hour or so, then rinse and dry the racks. Drain the tub immediately, or you'll end up with a major-league bathtub ring.

Oven spills

Pour salt on oven spills when they occur and while they are too hot to clean up. It will make the cleanup easier once they have cooled, and the salt will prevent the spill from smoking or flaming up.

Panty hose filter

If your washing machine drains into a laundry sink, attach one leg of an old pair of panty hose to the end of the washing machine drain hose to catch lint and prevent clogged drains.

Permanent marker stains

Tough stains from permanent markers are easily removed from most surfaces with rubbing alcohol.

Pet hair on carpet

To remove pet hair from a rug, try a window squeegee. Just pull the rubber edge toward you and let physics do the rest. Static electricity will cause the hair to cling to the rubber strip.

Picture frames

To clean a carved picture frame, reach in all the nooks and crannies by using an empty plastic squeeze bottle. Just squeeze a few times and you'll blow the dust away with a puff of air.

Potpourri alternative

Cinnamon can be a less costly alternative to store-bought potpourri. Place a tablespoon or two of cinnamon in a pot of water and bring to a boil. Reduce heat and let simmer. The cinnamon fragrance will make every room in your home smell clean, fresh, and delicious.

Quick clean

Wear white canvas work gloves sprayed with polish to speed up cleaning. Wash and reuse each week.

Quick refills

Keep a squeeze ketchup bottle full of water on your ironing board for handy refills.

Range drip pans

Before cooking on the range top, give the stove's burner drip pans a light misting with vegetable spray. Any spills will clean up fast with soapy water.

Range hood filter

Many metal mesh filters found in range hoods can be removed and washed in the dishwasher on the normal, hot-water wash cycle. Wash as a separate load to provide for plenty of water action.

Raw egg

Dropping an egg on the floor can create a real mess. It'll be easier to clean up if you lightly sprinkle the egg with salt, then let it sit for 20 minutes. A damp paper towel will pick the mess right up. Or skip the salt and waiting period and just suck the whole mess up with a turkey baster.

Refrigerator

Place waxed paper on each shelf and in the crisper drawer of your refrigerator. This will dramatically cut cleaning time because when the shelves get dirty you can simply change the paper.

Refrigerator mildew

To prevent mildew from forming in the refrigerator, wipe the inside with white vinegar. The vinegar acid effectively kills mildew fungi.

Refrigerator odor

Saturate a couple of cotton balls with pure vanilla extract and place them in a bowl in the refrigerator to eliminate refrigerator odors. Another way to remove odors: Place pieces of cut-up apple in the refrigerator or freezer for an hour or so.

Remove contact paper

A warm hair dryer can remove contact paper from a shelf. If there's any glue left behind, use rubber-cement thinner, Soilove, or WD-40 aerosol lubricant.

Remove lime buildup

Apply a paste of cream of tartar and vinegar to faucets to remove lime sediment easily.

Rubber gloves that stick

Rubber gloves difficult to put on? Sprinkle a little baby powder or some baking soda in them first.

Rubbing alcohol

Moisten a cloth with rubbing alcohol and wipe away the grime from doorknobs and light-switch plates.

Rug and carpet deodorizer

Sprinkle liberal amounts of baking soda over a dry carpet; then wait 15 minutes before you start to vacuum.

Rust

Remove rust from pots and pans with white vinegar. For quick action, heat the vinegar. Or remove rust from household items by soaking them in a cola soft drink.

Rust stains

To remove rust rings or stains from porcelain fixtures, make a paste of cream of tartar and hydrogen peroxide. Apply a small amount to the stain and gently scrub with an old toothbrush. Repeat as necessary. Rinse thoroughly.

Scales for the home

Three scales worth their weight in gold in any home: A 25-pound scale in the laundry room so wash loads are right; a 5-pound scale in the kitchen to measure food portions for serving, freezing, and storing; a 300-pound scale for weight control. The kitchen scale will also serve to weigh mail. No more wasting postage stamps trying to make sure you've used enough.

Scouring powder

Scouring cleanser is often wasted because holes in the containers are too numerous or too large. To keep the cleanser from coming out too fast, cover half of them with tape.

Septic tank

If you have a septic tank or recreational vehicle holding tank, flush a cup of baking soda down the toilet periodically.

Shellac

Clean paintbrushes of shellac and shellac-based products with rubbing alcohol.

Shower

Wipe ceramic tile clean with a solution of automatic dishwasher detergent and water.

Showerhead

To clear lime deposits out of faucets, pour white vinegar into a plastic sandwich bag. Tie the bag to the faucet so the entire faucet end is submerged in the vinegar. Leave on for several hours.

Silk flowers

Pour a half cup of raw white rice into a paper bag. Add your silk flowers. Close the top of the bag and shake for a couple of minutes. Carefully remove flowers, making sure the rice stays in the bag. Your flowers will come out dust-free and looking like new.

Silver polish

Toothpaste removes tarnish from silver. Just make sure you use a nonabrasive toothpaste, apply with a wet cloth, rub into a foam, then rinse off completely. Remove every trace of the paste because any toothpaste allowed to remain in cracks and crevices will dry as hard as cement.

Silver polishing

Polishing silver while wearing rubber gloves promotes tarnish. Instead, choose plastic or cotton gloves.

Sink stains

To remove mineral deposits caused by a dripping faucet, place a slice of lemon on the area and leave it there overnight. The next day, remove the lemon and wipe the area clean.

Soap scum

Apply a dab of ordinary cooking oil to a damp sponge and use it to remove soap scum from your shower doors. Rinse the doors well. Cooking oil will also prevent soap scum buildup.

Sour sponges

To sweeten sour-smelling dishcloths and sponges, soak them in a water and baking soda solution.

Sponges

Quickly freshen and disinfect your sponges by putting them in the dishwasher along with all the dirty dishes. Clip to the top shelf to keep them from falling to the bottom and getting scorched on the heating element.

Stained woodwork

To clean painted woodwork stained by grease and smoke, dissolve old-fashioned, dry laundry starch in water according to package directions. Paint it on, and when dry, rub with a soft brush or clean cloth. This removes the stains without harming the finish.

Stainless steel pans

First rinse the pan with white vinegar inside and out. Then shake on enough salt to cover. Rub lightly. This cleans the pan and keeps it shiny.

Stainless steel sink solutions

(1) Rub stainless steel sinks with olive oil on a soft cloth to remove unsightly streaks. (2) Remove streaks or heat stains from stainless steel by rubbing with club soda. (3) Pour some baking soda on a sponge to scour a stainless-steel sink; it is nonabrasive. (4) Remove hard-water spots from a stainless steel sink with a sponge dipped in a mixture of 3 teaspoons of laundry detergent to 1 cup of warm water.

Steam iron

Clean the clogged-up steam ports in your iron with a bent-open paper clip; then fill reservoir with a mixture of ⅓ cup of white vinegar and 1 tablespoon baking soda that has been well blended. Allow to steam. Empty reservoir by turning upside down over the sink. Follow with plain water and allow to steam. You may have to allow 3 to 4 reservoirs of water to steam through to remove all traces of vinegar.

Steel wool pads

After using an SOS or similar brand scouring pad, to keep it from rusting just set it back in the box with the unused pads. It won't rust. This way it can be used until it is used up, not rusted out.

Stickers and labels

Sticky labels on glass or plastic containers or mirrors come off easily with rubbing alcohol or cooking oil. If neither is handy, use your laundry prewash treatment, or, as a last resort, nail polish remover may work. But be careful; it might remove more than the offending label.

Sticky lock

Graphite from an ordinary soft pencil can be used to lubricate a resistant lock. Rub the key across the pencil point, then move it in and out of the lock several times.

Storage

If you have a table with no storage space by the front door, replace it with a bureau that has drawers galore.

Stuffed animals

To freshen up a stuffed animal that can't be laundered, give the toy a "shower" with baking soda. Sprinkle it on, work it in, allow to sit for a while, then shake well or vacuum the baking soda away.

Sudsy scrubber

Cut a slit in the side of a sponge and place soap slivers inside to make a sudsy scrubber.

Sweep up ashes

Use a spray bottle filled with water to very lightly dampen ashes before you start to sweep.

Table linens

Spray table linens with a fabric protector a few days before you plan to use them. The inevitable spills will be less likely to stain, and spills will simple bead up so you can remove them quickly.

Tame harsh detergent

To make liquid dish detergent easy on the hands, add 3 tablespoons of white vinegar to a full bottle and shake well. As a bonus the vinegar will help make your dishes shine.

Tarnish remover
Place a piece of aluminum foil, shiny side up, on the bottom of a glass bowl or pan. Fill the container with boiling water and a few teaspoons of baking soda. Drop silver pieces into this bath, making sure they touch the foil, and the tarnish will disappear.

Tar, sap
Petroleum jelly easily removes tar and sap from the soles of your shoes.

Tea kettle
To remove hard-water and lime buildup in a teakettle, pour in 2 cups of vinegar and bring to a boil. Let simmer for about 10 minutes, then rinse well.

Telephone
Use a clean, soft cloth dipped in a bit of rubbing alcohol to remove grease and grime from your telephone. Use an ordinary cotton swab dipped in alcohol to clean around the buttons.

Television reception
If your TV is getting ghostly reception, try moving the VCR away from the set. VCRs often pick up radio waves.

Thermos
Here's an easy solution that will work with a sour-smelling thermos. Fill the container with a quart of water and 4 tablespoons baking soda and let it sit overnight. In the morning, wash as usual. Do this every week or so as preventive maintenance.

Tidy for the evening
After dinner, set a timer for 5 minutes and have everyone in the house pick up and put away the day's accumulated clutter.

Toilet
To remove stubborn hard-water deposits from a toilet bowl, first remove as much water from the bowl as possible by either plunging it out or pouring a big bucket of water into the bowl. Heat a gallon of white vinegar to boiling and carefully pour it into the almost empty toilet bowl. Allow it to stand for a few hours or so or until completely cool. Scrub with a brush and flush to clear.

Toothbrush holder
To remove gunk from the toothbrush holder, roll up a paper towel, wet it with cleaner, then slide it right through the holes.

Trash can
Sprinkle baking soda in the bottom of the trash receptacle before putting in the plastic bag.

Tub caulking
Use rubbing alcohol to clean silicone caulking around bathtubs.

Under-bed dusting
Wrap an old cotton T-shirt around the bristle end of the broom for cleaning under beds.

Upholstery
In a pinch use shaving cream as an upholstery cleaner. It is very effective. Use it to spot-clean small areas.

Vacuum attachments
Coat vacuum cleaner attachments with a thin layer of petroleum jelly to make them easier to attach and remove.

Vacuum refrigerator interior
When vacuuming the kitchen floor, take a couple of minutes to suck up crumbs and other dried debris from refrigerator shelves and food bins while narrow vacuum attachments are handy. Check the freezer area, too, where crumbs have a way of collecting.

Vases
Narrow-necked, hard-to-clean vases and other glassware will sparkle when you clean them with denture-cleaning tablets. Put one or two tablets into the container and fill with water. Wait a few hours. Rinse clean.

Vases
To remove mineral and hard-water deposits from vases, scrub with a wet cloth that has been dipped into salt. Follow with warm water and soap.

Vinyl shelf lining
Use pieces of vinyl flooring to cover shelves. This product can be cut to size and is easily removed to clean. Vinyl flooring is also very durable and comes in a variety of colors and patterns. Do not glue or attach in any way; just lay it on the shelf. Put the vinyl in the sun to soften it before cutting.

Wastebaskets
Use a plastic wastebasket as a bucket for mopping the floor, and you'll get two jobs done at once.

Watch crystal
Toothpaste cleans a nicked and scuffed watch crystal.

Wax mop

Has floor wax made your favorite mop stiff and foul-smelling? Soak it for a half hour in a gallon of water mixed with ½ cup of nonsudsing household ammonia. It will look brand new. To prevent repeat performances, clean wax mop thoroughly with an ammonia-water mixture after each use. Never clean a wax mop with soap or detergent, and use it only for the purpose of applying liquid floor wax.

Wax that fiberglass

For a brilliant shine and easy cleanups, give freshly cleaned tile and fiberglass shower walls a coat of car polish. Do not wax the shower floor or bathtub. It will become dangerously slick, and I don't have any good tips for coping with a broken back.

Wet carpet

When pipes break and the carpet is soaked, put rubbing alcohol in the carpet steam cleaner to rinse away mildew and speed drying. Use approximately 8 ounces per tankful.

White grout

Mix a paste of baking soda and hydrogen peroxide. Using an old toothbrush, apply paste to grout and give a little scrub. Leave on for a few minutes; rinse. For stained grout between floor tiles, try rubbing the area lightly with folded sandpaper.

White rings on wood furniture

Rub with a mixture of mayonnaise and white toothpaste. Wipe the area dry, then treat the entire surface with furniture polish.

Wicker furniture

Dust wicker furniture with a stiff, clean paintbrush.

Window frames

Use cream silver polish to shine aluminum window frames.

Window screens

First, run a dry sponge over the screen to remove any loose dust. Then, with the screen propped at a slight angle against a tree or wall, pour a solution of sudsy ammonia and water (1 cup to 1 gallon) across the top. When it starts to dribble down, rub with a scrub brush, using an up-and-down motion. When you finish, turn the screen over and repeat on the other side. Use the garden hose to rinse it, and place in the sun to dry.

Windowsills

Clean spotted windowsills with a cloth soaked with rubbing alcohol.

Window washing

Rather than use paper towels to clean mirrors and windows, use newspaper. It cleans much better than the paper towels with less streaking, and the ink never comes off on the glass. (It may on your hands, but they can be washed.)

Window washing

Never wash windows on a bright, sunny day. Choose an overcast day instead. The windows will dry more slowly and will have fewer streaks.

Window washing

Use vertical strokes when washing outside and horizontal strokes when washing inside. This way you'll know which side the streaks are on.

Wood cabinets

Dirty wooden cabinets can be cleaned with a mixture of 10 parts water and 1 part ammonia or Murphy's Oil Soap, either of which will strip old polish or wax and accumulated dirt. Then spray or rub with wax.

Wood furniture

Never use a cleaning solution that contains ammonia on your wood furniture because the ammonia may dissolve or affect the finish. Murphy's Oil Soap is a good product for cleaning wood. Find this in the home care section of your supermarket.

Wood paneling

Clean wood paneling with 1 ounce of olive oil mixed with 2 ounces of white vinegar and 1 quart of warm water. Emulsify in a blender. Wipe paneling with a soft cloth dampened in the solution, then follow with a dry cloth to remove yellowing from the surface.

Woodwork

Apply a thin layer of paste wax to doorjambs, windowsills, and other woodwork that collects fingerprints and smudges. Cleaning will become a breeze.

HOUSEHOLD FORMULAS

All-purpose cleaner

Pour 1 cup ammonia, 1 cup washing soda (available in the supermarket laundry section), and enough warm water to fill a gallon-size plastic jug; shake to mix. Label container and keep out of reach of children. This cleans countertops, painted woodwork, tile, appliances, vinyl floors, and even some painted walls.

All-purpose cleanser

Borax and baking soda mixed makes an effective nonabrasive cleanser for removing mold and mildew from tile grout.

All-purpose household cleaner

Mix ½ cup white vinegar, 1 cup ammonia, ¼ cup baking soda, and 1 gallon lukewarm water. Label and keep out of reach of children. Use straight in a spray bottle. No rinsing necessary.

Aluminum pot cleaner

Mix together ¼ cup cream of tartar, ¼ cup baking soda, ¼ cup white vinegar, and 2 tablespoons liquid soap. Store mixture in a container with a tight-fitting lid. Label and keep out of reach of children. To use: Rub a small amount of the cleaner onto the aluminum pan and scour with fine steel wool.

Antistatic spray

Mix 1 part liquid fabric softener and 20 parts water in a spray bottle set to spray a fine mist. Use as you would commercial aerosol antistatic spray by spraying on clinging petticoats, panty hose, socks, and dresses.

Basic fabric stain remover

Mix 1 cup Cascade (powdered) and 1 cup Clorox 2 with very hot tap water in a large pail or container. Soak stained articles overnight. Wash as usual.

Basic scouring powder

For a basic scouring cleanser, mix together 1 cup baking soda, 1 cup borax, and ¾ cup salt.

Bubble bath

Mix 2 cups vegetable oil, 10 drops perfume (optional), and 2 tablespoons shampoo; beat at high speed for 2 to 3 minutes to emulsify. Keep in a tightly closed bottle. Use about 3 tablespoons in each bath.

Ceramic tile and grout cleanser

Pour 1 cup baking soda into a gallon plastic jug. Add 1 cup ammonia (sudsing or nonsudsing), ½ cup vinegar, and enough warm water to fill the gallon jug. Swish the jug to mix ingredients before it is completely full. Label and keep out of the reach of children.

Cockroach killer

Mix ¼ cup shortening with ⅛ cup sugar. In a separate container mix ½ pound of powdered boric acid (available at drugstore) and ½ cup flour. Add to shortening mixture. Stir well with enough water to make a soft dough. Form into small balls the size of a marble, and place them in those out-of-the-way corners and dark places where roaches love to hide. Sounds crazy, but this really works better than most commercial products.

Craft clay

Mix 2 cups baking soda, 1 cup cornstarch, and 1½ cups water. Heat in a saucepan over medium heat, stirring constantly. Mixture will become thin and smooth at first. Cook, stirring constantly, until mixture is too thick to stir. Turn the mixture out onto a cookie sheet to cool. Cover with a damp cloth. When cool, knead until smooth. Store in a tightly closed plastic bag in the refrigerator for up to 2 weeks. Clay will harden at room temperature. Most items made with this clay will be dry after 24 hours. If desired, you can preheat the oven to 350 degrees, turn it off, and then put the clay into the oven to dry, turning the pieces occasionally.

Dishwasher soap extender

This is for your automatic dishwasher and extends your favorite brand by 50 percent. Mix 1 cup borax and ½ cup baking soda with 3 cups of your favorite dishwasher detergent. Store in a clean, tightly closed container. Use it in the same quantity as you use straight dishwasher detergent. It also acts as a spot stopper. Caution: If you have a home water-softening unit, do not use this formula. It will react with the chemicals in your water and could permanently etch fine glassware.

Dry carpet cleanser

Mix 2 cups baking soda, ½ cup cornstarch, 4 to 5 crumbled bay leaves, and 1 tablespoon ground cloves together; store in a container with a tight-fitting lid. Label and keep out of reach of the kids. To use: Shake a generous amount of cleaner over the area to be cleaned. Scrub mixture into heavily stained areas with a stiff brush. Leave overnight. Vacuum thoroughly in the morning.

Eyeglass cleaner

Mix ⅓ cup isopropyl rubbing alcohol with 1 cup water. Put in spray bottle.

Furniture polish

Mix 3 parts olive oil with 1 part lemon juice or vinegar in blender. Blend on high to emulsify, and apply with a clean, soft cloth.

Garbage disposal cleaner

Mix 1 cup chopped lemon, orange, or grapefruit (rind and all); 1 cup baking soda; and 1½ cups water. Pour into an ice cube tray and freeze until solid. Remove cubes, place in plastic bag if you don't intend to use them immediately, and label them. To use: Turn on your disposal unit, dump in 6 to 10 cubes, and let the machine grind them up. Rinse with cold water.

Glass cleaner

Add 2 tablespoons cornstarch and ½ cup white vinegar to 1 gallon of warm water.

Glass cleaner

Fill a spray bottle with nonsudsing household ammonia and rubbing alcohol in a 50:50 ratio. Label and keep out of reach of children. This solution is also great for chrome and cleaning fixtures in the bathroom and kitchen. What this lacks in fragrance it more than makes up in cleaning and disinfecting power. May damage painted surfaces.

Glass cleaner

Mix 1 cup white vinegar, 1 cup ammonia, 1 tablespoon mild detergent, and enough warm water to fill a clean, gallon-size plastic jug. Label, keep tightly capped, and keep out of reach of children. To use: Pour solution into a spray bottle. Spray the window, wait 30 seconds, then wipe the window thoroughly with newspapers, turning paper often.

Identify cleaners

Add a tiny drop of food coloring to a cleaning mix in a spray bottle in order to distinguish the contents from other sprays. This will not affect the cleaner.

Kitchen disinfectant

We now know how important it is to disinfect cutting boards and countertops. Instead of buying expensive kitchen disinfectants for countertops and cutting boards, make your own: Combine 1 teaspoon liquid chlorine bleach per quart of water. Flood food-cutting surface with the solution, let stand several minutes, then rinse.

Laundry pretreatment

In a spray bottle combine ½ cup white vinegar, ½ cup household ammonia, ½ cup Wisk (commercial liquid laundry soap), and ½ cup water. Spray on spots and launder as usual.

Laundry starch

Dissolve 1 tablespoon cornstarch in 1 pint of cold water. Place in a spray bottle. Shake well before using. Clearly label the contents of the spray bottle.

Liquid hand soap

Grate lots of soap slivers on a cheese grater, mix with water (the amount depends on how much soap you have, but generally speaking you want about 1 part grated soap to 3 parts water), and melt in microwave or on the stove. Beat with a rotary beater until smooth. If you don't want to bother with slivers but want to make your own liquid soap, follow these instructions using a full bar of soap and 3 cups of water.

Liquid hand soap for kids

If your small children are really into washing their hands and go fairly nuts with the soap dispenser, make up a special batch of handwashing soap just for them: Mix 10 parts liquid dishwashing detergent or generic shampoo to 1 part water.

Mirror and glass cleaner

You can make an excellent mirror and glass cleaner, which also works well on chrome, by mixing 4 tablespoons fresh-squeezed, strained lemon juice with 1 gallon of water. Fill sprayers. This works well and is inexpensive.

Stuck photos

If photos have marks (even permanent marker), sticky stuff, dirt, or they are stuck together, clean them with 91 percent or more isopropyl alcohol, and carefully pry them apart. Dry them printed side up and not touching other photos. Anything less than 91 percent alcohol will ruin the photos because it contains too much water.

Window cleaner

Mix ¼ cup ammonia and ½ cup white vinegar with 1 gallon warm water. Work in a well-ventilated area.

Windshield washer fluid

Mix 3 cups isopropyl alcohol, 1 tablespoon liquid detergent, and 10 cups water. Pour alcohol and detergent into a clean, gallon-size plastic jug. Fill with water, cover, and shake well to mix. Label, cap tightly, and keep out of reach of children. Shake well, then pour into your car's windshield-washer compartment. You can use this in your car year-round because the alcohol will prevent it from freezing in the winter.

HOUSEHOLD TRICKS

Address location

When driving in an unfamiliar neighborhood with only a street address to help you locate your destination, remember this: East is even and so is south. If the address number is even like 124 Elm Street, it will be on the east side of the street or the south side. Conversely, 123 Elm Street will be on the west side or the north side.

Batteries for pennies

Check with your local photo center about buying the slightly used batteries that remain once a disposable camera is opened and the film is developed. Some centers sell these batteries for as low as 10 cents each, but it's the kind of thing you have to know about. So now you know!

Bubble gum on upholstery

To remove bubble gum from upholstery, make a loop of duct tape around your fingers with the sticky side out. Press on the gum and jerk it up quickly. Repeat until all the gum is pulled away.

Coffee filters

As a substitute for paper towels, coffee filters will shine glass, mirrors, and chrome perfectly without lint or streaky marks.

Dryer sheets

Save and use your fabric-softener sheets to shine shoes to a high gloss.

Dryer sheets

Save and use your fabric-softener sheets to remove dust and static from TV screens.

Funky envelope

Need to mail something but you don't have an envelope that's large enough? You can use a small paper bag. If it is larger than 6 by 9 inches you will need to add additional postage. The maximum size allowable is 6⅛ by 11½ inches. The top can be folded down to meet length requirements and stapled or taped.

Handy pencil sharpener

In a pinch you can sharpen a pencil on a piece of sandpaper, if you work at it for a few minutes.

Help for home business

If you are starting a home business, check with your local community college or university. College art classes will design business logos as part of a class project, marketing classes will often help with brochures, and photography classes will take pictures.

Indentations in carpet

Here is how to make those carpet indentations rebound: Place an ice cube in each indentation. Let it melt, then wait about 12 hours before blotting up the moisture. Gently pull up the carpet fibers using a kitchen fork.

Magnetic photo album nightmare

A warm hair dryer can loosen photos that have become stuck within the pages of a magnetic photo album.

Moving boxes

Before you tape a box shut, run a piece of string along the path where you'll be placing the tape. Press the tape over the string to seal the box, leaving a bit of the string hanging loose. When it's time to unpack, just pull on the string to rip the tape.

Out of glue?

Clear nail polish makes a good emergency glue for small items like stamps, recipe clippings, etc.

Packaging material

When mailing something breakable to family or friends, use intact rolls of toilet tissue as filler to cushion the item. It's lightweight and inexpensive filler—and something the recipient can use. If you remove the center cardboard tubes, the rolls become more flexible.

Postage stamps

Postage stamps in any quantity and any denomination can be ordered through the mail. The U.S. Postal Service even provides a postage-paid envelope in which to send the order. There is no service charge, you pay only the cost of the stamps you order, and they always send a postage-paid envelope with the order. This saves a lot of time and eliminates the frustration of standing in line at a small post office that never has the stamps you want in the first place. You can get the initial order form at the post office.

HOUSEHOLD TRICKS

Quick pickup

Pick up spilled nails, screws, or pins with a strong magnet wrapped in a paper towel. When the spilled items attach to the magnet, gather the towel corners over the pieces and pull that tidy bundle away from the magnet.

Rechargeable batteries

Use rechargeable batteries wisely. Always put them in often-used items like toys, remote controls, or portable music players. Do not install them in appliances like smoke detectors, flashlights, or other items that you use infrequently or have to count on in an emergency. Rechargeable batteries lose about 1 percent of their charge each day and will completely uncharge in 100 days if not used. Don't leave them in something for months and months without checking the charge.

Recycling with style

For just a few bucks you can order a rubber stamp that reads something like: "Personally Recycled by (your name)." Now you can collect paper that has been printed on one side only, like computer run, flyers, and junk mail. Just cut it to size, stamp it, and have your own personalized notes and stationery.

Remove a knot in a jewelry chain

Lay the chain on a flat surface and, with a straight pin in each hand, gently work the knot out. If the knot is really tight, apply a single drop of baby oil or cooking oil to the offending area and repeat the procedure.

Rocking chair

If a rocking chair is wearing the finish off your wood floor, put a strip of adhesive weather-stripping tape on the runners.

Roll ends of paper

Local newspapers and large printing companies occasionally print pages on lovely pastel-colored paper. The roll ends are typically given away or sold for $1 to $2, depending on the weight. This type of paper works very nicely for wrapping gifts, table covers, and art projects. Call ahead to make arrangements.

Silver chest

Don't throw out that old tarnish-retardant silver chest designed to store silverware. It will make a wonderful jewelry box. Earrings clip to the band designed to hold knives; chains, rings, and brooches fit nicely in the open spaces; and you won't have to worry about tarnish because of the specially treated material that lines this type of chest.

35mm film canisters

Poke holes in the bottom of 35mm film canisters to make salt and pepper shakers for lunch boxes or camping trips.

Warped candles

To straighten those droopy, warped candles, dunk them in a pan of warm water until they are just pliable enough to bend back to their original shape.

Warped vinyl records

To straighten a warped phonograph record, place the record between two pieces of sturdy glass and set the glass in direct sunlight for two hours.

KITCHEN

Aluminum cookware

To remove stains and discoloration from aluminum cookware, fill cookware with hot water, and add 2 tablespoons cream of tartar to each quart of water. Bring solution to a boil, and simmer for 10 minutes. Wash as usual and dry.

Bag of ingredients

Keep all the items you buy for special occasions, such as a dinner party or holiday baking, in a grocery bag that you store in the refrigerator or the basement so you just can grab the bag when you're ready to start cooking.

Bakeware

Use heavyweight, dull aluminum pans for best baking. Dark pans cook too quickly, shiny surfaces reflect heat, and neither gives you the good, even baking results you want.

Baking pans

Nonstick baking pans are not worth the extra cost. You still have to grease them, and the nonstick coating scratches off easily.

Banana tree

A banana tree is a great invention that prevents bananas from bruising so they will last longer. They're also quite expensive. So, purchase a big cup hook and screw it into the underside of an upper cabinet. For a total cost of about 10 cents, your bananas can hang properly and be up and out of the way.

Blades

For easy cleanup, coat the grater, the knife blade of a food processor, and the beaters of an electric mixer with vegetable cooking spray before using.

Blender

To clean the blender, fill it less than halfway with hot, soapy water; replace the lid; and turn the machine on at the lowest speed for a minute or two. Rinse the blender thoroughly, then towel-dry it before using again.

Bowls and lids

To save space and promote neatness in the kitchen, nest all plastic storage containers, and place the lids in a resealable plastic bag. Hang the bag of lids from a hook inside a door.

Box opener

If you have a difficult time opening a pantry or laundry box that says "Press here to open," instead of pressing there with your thumb (which rarely works) use a juice-can opener.

Broiler pan

To clean a messy broiler pan, sprinkle it with dry laundry detergent while it's still hot. Cover the surface with a short stack of wet newspapers. Leave in oven that has been turned off with the door closed. This will produce a steam cleaning effect while you eat. Throw the newspaper away, and the residue should come off quickly with very little effort.

Broiler pan

Make cleanup easy by spraying the clean broiler pan with nonstick vegetable spray before beginning to cook.

Burned-on mess

To remove burned-on crud from pots and pans, put enough water in the pot to cover the yuck. Add 2 tablespoons powdered dishwasher detergent. Boil for 15 to 20 minutes. While you're at it, put the rangetop burner plates in the boiling solution to clean them too.

Casserole transportation

To prevent spills when transporting a casserole dish, stretch one rubber band from each handle to the knob on top of the cover. The lid stays secure and will be easy to carry.

Clean or dirty?

Never sure whether the dishes in the dishwasher are clean or dirty? Place an uncapped spice bottle upright in a front corner of the top rack. When dishes are clean, it will be full of water. Empty the bottle when you unload.

Clips

Instead of purchasing plastic "chip clips," keep a supply of sturdy clothespins on hand. Hot-glue magnetic strips to the back of some of the clothespins to be used in the refrigerator and stored on the door. If a bag will not stand on its own, clip it shut, and hang it from an inside refrigerator wall. Clothespins work great for keeping bags of chips, cookies, rice, flour, and coffee closed tightly.

KITCHEN

Coffee filters

Unbleached tan coffee filters last longer and are stronger than the bleached white type. They can be rinsed out and reused several times before discarding.

Coffee stains

Remove coffee and tea stains by scrubbing pots or cups with baking soda and a plastic scouring pad.

Colander

Keep a colander in the sink and scrape plates into it at dishwashing time. It's more efficient than standing over the garbage pail, and the liquids will go down the drain rather than into your wastebasket.

Containers

Short on refrigerator containers for small portions or leftovers? Cut a waxed milk carton down to size and then cover with foil or plastic wrap.

Cookware

When food begins to stick on your nonstick skillet, fill the cookware with a solution of 3 tablespoons nonchlorine bleach, 1 teaspoon liquid dishwashing detergent, and 1 cup water. Let the solution simmer in the cookware for 15 to 20 minutes. Wash and dry as usual. Recondition the nonstick finish with cooking oil or shortening before using.

Counters

Use equal parts white vinegar and water in a spray bottle to remove soapy film from countertops.

Cutting board

After scrubbing and disinfecting your wooden cutting board, season it by rubbing on a coat of mineral oil. Do not use vegetable oil because it may turn rancid.

Dental floss

In the kitchen, dental floss can do the job of a sharp, serrated knife—and with better results. Stretched taut between your hands, a length of floss can split a cake into layers without a turntable and with a minimum of crumbs. It will also slice a log of soft fresh cheese into rounds that stay intact, instead of crumbling into bits. Cut creamy cheesecake with dental floss. Stretch a length of floss over the top of the cake and, holding it taut, bring it down top to bottom through the cake to cut it into halves. Repeat until you have the desired number of pieces.

Deodorizer

Lemon juice cleans, deodorizes, and bleaches out the stains on wooden cutting boards and wooden utensils.

Dishwasher

If your dishwasher interior has rusty stains, try running a cycle with no dishes, and instead of automatic dishwasher detergent, fill the cups with Tang Instant Breakfast drink. The citric acid works miracles.

Dishwasher

To assure your dishes come out sparkling clear with no soap or hard water residue, pour a cup of white vinegar into the dishwasher during the final rinse.

Dishwasher

Hang onto those mesh bags that onions and other produce come in. Instead of dropping small things like cookie cutters, container lids, and the sponge into the silverware compartment of your dishwasher, put them in the mesh bag, tie it shut, and place it in the regular-size compartment for an easy wash.

Dishwasher

Don't be tempted to use soap meant for dishes or laundry when you run out of dishwasher detergent, or you'll wind up with a mountain of bubbles. If someone else makes the mistake, here's how to get rid of the mess: Open the dishwasher, slide out the bottom rack, and sprinkle salt on the suds, which will immediately reduce their volume. Pour 2 gallons of cold water into the bottom of the dishwasher and advance the cycle until you hear the machine begin to drain. Repeat until only a few suds remain. As a last step, run an entire cycle without any detergent.

Dishwasher detergent

Haul out your dishwasher's owner's manual and learn how much detergent you should be using. You may be surprised to find you've been using too much.

Dishwasher spots

No matter which dishwashing detergent you use, glasses often come out of the dishwasher with spots. Solution: Mix equal parts water, vinegar, and lemon juice in a spray bottle and spray the glasses before putting them in the washer.

Disinfecting

To disinfect a wood chopping block that can harbor harmful bacteria, mix a solution of 3 tablespoons bleach to 1 quart of water and pour it over the wood. Wait a few minutes before rinsing well. This also works with a plastic cutting board.

Double boiler

Here's a way to save a little money on your electricity or gas bill: Cook with a double boiler or steamer. For example: Boil pasta in the boiler's bottom pot and steam vegetables in the top section.

Drainboard

If you only occasionally handwash dishes such as delicate crystal, china, or a messy pot, don't waste money purchasing a drainboard. Place just-washed items on the top rack of your empty dishwasher where they can drain and air-dry.

Draining

When deep frying, use only one paper towel with a thick section of newspaper under it on which to drain the food.

Drain maintenance

To eliminate odors and keep grease from building up in your kitchen plumbing, regularly pour a strong saltwater solution down the drain.

Dryer sheets to the rescue

Don't throw away all of your used laundry softener sheets. When you have an impossible-to-clean casserole dish or pot, toss one or two of the used sheets into the pan, fill with hot water and presto! In 20 minutes it wipes clean, no scrubbing needed. Store them in an empty tissue box.

Electric can opener

To clean that cruddy electric can opener blade, soak an old toothbrush in vinegar, hold it under the blade wheel, and operate the machine.

Enamel cookware

If your enamel cookware has unsightly stains, fill it with a mixture of equal parts household bleach and water and allow to sit overnight. Rinse well.

Fires

Never waste precious time pouring water on cooking fires. Use baking soda or salt instead.

Flatware

To remove thick, caked-on stains from your good silverware, rub the utensils with a clean cloth that has been dipped in wet salt.

Flatware

Save time by presorting forks, knives, and spoons as you load them into your dishwasher's utensil compartment.

Flour sifter
A kitchen strainer works just as well as a flour sifter. Lightly press flour or powdered sugar through with the back of a wooden spoon or gently shake back and forth until the dry product has worked its way through.

Food containers
Remove smells from food containers: Fill with water and several tablespoons of baking soda. Let sit overnight. Wash and rinse.

Food list
Place a chalkboard on the refrigerator. List what snacks or leftovers are available inside. This will prevent family members from eating things you're planning to have for dinner. And it will keep them from opening the refrigerator to search for snacks that may or may not be there while all the cold leaks out.

Food list
If your supermarket receipt clearly lists every item you purchased by name, post it on the refrigerator door. It lets everyone know what you bought so they can decide quickly what they want.

Food stains
To remove food stains from countertops, cover stains with a paste of baking soda and water. Let it sit a few minutes, then wipe with a cloth or sponge.

Freezer
Use a hair dryer to quickly defrost your refrigerator's non-frost-free freezer. Or rotate two pans filled with boiling water; one goes into the freezer compartment while the other goes back on the stove for reheating. When you've completed defrosting the freezer, spray a few coats of nonstick cooking spray on the top and sides of the freezer. The next time you defrost, the ice will fall right off.

Freezer list
Keep a current freezer inventory list posted to the outside of the freezer door. The longer you leave the door open while you look to see what's in there, the more cold air escapes, and the harder the freezer has to work.

Frosting spreader
Use a 6-inch scraper or putty knife, which you can buy in hardware stores or lumberyards, as a spreader for icing the side and top of a layer cake. It's smaller than a spatula and much easier to hold straight. Position the scraper perpendicular to the side of the cake that you've placed on a lazy Susan, hold it gently, and rotate the

cake's turntable. The scraper also works beautifully on square and triangular cakes because it can make sharp, perfect corners.

Funnel

Make an emergency funnel out of aluminum foil.

Garbage disposal

To purge your garbage disposal, fill the sink with water, remove the drain stopper, and turn on the disposal for a few seconds until the water is gone.

Garbage disposal

To clean the garbage disposal, dump in a tray of ice cubes made from white vinegar and water. Turn on the water and operate the disposal as usual. Or dump in a tray of regular ice cubes and a handful of lemon rinds and operate the disposal as usual.

Glass bakeware

Glass bakeware conducts and retains heat better than metal, so oven temperatures should be reduced by 25 degrees whenever glass containers are used.

Glass chips

Keep a fingernail sanding block (available from a beauty supply store or drugstore cosmetic counter) on hand. Use it to sand, polish, and smooth out chipped corners and edges of glassware and glass baking dishes. With just a few minutes of gentle sanding and polishing with the block, the jagged dangerous edge or corner will be smoothed out and the glass piece will be restored to usefulness.

Glassware

To unstick two stacked glasses, pour cold water into the inside glass. Place both glasses in warm water up to the rim of the outer glass. Remove glasses from water, then gently pull apart.

Graters

An old toothbrush is perfect for quickly cleaning the holes in cheese and vegetable graters.

Grease fire

Smother a grease or oil fire in the kitchen by sliding a pan lid over flames. Never carry the pan outside.

Grease fire

To douse flames from grease fires, keep a box of salt handy near your stove.

Grilling

Don't place the grilled food back on the same platter it was on before cooking. Wash the platter after it has held raw meat, or use a separate plate for serving grilled food.

Jar with a pouring spout

You can easily turn any canning jar into a pouring jar with a spout: Take an empty round salt box that has a little metal pouring spout in the top. Remove the lid and ring from the canning jar. Using the lid part as a pattern, cut a circle from the top of the salt box. Discard the canning lid and replace it with the circle from the salt box. Screw on the ring, and you have a great pouring spout that can be closed. A canning jar with a spout makes a great storage container for sugar, cornmeal, etc.

Lifting a label

To remove a label that you want to save because it contains a recipe or coupon, wet a paper towel and wrap it around the jar or can. Place the container—paper towel and all—into a plastic bag, and zip or twist-tie shut. Let stand overnight, and the label will come right off.

Lunch supplies

For the lunch crowd, store all sandwich and lunch fixings in the same refrigerator drawer; keep some plastic and brown bags there too.

Measuring caps

The big round measuring lid from a container of liquid laundry detergent doubles as an adequate liquid measuring cup. Look inside and you will likely see marks indicating ¼-, ⅓-, and ½-cup measurements. Save a few of these big bottle lids because they also make dandy cookie cutters.

Measuring devices

The tall lids on some liquid laundry detergent bottles make great biscuit cutters when washed thoroughly. Also, the dosage cups found in over-the-counter cold medicines come marked with 1 and 2 tablespoon lines and work especially well for measuring liquids such as oil and milk.

Messy bags

Instead of throwing out those plastic bags from the grocery store, cram them into an empty, paper-towel tube. They'll store neatly in a drawer or cupboard. If you want to get fancy, cover the tube with contact paper or wallpaper that coordinates with the kitchen decor.

Messy jobs

Before starting a messy kitchen job like peeling potatoes or grating cheese, cover the counter or sink with a ripped-open brown grocery bag.

When finished, just roll up the mess and dispose of it in one step to the garbage can.

Microwave
To zap microwave odors and steam clean the interior, place two cups of water with two tablespoons lemon juice in a microwavable bowl. Place in the microwave and heat on high for 12 to 15 minutes. The mixture will bubble, boil, and steam. Carefully remove the bowl and wipe the interior with a clean sponge.

Nonskid
Cut the fingertip from an old rubber glove and slip it over the end of your broom handle. Now it won't slip when leaned against the wall.

Nonstick colander
Coat your colander with nonstick vegetable spray before using to drain pasta; this will keep the pasta from sticking.

Oil bottles
Since oils can become rancid more quickly when exposed to light, use designer water bottles made of colored glass to store oils.

Oil bottles
Transfer cooking oil from large, clumsy jugs to squeeze-type plastic bottles, and you'll have a lot more control over the amount of oil you use in pots or on salads.

Organizers
Plastic berry baskets make terrific holders for powdered soups, drink mixes, and envelopes of seasonings that seem to collect around the pantry.

Oven
Preheat oven only if the recipe tells you to. Casseroles and roasts don't suffer from starting out cold, but breads, cakes, and pies do.

Oven fire
Leave the oven door shut and turn off the heat to smother an oven or broiler fire.

Pantry shelving
Create more pantry storage by laying a narrow board across two tall soup cans.

Parchment paper
Instead of paying about 20 cents a sheet retail, inquire at a commercial bakery if they will sell parchment paper to you at their cost, which is more like 3 cents a sheet.

PASS the fire extinguisher
Everyone in the family needs to know how to operate a portable fire

extinguisher. Just remember the word *PASS. P:* pull the pin to release the locking mechanism. *A*: aim low, at the base of the fire. *S:* squeeze the handle. *S:* sweep the spray from side to side, as if you were hosing down a sidewalk.

Pastry brush

A new paintbrush is perfect for brushing glaze on bread and pastry dough before cooking, or melted butter on corn or dinner rolls.

Pizza stone

Instead of spending $25 to $35 for a pizza stone (also called a baker's stone), pick up one or two large unsealed terra cotta tiles from the home improvement center for about $1 each. Place on the oven rack, which you've positioned at the lowest point in the oven. Preheat oven with tiles in place to 450 to 500 degrees. Slide pizza or bread directly onto the tiles. This works just like an authentic pizza oven and produces a crisp and delicious crust.

Plastic bags

Stuff plastic bags into an empty tissue box for neat storage and quick retrieval.

Plastic wrap

When you can't find the end of the plastic wrap, put a piece of cellophane tape, sticky side out, around your index finger. Run the taped finger around the roll until the wrap lifts up.

Plastic wrap

Store plastic wrap in the freezer. The cool air will keep it from clinging to itself and makes it a lot easier to work with.

Plastic wrap

Plastic wrap will cling better if you moisten the rim of the bowl or pan you are covering with a bit of water.

Potato peeler

Uses for a potato peeler: (1) Need just a little grated cheese for a topping? Use your potato peeler instead of a grater and save time on cleanup. (2) A peeler can double as an emergency pencil sharpener. (3) Shave off small pieces of butter or margarine from a frozen or hard stick by "shaving" it with a potato peeler. (4) Pit cherries with a potato peeler.

Prevent cooking fires

Keep an eye on your cooking and stay in the kitchen. Wear short or close-fitting sleeves. Watch children closely. Teach children to cook safely. Clean cooking surfaces to prevent grease buildup. Keep curtains, towels, and pot holders clear of flames and hot surfaces. Store gasoline, solvents, and cleaners away from the heat source.

Quick funnel

Need a funnel but don't have one handy? Make one yourself by cutting the corner out of a plastic lunch bag.

Recipe album

Keep recipes clean and easy to use by storing them in small photo albums. They stay open and lie flat, and the pages can be wiped off easily. They're especially great for recipes printed on thin paper from magazines or newspapers.

Recipe card

A recipe written in ink on a card won't smear if you rub a piece of white paraffin (a candle will do) over the card to coat the surface.

Recipe holder

To keep recipe cards clean, clip them to a clothes hanger, the kind you use for skirts, and hang it from a cupboard doorknob.

Refrigerator

A lazy Susan on a refrigerator shelf can assure access to items often forgotten in the back.

Ring hook

Hang a small hook near your kitchen sink to hold rings, watches, or other jewelry you remove when washing, cleaning, or cooking.

Scale

Here's how to make sure your kitchen measuring scale is accurate: Place nine pennies on the scale. They should weigh 1 ounce.

Scouring pads

Cut scouring pads such as Brillo or SOS in half or quarters. Now you can use a new smaller pad every time, throw it away, and avoid a rusty, yucky mess.

Season cast iron

To season a new or newly-scrubbed cast-iron pan, coat it with mineral or vegetable oil and place it in a warm (200-degree) oven for a few hours. The oil will slowly soak into the pan.

Sink stopper leaks

To stop water from leaking out of the kitchen sink while you're doing dishes, put a piece of plastic wrap between the drain and the drain stopper. This is also a handy trick to remember if you're soaking something overnight.

Spaghetti measurer

An empty 35mm film canister makes a perfect spaghetti measurer. Stack uncooked spaghetti into a canister. A full canister makes spaghetti for two—no waste, no guessing.

Spaghetti server

Invest in the gadget called a spaghetti fork or spaghetti server. It looks like a weird spoon with claws and makes serving a whole lot easier. You can also use tongs or two large forks.

Spice jars

Attach tops of empty baby-food jars to the underside of shelves. Fill the bottles with spices or small objects and screw them into their tops.

Spices

Fill a drawer near your food preparation area with spices. This is an excellent way to utilize drawer space. Label the jar tops for easy identification.

Splatter guard

Lay a washable rolling window shade in the space behind your rangetop. When you cook, pull the shade up and attach to a mounted cup hook to protect the wall from splatters.

Splatter guard

Avoid splatters while using your electric mixer by punching holes in a paper plate; insert beaters, and keep the surface of the plate even with the top of the bowl.

Stained plastic

Put stained, plastic storage containers and kitchen utensils outside to whiten in the sun. Even tomato stains will disappear.

Syrup bottles

Before placing an opened bottle of pancake syrup or honey on your pantry or kitchen cabinet shelf, place a cupcake baking cup under the bottle to catch the drips. This will keep surfaces clean.

Tea kettle

Place an agate marble in your tea kettle and you'll never have to clean out lime deposits.

Teapot stains

Place a denture tablet in a porcelain teapot of warm water to remove stains.

Tea stains in china cups

To remove stains from china tea cups, pour an equal amount of salt and white vinegar in cups and let stand. Rub off stains with a soft cloth and rinse with clear water.

KITCHEN

Tight jar lids

To loosen a stuck jar lid, hold the jar upside down and pour warm vinegar around the neck at the joint between the glass and the top.

Tight lids

When you can't remove a too-tight lid from a jar, this handy hint may do the trick: Take a heavy-duty rubber band, put it around the lid, and twist. Because the rubber band gives you something to grip, the lid should come off easily.

Towels

Paper towels are expensive. Use cloth towels and sponges instead.

Trash can liners

Store the roll of tall kitchen bags in the bottom of your kitchen trash receptacle. Now no one has a reason not to put a new bag in when the full one is removed.

Uneven heat

If your oven has hot spots (places that seem to cook faster than others), you can avoid burning by changing the position of the food in the oven often and by using thicker or double-ply baking pans.

Utensil holder

Put large cooking implements such as wooden spoons and spatulas in a terra-cotta flowerpot to be left out on the kitchen counter.

Vegetable bin liners

Place paper towels in the bottom of vegetable bins to absorb water.

Vinyl wrinkles

To remove the wrinkles from a new plastic or vinyl tablecloth, toss the tablecloth in the dryer with a damp cloth (for moisture), set on the lowest heat possible, and let tumble for *only* a minute or two. To be on the safe side (putting plastic in a clothes dryer sounds like a fire hazard just waiting to happen), do not leave it unattended. Stand there for the short time it takes to do this, so you can personally take out the beautifully wrinkle-free tablecloth.

Waxed produce

Some vegetables, such as bell peppers and cucumbers, are coated with wax before they're shipped to the store. Waxing is done to extend shelf life, seal in moisture, and improve appearance. The waxes are safe to eat, but may contain pesticide residue, so wash carefully all waxed vegetables and fruit.

Wooden bowls
Freshen wooden salad bowls and cutting boards. Sprinkle the surface with salt and rub with half a lemon.

LAUNDRY

Air-dry

Occasionally dry 1 or 2 loads of laundry outdoors instead of in the clothes dryer. You'll save about $1 per load, and over a year's time that could add up to some serious cash.

Air-drying unmentionables

Heat deteriorates hosiery and misshapes bras, so air-dry whenever possible.

Antisuds

Cut excess suds when handwashing clothes by adding a splash of vinegar to the rinse. Rinse again in plain water.

Baby formula stains

Unflavored meat tenderizer will remove some milk and baby formula stains from fabric. Make a paste of the tenderizer and cool water, rub on the spots, allow to sit, and wash as usual. The meat tenderizer contains an enzyme that breaks down the protein that is in milk and formula.

Baby shampoo for delicates

Instead of using expensive cold-water detergents for delicates and fine sweaters, use baby shampoo. The results with be the same, and the cost is considerably less.

Bag the rugs

Cotton and synthetic braided throw rugs are generally machine-washable in cold water on a gentle cycle. However, the agitation of the machine can be hard on these types of rugs, so to keep them intact, put the rug into a pillowcase and close it with a safety pin. Throw the rug, case and all, in the washing machine for a gentle yet effective cleaning. Be sure to test that the rug is colorfast prior to laundering.

Baking soda in the hamper

Sprinkle baking soda into the laundry hamper to minimize odors from soiled clothing.

Baking soda in the laundry

Add ½ cup baking soda to the laundry wash cycle, and you can expect your liquid laundry detergent to get a boost in its enzymatic and cleaning action.

Blood stains

Presoak in cold or warm water for at least 30 minutes. If the stain remains, soak in lukewarm ammonia water (3 tablespoons ammonia per gallon of water); rinse. If the stain still remains, work in detergent and wash, using fabric-safe bleach. If the stain still remains, use Soilove.

Brilliantly white

If you want to keep your white laundry stain-free and brilliantly white without using chlorine bleach, here's the secret: Fill the washing machine with the hottest water available. Add 1 cup Cascade automatic dishwasher powder and 1 cup washing soda (find this in the supermarket laundry section). Add washable whites and allow to agitate for a few minutes. Turn the machine off and allow to soak at least 3 hours (overnight is fine). Finish the cycle and dry as usual.

Cheaper dryer sheets

As a cheaper substitute for dryer sheets, dampen an old washcloth with the liquid softener, throw it in the dryer with a load of clothes, and you'll have static-free, good smelling, soft laundry. Wash and dry the cloth every couple of loads so it will continue to absorb the solution.

Cocoa and chocolate stains

To remove cocoa and chocolate stains, scrub the stained area immediately with ammonia. If the stain remains, soak the stained clothes overnight in carbonated water, then wash them.

Coffee stains

The key to treating coffee stains is to get at them as quickly as possible. If the garment must be dry-cleaned, don't waste any time getting it to the cleaner. If it's washable, immediately rinse in cold water and apply a good prewash treatment as soon as possible. Wash the garment in warm, soapy water; rinse and allow to drip-dry. Don't put it in the dryer just in case all the stain didn't come out (which sometimes happens with coffee) and you need to repeat the process. The dryer will set the stain, and then you'll be stuck.

Coin-operated laundry

Use more than one machine at a time when at the laundromat, and you'll be out of there in half the time or less. To help remember which machines are yours, place a small refrigerator magnet on top of each washer and dryer. No more embarrassing mix-ups.

Cold water

The bulk of your laundry is only minimally soiled. Modern-day detergents clean very well with cold water as well as warm. Your colors will last longer, too, if you use cold. The average family can save about $200 per year by switching to cold water when possible. And always rinse clothes in cold water. The temperature of the rinse cycle does not affect cleaning. Exception: Health professionals recommend that bed linens and towels be laundered in 130 degree water to make sure nasty bacteria and stubborn germs are properly laid to rest.

Color setting

White vinegar sets the color in washables. The first time you wash dark and bright colors, add 1 cup of white vinegar to the wash water.

Complete outfits

If you iron your kids' school and play clothes, place complete outfits on hangers with socks, barrettes, belts, and other accessories tucked in a pocket. This saves a lot of time and frustration when it's time to get up and get ready to go.

Corduroy

Keep corduroy looking brand-new. Wash inside out and according to label directions. If necessary, iron corduroy inside out to avoid crushing the pile.

Corduroy and lint

To remove lint from corduroy garments after laundering, take them out of the dryer while they're still damp and brush vigorously with a clothes brush. The next time you wash the items, keep them lint-free by turning them inside out before laundering.

Cut the drying time

When you have a heavy load in the washing machine, towels for instance, reset the machine for an extra spin dry. The drying time will then be reduced considerably.

Delicate items in the machine

Machine wash hosiery and other delicate items in the washing machine by first putting them into a pillow case and closing it with a safety pin.

Dry a bunch

Don't dry only one load of laundry. Do several loads if you can, one right after the other. It takes a lot of energy to get the dryer from room temperature to hot, so while it's at that level, take full advantage and save energy.

Dryer repair

If your clothes dryer seems to take twice as long to dry a standard load, try these two tips before calling the repairman: (1) Go outside, remove the vent cover and clean out any lint that missed the trap and has become stuck at the vent opening. (2) Pull the entire dryer away from the wall. This will alleviate a possible "kink" in the accordion tubing, which can impede efficient operation.

Dryers are hard on clothes

Dryer lint is visual proof of just how destructive to clothes that convenience can be. And if that's not enough, the heat causes gradual shrinking (expect even your preshrunk garments to lose another 5 percent). Whenever possible, air-dry your clothing. You'll cut energy costs and prolong the life of your garments. When you do use the dryer, turn dress garments inside out to minimize the pilling on the outside.

Dryer sheet dispenser

Mount a paper towel holder next to the clothes dryer to dispense a roll of fabric-softener sheets for easy access. And keep an empty tissue box close by to stash the used dryer sheets, which can be recycled.

Dryer sheets

There is no need to throw out your fabric softener sheet after one use. One sheet will work just fine for 2, often 3 loads of laundry.

Drying comforters

When drying a comforter or pillow in the clothes dryer, toss in a couple of clean tennis shoes. They will bounce around on the items and keep them from bunching up.

Dry the shower curtain

Yes, you can dry a plastic shower curtain in the dryer. Set the temperature to low and add one or two dry towels. Conventional wisdom says plastic in a clothes dryer presents a potential fire hazard. So don't even think about walking away. Stand there for the two minutes it takes to remove the wrinkles and dry the shower curtain.

Emergency ironing board

Need an emergency ironing board? Use a kitchen breadboard covered with a dish towel.

Foam pillows

Handwash foam-filled pillows in mild detergent, then roll in a towel and squeeze out excess water. Machine drying could cause a fire so always air-dry foam-filled pillows away from heat.

Fruit stains

Stains in fabric from fruits, berries, and juices should be sponged immediately with cold water. Then if it's safe for the fabric, hold the garment over the sink and pour boiling water through the stain. Follow by working laundry detergent into the stain and rinse.

Grass stains

To remove grass stains from clothes, spot-treat the stain with a shampoo made for oily hair.

Grass stains

Pretreat minor grass stains on washable fabric with full-strength rubbing alcohol. Rub gently and launder as usual. For more serious grass stains, use Soilove according to the directions on the label.

Handwashables in the shower

Take your delicate items that require handwashing into the shower with you. Instead of laundry detergent or Woolite, wash them with your shampoo.

Hydrogen peroxide and scorch marks

The best way to remove scorch marks from white cotton is with 3 percent hydrogen peroxide, which acts like bleach. Using an eyedropper, saturate the scorched area, and allow to sit for 15 to 20 minutes. Repeat until the marks have disappeared, then flush the fabric with water.

Ink remover

Place the ink-stained fabric over several thicknesses of paper toweling. Combine 1 tablespoon white vinegar, 1 tablespoon milk, 1 teaspoon lemon juice, and 1 teaspoon borax in a small bowl, and "paint" the spot. Wait for a few minutes, then sponge the area with cool water. Repeat until the stain is gone.

Ink spots

A quick, easy, and cheap way to get ink spots out of washable clothing is to soak the stain in milk. Wash as usual.

Inside out means longer wear

Reduce fading and pilling: Turn clothing wrong side out before washing and drying to reduce friction on the right side of the garment.

Ironing pleats

Use bobby pins or clothespins at the bottom of each pleat to hold it flat while you iron.

Last-ditch effort for impossible stains

After you've tried every method you know of to remove impossible stains such as mildew from fabric, try this right before you chuck the item into the rag bag: With a cotton swab apply a commercial mildew stain product like Tilex directly to the stain. Let stand for about a minute and wash immediately. This will work on colorfast or white fabrics, but will leave a huge bleach mark on noncolorfast items. This is a last-ditch, severe action—so beware.

Laundry products

Measure detergent for both washing machine and dishwasher. If you just dump it in, you are probably using way too much.

Less bleach

You can cut the amount of chlorine bleach used in your wash by half when you add ½ cup baking soda to top-loading washing machines or ¼ cup to front loaders.

Lightly scented

If you do not like to spray perfume directly onto your clothes or skin, try giving your ironing board a squirt or dab before pressing your blouse, trousers, or skirt. The steam from the iron draws just the whisper of the scent, and it clings to the fabric all day.

Lint on dark clothes

Use a bit of white vinegar in the final rinse water to keep lint from clinging to dark clothes.

Lipstick stains

Use hairspray to remove lipstick stains from clothing. Spray it on, let it sit for a minute or two, and wipe carefully. Launder as usual.

Little League uniforms

Clay dirt from baseball fields gets on clothes and uniforms and is just about impossible to remove. Try this: Brush off any dry clay remaining on the fabric. Treat heavily stained areas with Soilove, then soak the garments overnight in a solution of enzyme-action detergent (like Biz), following package directions. The next morning, launder the clothes. If stains remain, repeat the whole process. Or, if the fabric is white, use chlorine bleach as a last resort.

Locking hangers

Protect the clothes you hang outdoors from taking off in a strong wind: Put each piece of clothing on two hangers, hooks reversed, to keep the hangers from falling.

Makeup stains

Here's a wonderful prewash treatment for cleaning makeup from collars: Mix equal amounts of white vinegar and liquid dishwashing detergent like Dawn or Joy. Rub into the soiled collar or other soiled spots and toss into the washing machine. Launder as usual.

Marks from clothes rack

If the bars of your wooden clothes-drying rack leave brown stripes on your clothes, you can solve the problem easily by covering the bars with aluminum foil.

Mending kit for laundry

Create a mending kit for the laundry room. Thread several sewing needles with basic colors, stick them into a pincushion, and hang it near the dryer.

Mildew stains

To remove mold or mildew stains from most white fabrics, soak the garment for an hour or so in a solution of 1 tablespoon vinegar, ½ cup liquid bleach, and 2 quarts hot water. Wash and dry the garment as usual.

Monthly maintenance

Take care of your washing machine, and you'll add years to its useful life: To unclog hoses and flush out all the minerals and all the gummy buildup, fill the machine with hot water (no clothes), pour in 1 gallon of distilled white vinegar, and allow to run though an entire cycle.

No more sorting

Keep 2 hampers in a central location, 1 for whites and 1 for darks. You'll save lots of time because the laundry will be already sorted.

One last washing

When using the last quantity of liquid laundry soap, fill the empty bottle all the way to the top with water and replace the lid. Shake vigorously, and use the entire contents with your next load of laundry. You'll get one last wash from a bottle that normally would have been thrown away.

Perspiration challenges

Perspiration odors in washable clothing can be removed by wetting the area and rubbing in baking soda before laundering.

Perspiration stains

To remove perspiration stains, add 4 tablespoons of salt to 1 quart of hot water, and sponge the fabric with the solution.

Petroleum jelly as stain treatment

Soften hardened paint, tar, and rubber cement on washable fabrics with petroleum jelly. Launder fabrics treated in this way immediately after application.

Presoak manually

Instead of using the presoak and prewash cycles on your washing machine, which use additional water and energy, use the regular cycle, but turn it off after the clothes agitate a few minutes. Let them soak for an hour or overnight, and then resume the rest of the cycle.

Refrigerate the ironing

If you run out of time for ironing before you finish, stuff any clothes you've dampened into a plastic bag and store the bag in the refrigerator. This keeps the clothes from mildewing and saves the time it would take to redampen them.

Remove candle wax

To remove candle wax from a tablecloth, use a dull knife to scrape off as much wax as possible. Place the fabric between two blotters or facial tissues and press with a warm iron. Remove color stain with nonflammable dry-cleaning solvent or Soilove. Wash with detergent in the hottest water that is safe for the fabric.

Remove stickers and labels

When stickers go through the wash on your kids' clothes and become welded on during the dryer phase, remove them with duct tape: Press the duct tape to the stickered area, then rip it off quickly and with great gusto. This works equally well with those "Hello! My Name Is . . ." stickers that have been known to work their way through the family laundry process too. Any sticky residue may be removed with a quick spritz of Soilove.

Rust on fabric

To remove rust stains from washable fabric, shake ordinary table salt on the stain and wet with lemon juice. Allow to set overnight, then wash normally.

Scorch marks

If you happen to scorch a cotton garment when ironing, here's a possible solution, depending on the severity of the burn mark: Soak the whole garment for 30 minutes to 1 hour in a solution of 1 part hydrogen peroxide to 3 parts warm water. Don't try to spot-clean the scorch mark because the peroxide solution may alter the fabric color slightly. Soaking the entire garment will allow the slight color alteration to be uniform. Rinse in warm water and hang to dry. Press the item when it's still slightly damp, and be sure to use the medium setting on your iron this time.

Shampoo on collars and cuffs

Use shampoo to pretreat dirty collars and cuffs. Scrub gently with an old toothbrush. Shampoo is meant to clean body oil, which is exactly what that ring is.

Shampoo to save

Instead of buying delicate-wash products like Woolite for sweaters and washable silks, use regular shampoo instead. Caution: When using as a laundry product, do not use specialty formulas for dry or oily hair.

Smoky-smelling clothes

When clothing or fabrics smell smoky, throw the items in the dryer on fluff cycle for about 20 minutes along with a small towel or cloth dampened with lemon-scented household ammonia.

Socks

Pin kids' dirty socks together before dropping them in the laundry. The time invested will be more than returned when you're sorting later.

Speed drying time

A dry towel in the dryer with a very damp load will speed drying time. The towel will absorb a lot of the moisture.

Spot remover for wool and silk

An excellent spot remover for wool and silk is Murphy's Oil Soap (available in the household cleaning section of the supermarket). Use directly on the fabric and allow it to soak in. Wash as usual. Murphy's is also great for cars, floors, and, of course, wood furniture and cabinets. Always test on a inconspicuous spot like an inside seam.

Spray starch

If you use a lot of spray starch around your house, you've likely discovered those aerosol cans of spray starch don't last very long. Cheaper and better: Purchase concentrated liquid starch such as Sta-Flo and mix it in a spray bottle, 1 part starch, 2 parts water. In this way a 32-ounce bottle of starch equals 3 ½ cans of aerosol starch for a fraction of the cost.

Stubborn smoke odors

If you can, wash the smoky-smelling duds and add 1 cup baking soda to the wash cycle. If laundering doesn't do the trick, check whether your dry cleaner offers a process called ozone treatment, which removes smoke odor. It does cost considerably more than regular cleaning, but it might be worth the cost if the clothes are of particular value.

Sunscreen stains

That ring around the collar on shirts and blouses may be your sunscreen, so make sure you pretreat it with a stain treatment that is designed to break down and remove grease and oil. Wash as usual using the warmest water that is safe for the fabric. Don't put the garment in the dryer before checking to see if all the stain has been removed. If it hasn't, the heat of the dryer may set the stain. Repeat treatment as necessary.

Test for colorfastness

Will your new blue blouse run in the wash? Take a light-colored, wet washcloth and rub an inside seam of the blouse. If any color rubs off, the garment will run. Handwash or dry-clean instead.

The sock solution

No more lost socks. Make each family member—even baby—a drawstring sock bag to keep in their room. All dirty socks go in, and the bag is thrown into the wash. After drying, the bag, still full, is returned to its owner intact.

Too much detergent

If items come out of the laundry stiff, you're probably using too much detergent. Don't use more than the manufacturer advises, and add a cup of vinegar to the rinse water to help soften your clothes.

Vinegar removes deodorant stains

Vinegar applied to clothing stained by deodorant removes the spots from most fabrics. Soak the soiled area in the vinegar, then launder the garment as usual.

Wash the shower curtain

Wash plastic shower curtains in the washing machine, adding ½ cup baking soda or ½ cup vinegar to your regular liquid laundry detergent plus 1 bath towel. The agitating motion will turn it into an automatic scrubber.

Yellowed linens

To remove that disgusting yellow from old linens that are supposed to be white: Dissolve ¼ cup automatic dishwasher detergent (like powdered

Cascade) in a large stainless steel (not aluminum) pan filled with boiling water. Carefully add linens and allow them to soak, off of heat, for 8 hours. Rinse; launder as usual.

Yellow stains

Denture-cleaning tablets will remove yellow stains from fabric. Find a container big enough to hold the stained fabric. Fill the container with warm water and the number of tablets according to the ratio described on the package. After the tablets dissolve, add the stained item to the solution and soak until the spots are gone.

A home for the table leaf

Hang the table extension leaf on the closet wall behind your clothes. It won't take up room, and it will be out of sight and protected from scratches.

Address book

Keep an address book listing the first names of your kids' friends, followed by their numbers, addresses, and their mothers' first names. If the kids want to call a friend, they don't need to remember the mother's last name; and if the mother's last name is different from the friend's, it's easy to locate the mom by referring to her child's first name.

Artists' paintbrushes

Slip tiny artists' paintbrushes into drinking straws to protect them.

Belt holder

For a great belt holder, install a row of big cup hooks along the bottom of a wooden hanger.

Belt the ladder

Nail a sturdy, old leather belt to the garage wall. Store the ladder by wrapping the belt around its top step and buckling it closed.

Blanket storage

Eliminate the question of where to store extra blankets. Keep them between the mattress and the box spring.

Boxes inside out

For mailing packages it's best to reuse boxes instead of purchasing them for 80 cents or more at a packaging store. Oftentimes however, there is already printed material on the box itself. Instead of wrapping it with brown paper, simply disassemble it, then reassemble it "inside out," secure it with packing tape, and it's ready to go.

Box under the bed

Keep a cardboard storage box in each bedroom (under the bed is good), and use it to collect outgrown clothes and toys. Full boxes means it's time for a yard sale or a trip to the Salvation Army or consignment store.

Bug banquet
Insects are attracted to the glue in cardboard cartons and brown paper bags, so when you keep things stored in them it's the same as inviting the bugs to a banquet. Seal items in plastic before placing them in cardboard boxes and paper bags.

CD storage container
Keep your compact discs neatly organized by storing them in the perfect-sized container—an empty shoebox. Place them upright in the box so the titles are visible, and you'll be able to easily flip through them to find the ones you're looking for. The box can be covered with contact paper or painted.

Closet dust protectors
Convert extra pillowcases (king-size are extra long) into garment bags to protect the clothes hanging in your closet, especially those that are out-of-season. Just cut a hole in the top and insert the hangers.

Closet mirror
Attach a mirror on the closet ceiling so you can keep track of top-shelf contents.

Dealing with the mail
As soon as you get the mail, read it and sort it into one of these categories: pay, answer, file, and dump. Then do it.

Dejunk
Dejunk drawers and closets in one room each week until you're done. Prepare one box for charity, one for items in need of repair, and one for a garage sale.

Don't forget
If you're worried about remembering something, wear your watch on the wrong wrist. It doesn't look as silly as a piece of string tied to your finger, but it works just as well.

Double the closet space
Hang a length of chain from a strong hanger. Each link can hold one hanger, which takes up much less space and effectively doubles or triples your closet space.

Drawer organizer
Keep your earrings, small bracelets, and necklaces in the separate compartments of a plastic ice tray. The tray fits in a dresser drawer so jewels stay neat and out of sight.

Everything in the bag
The perfect solution for organizing all the little stuff that clutters the rooms in your home is a large, clear plastic shoe bag—the kind with lots

of pockets. All of its contents are clearly visible, neatly separated, and easily portable. Hang one on the back of the door in the nursery, kitchen, bedrooms, and bathrooms.

Fake vent

Cut a hole at the approximate location and of the size of a heat vent in the wall, and attach a vent cover. Paint it to match all the other heat vents, and you'll have a great hideaway for your treasures.

Family filing system

Establish a color-coded family filing system. Use red folders for kids' school papers, blue for car and home documents, green for finances, yellow for medical, and orange for personal items.

Family in-boxes

Designate a colored file folder or plastic in-box for each of your children. When they come home from school, have them place important papers, forms, and other school information in their special place. And they'll know where to find the papers and items they need to return to the teacher the next day.

For the keys

Keep a pretty, decorative bowl on a table near the front door to hold house keys. You'll always know exactly where they are.

Frozen policies

Do not keep wills or life insurance policies in a safe-deposit box. It is not unusual for a safe-deposit box to be sealed at the time of death, making it very difficult for the survivors. Instead keep them in a fireproof safe, or wrap them in plastic and put them in a sealed container in the freezer. They will be easily accessible and protected in case of fire.

Grocery bag method

Take a large brown grocery bag and load into it all the clutter that's driving you nuts. Stash it in a cupboard or another out of the way place. If family members are missing something, send them to the bag. Anything not retrieved in 2 or 3 weeks can be considered a likely candidate for the trash—just in time for another clean sweep of the house.

Hang 'em high

Hang shoes from screw-in doorstops installed on the inside of the closet doors.

Home filing system

Set up temporary files labeled "To be filed" and "To be tossed." In the first, place items that need to be saved permanently. In the second, put dated material. Once a month, file the first and dump the second.

Important papers

Roll your important papers and store them in cardboard tubes. They can be tucked away and will stay crease-free.

Jewelry chains

Prevent chains from tangling and knotting in your jewelry box this way: Cut a drinking straw to half the length of the chain, slip the chain through it, then fasten the catch.

Key holder

Remove the spine from an old 3-ring loose-leaf notebook to hold those extra keys. You can attach it to a wall or cabinet.

Lace bolts

Fabric stores often give away empty, plastic lace bolts. They work perfectly for storing strings of Christmas lights, extension cords, ribbon, and yarn—anything that has a way of turning into a tangled mess.

Linen roll-up

Use the cardboard tubes from long rolls of holiday or birthday wrapping paper to store crease-free, freshly ironed dresser scarves and table runners. Simple lay the tube over one end of the item and roll it up. Secure with a piece of ribbon or string.

Milk cartons

When you know you will be moving, start saving waxed milk cartons. They are just the perfect size for packing odd-shaped dishes, vases, knick-knacks, jars, small sculptures, even silverware; and when closed, they stack neatly inside a larger box.

Musty suitcases

To restore a musty suitcase, fill it with crumpled newspaper, then close it up. Change the paper every 2 to 3 days until the odor is gone.

Neat cords

Keep extension cords neat. Stuff the looped cords into individual cardboard tubes.

Office organizer

Glue a cluster of several different short lengths of PVC piping together. Put end caps on the bottom of each and you have an organizer for pencils, pens, and other invaluable home office tools.

Organize the laundry

If your children wear different sizes of similar underwear, socks, and T-shirts, doing the laundry can be enough to send you to the funny farm because everything looks alike. Clearly, your family needs to get color-coded and the sooner the better. Pick up a variety of fabric paints so you have a different color for each member. Mark the toes of socks and the labels on underwear and T-shirts with the owner's color. Now folding and sorting laundry will be so easy, even the kids can do it.

Packing fragile things

Crumpled-up plastic bags make wonderful packing material for fragile items and gives the recipient a little extra bonus.

Pants racks

Install towel racks on the back of closet doors for hanging slacks.

Photocopy wallet contents

Make a photocopy of everything in your wallet. Now if you lose your wallet, you'll have a record of the important information so you can move quickly to have things replaced or canceled as will be necessary.

Plastic grocery bags

Save and organize plastic grocery bags neatly and compactly inside a cardboard tube from a roll of paper towels or waxed paper. Stuff the plastic bags into the tube and store in cupboard or drawer. Keep one under the car seat. It will come in handy.

Rolling storage

Attach casters to the bottom of an old dresser drawer and use it for storage underneath a bed.

Roll up chalkboard

Paint an ordinary window shade with chalkboard paint and mount it on the wall in front of your garage workbench or in your utility room. When you need to make a note of something, just pull it down.

Safe storage

Spray the inside of a mayonnaise jar white. Store it in the refrigerator as a hiding place for money or valuables.

Saw blades

Store circular saw blades in an old record album jacket.

Screwdriver caddy

To make a great screwdriver caddy, tightly coil a roll of corrugated cardboard and stuff it into a 2-pound coffee can. Poke all your screwdrivers between the corrugations.

Socket nuts

Find a nut to fit each socket of your set. Glue the nuts in a row in a tool tray. Now store each socket on its own nut, and it will stay secure and in place.

Store in the luggage

Suitcases, which spend the greater portion of their functional lives completely useless and taking up space, should be considered for storing almost anything, from holiday decorations to out-of-season clothes.

Table linens

Use a multiple skirt hanger to organize place mats, cloth napkins, and folded tablecloths. Hang it in the entry closet, and they'll always be neat and wrinkle-free.

The well-labeled video

After you record a TV program, cut out the synopsis of the show from the newspaper and tape it to the cassette case. Later, when you are ready to view the tape, you'll have all the information about the program right at your fingertips.

Tissue box for the car

Empty tissue boxes make great car totes. They can be used to hold all the loose items that roll to the front of the car when the brakes are applied (i.e., bottle of lotion, spare change, kiddie toys, cassette tapes). Let the kids fill one of these little boxes with stuff for long car trips.

Tool protector

Staple a pocket protector to your workbench so you can keep track of those really small tools that have a way of disappearing.

Velcro the remote

Attach a self-stick Velcro strip to the side of your TV and another to the back of the TV remote control.

Wrinkle-free

Throw wrinkled clothes into the dryer along with a wet towel. Turn it on for a few minutes and all the wrinkles will iron themselves away while you're getting ready.

American flags

The U.S. Government is an inexpensive source for cheap American flags. Flags that have been flown over the nation's capitol can be purchased through one's senator or congressperson. Flags come in either nylon or cotton and in a variety of sizes. A 3-by-5-foot nylon flag runs about $10, which includes shipping and handling. Call your senator or representative's office to receive an order form.

Barbecue cover

Fold an old vinyl tablecloth in half, and sew up the sides to make a cover for your outdoor barbecue grill.

Barbecue fire

For a fast, hot, and fume-free blaze, set a dry pinecone in the bottom of the barbecue. Build a pyramid of charcoal around it. Start your fire by igniting the pinecone.

Beach bag

Take a large zippered storage bag to the beach with ¼ cup of baking soda inside. Use it to bring home wet suits. Just put them in the bag and shake. The soda absorbs moisture and helps prevent mildew and scary smells until you can get the suits properly laundered.

Beach collection bags

Use mesh onion sacks for gathering shells at the beach. They're strong, waterproof, and they sift out most of the sand by themselves. When you get home, rinse the sack and its contents under an outdoor faucet, and you won't get a speck of sand in the house.

Beach towel and more

Sew a coordinating washcloth to a beach towel along three sides and use Velcro-type fasteners to close the fourth. Now you and your kids have an instant pocket for keys, coins, or suntan lotion.

Canvas awnings

If your outdoor canvas awnings are faded and ugly, refurbish them by first cleaning them well and then repainting with canvas paint.

Charcoal barbecue
To build a perfect charcoal fire for the barbecue, fill each slot of 2 or 3 empty cardboard egg cartons with briquettes. Set them in the barbecue, light the cartons, and you have a perfect charcoal arrangement with no lighter fluid required.

Charcoal recapture
After the food has cooked, don't let the coals burn themselves out. Scoop them up into an empty can and smother them by placing a nonflammable lid over the can. They can be used again.

Concrete stains
Commercial cleansers, such as Ajax and Comet, work well to clean concrete that has been stained by mold or leaves. Sprinkle cleanser on the cement, add water, and scrub with a stiff broom. Allow to sit for a few hours; rinse.

Floating keys
Tie a couple of corks to your key ring when you go boating.

Icy deck
If your wooden deck gets icy in the winter, you can make it safe: Sprinkle it with cornmeal. This provides traction and a snack for the birds when the ice melts.

Insect-free picnic
Keep flies from the picnic area: Put a vase filled with sprigs of lavender, mint, or elder in the center of the table. Be sure to rub the leaves frequently to release their scent.

Keep animals away
Sprinkle a small amount of household ammonia in the outdoor garbage cans. Animals will be repelled by the strong smell.

Moldy bricks
Wash bricks with a mixture of household bleach and water, a 50/50 mix for heavy deposits, a weaker mix for lighter ones.

Natural insect repellent
Pots of sweet basil placed strategically around the patio, swimming pool, or doorway repel flies.

Natural repellent
Crush bay leaves between your fingers and then rub your fingers over your skin to repel gnats. It's good for flies and mosquitoes too.

Nest-building material
Help the birds with their spring nest-building chores. Collect the lint from

your clothes dryer, tie it up in a ball with string, and hang it in the backyard.

Picnic basket cooler

Turn a picnic basket into a cooler by lining it with slabs of poly foam (from a fabric store) glued in place. As long as you only pack items that have been thoroughly chilled, they will stay cool for several hours longer than in the uninsulated basket.

Pool decals

Put bathtub decals on the bottom of a kiddie pool to make it less slippery.

Pool repairs

If your above-ground swimming pool develops tears and cracks, patch them using bathroom caulking, smoothing it onto the damaged, dry pool surface. Leave it on overnight, and it will dry to a flexible, waterproof surface.

Poolside towel rack

A folding clothes rack makes a great poolside towel rack.

Propane

Never sure how much propane is left in the barbecue tank? Make a streak down the side with a wet sponge. Moisture will evaporate from the upper, empty part more quickly.

Resin patio furniture

Make a good lather with dishwashing detergent, household ammonia, and warm water. Sponge the lather on and wash gently. Don't use an abrasive sponge. For heavy stains, use a solution of bleach and water (do not allow the bleach and ammonia to come in contact with each other). Restore the shiny finish by applying a coat of car wax.

Roll-on sunscreen

Sunscreen won't spill and will be much easier to apply if it's transferred to a roll-on deodorant bottle. Squeeze the neck of an empty bottle with pliers so the ball pops out. (Watch out because it can really fly.) Clean the bottle, pour in the sunscreen, and pop the ball back in.

Sand-free radio

When you go to the beach, carry the radio in a plastic zippered storage bag. You can operate it without ever opening the bag. It will stay sand-free and completely dry.

Shoveling snow

Spray vegetable oil on your snow shovel to keep snow from sticking.

Snow

If only a small amount of snow has covered your sidewalks, sweep the snow away with a broom instead of shoveling it. The job will be completed more quickly and with much less stress to your back.

Tablecloth

When entertaining outdoors, use a clean, bright beach towel for a tablecloth.

Wax the patio furniture

The bright colors of outdoor plastic furniture, kiddie gyms, etc., can fade from regular exposure to the sun. But you can prevent them from fading with a protective coat of car wax. The wax also repels dirt and grime, which makes for quick and easy cleanups.

White stains on terra-cotta pots

The white rings on the outside of terra-cotta pots, caused by minerals in the water, can usually be wiped away with white vinegar.

PEST CONTROL

All-purpose insect spray

Mix 1 chopped garlic clove, 1 small onion chopped, and 1 tablespoon cayenne powder to one quart of water. Allow to steep 1 hour, then add 1 tablespoon of liquid Ivory soap. This all-purpose insect spray remains potent for only one week, so use it up.

Ants

Repel ants by washing countertops, cabinets, and floors with equal parts water and vinegar.

Ants

Drive ants from the kitchen by sprinkling shelves or windowsills with cinnamon, cloves, or baking soda. Put it into crevices, too, and repeat occasionally.

Aphids

Mix 1 gallon water, 1 tablespoon vegetable oil, and 2 tablespoons Ivory liquid. Spray on plants where aphid damage is evident.

Bats

The next time you start to wonder what you can do to rid your property of bats, remember this: A single bat can catch and kill 900 insects an hour—as many as 3,000 in a night.

Citrus insect repellent

To prevent ants, spiders, and bugs from entering your home or another structure, spray the foundation and the grout within a foot of the wall with a mixture of ½ cup ground lemon (you can puree the lemon in a blender or foot processor), including the rind, and 1 gallon of water. Apply with a garden sprinkling can. Not only is the weak solution versatile, it's mild, cheap, and environmentally sound.

Cockroaches

A common entrance for cockroaches is the holes through which the plumbing enters under the kitchen or bathroom sinks. Plug these tightly with rags or steel wool, and you'll cause a permanent traffic jam on that roach freeway.

HOME

Cockroach killer

Mix ¼ cup shortening with ⅛ cup sugar. In a separate container mix ½ pound powdered boric acid (available at pharmacies) and ½ cup flour; add to shortening mixture. Stir well with enough water to make a soft dough. Form into small balls the size of marbles and hide in those out of the way places roaches love to hide. This recipe works far better than commercial products. Just make sure you keep this out of the reach of children.

Crickets

Mix 1 can beer, 1 cup Epsom salts, 1 cup detergent, 1 cup ammonia, and 2 cups water. Spray where grass damage is evident.

Cutworms

If your garden is infested with ants or cutworms, sprinkle used coffee grounds on the affected area.

Flea treatment for the home

Commercial flea exterminators charge anywhere from $300 to $1100 to treat your home with a product called food-grade diatomaceous earth. You can do this yourself with a flour sifter and a 5-pound box of diatomaceous earth for about $20. Sift onto your carpet with the sifter, brush or pound it in with a broom. Leave for 24 to 36 hours, then vacuum up. This is a nontoxic and environmentally safe treatment, but wear a face protector because it is fine as powder. The diatomaceous earth you get from a pool supply is *not* food-grade. It has been chemically altered and does not kill fleas. Check with a garden supply store or call Natural Animal Health Products 800-274-7387 to order by mail.

Fly and insect spray

Rubbing alcohol makes a great fly and insect spray. The fine mist evaporates quickly and is not harmful to anyone but the pests. This doesn't necessarily kill them, but it anesthetizes the little guys, so once they're asleep, dispose of them quickly.

Fruit flies

Set out a small dish of vinegar to which you've added a few drops of detergent to repel fruit flies.

Garbage cans

Sprinkle dry soap or borax into garbage cans after they've been washed and allowed to dry; it acts as a repellent to flies.

Hairspray for wasps

In a pinch use hairspray to kill wasps. As long as you get some of the product on their wings, they'll go down.

PEST CONTROL

Keeping ants at bay

Spread dried coffee grounds or whole cloves around the picnic area. If you are on a solid surface, draw a white chalk line around the perimeter. For whatever reason, ants won't cross that line.

Lemon repels ants

Squirt lemon juice on windowsills and doorways. Ants hate it and will absolutely refuse to come into your house.

Mice

Use peanut butter as bait for your mousetraps. You can reset the traps and catch several mice before you need to add bait.

Mosquito repellents

Plant basil and pansies around the patio and house to repel mosquitoes. Mint planted around the home repels flies. Keep basil well watered so that it produces a stronger scent. Dried ground basil leaves left in small bowls or hung in muslin bags are also effective.

Moths

Make sachets of dried lavender or equal portions of rosemary and mint. Place in closets, drawers, or closed containers to mothproof garments.

Natural repellents

Fill vases with geraniums or eucalyptus—bugs stay away from their scents.

Silverfish

To get rid of silverfish, put about ¼ inch of flour in a small, straight-sided glass. Run a strip of adhesive tape from bottom to top on the outside. Silverfish will travel up the tape and drop into the glass, but they won't be able to get back out. Place one of these traps in each room where you've seen silverfish.

Snails and slugs

To keep snails and slugs out of your garden, sink pie pans in the garden so that the rims are flush with the ground. Fill with beer. The slugs and snails will be attracted to the beer, which will be their final undoing. (This is a lovely object lesson for kids who think it's cool to drink beer!) Simply empty the pie pans when they get full.

Snails

Snails will turn around and go the other way rather than cross a protective border of sand, lime, or ashes.

Spiders

To discourage spiders, spray rubbing alcohol on windowsills.

PEST CONTROL

Squirrel ladders

To keep squirrels out of your attic, get rid of any tree branches that hang over your house and outbuildings so they can't use them as ladders.

Tacky flyswatter

For fruit flies and other tiny flying insects that a regular flyswatter just seems to miss, put a few strips of double-backed tape on your flyswatter.

Tape that sucker

Don't squash a bug that is crawling on your wall, drapes, or anywhere else it can stain. Just "apply" a strip of tape; the bug adheres to it and can be disposed of.

Wasp repellent

Toilet-bowl deodorizers nailed by the door, placed near wastebaskets, or set on a windowsill will keep wasps away. They hate the smell.

Whiteflies, spider mites, mealybugs, cinch bugs, and aphids

Mix 3 tablespoons liquid Ivory soap in a gallon of water and mix well. Fill a sprayer with the soapy solution and mist the leaves of plants and bushes to kill these little pests.

SEWING & MENDING

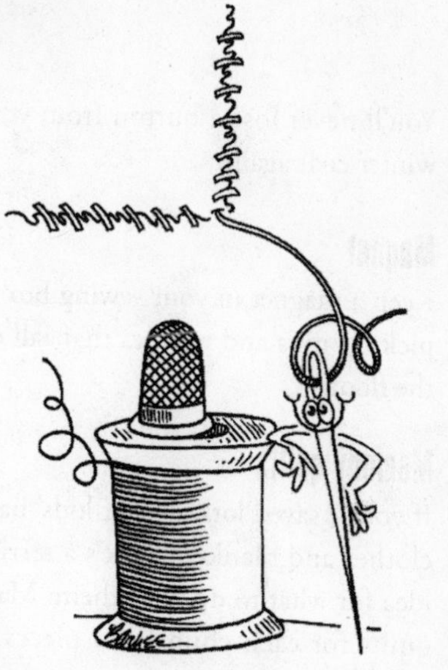

Button glue

Before sewing, place clear fingernail polish on the center of a button, on the side toward the fabric. Then once the button has been securely attached to the garment, place another dab on the top center. This will help keep that button from going anywhere for a long, long time.

Buttons that give

Place a toothpick between the button and fabric as you sew. When the button is secured, remove the toothpick. This gives the button a little slack and will make it easier to operate.

Buttons to spare

Sew extra buttons into the seams of jackets and pants. If you need a spare, you'll always know right where it is.

Button tricks

When attaching a four-hole button, stitch through two holes, then knot the thread before you sew through the other two holes. If the thread breaks on one side, the button won't come off.

Collars

Take off the frayed collar of a shirt, turn it over, and carefully sew it back. With a "new" collar the whole shirt should have a new life.

Dryer sheets for appliqué

Another use for dryer sheets: Use these sheets, new or used, as interfacing when appliquéing a quilt. They form the layer between the cutout and the quilt top. They keep the quilt fresher longer between washings and airings, add incredibly lightweight insulation, and extend the life of the quilt.

Dusting the insides

When the bobbin apparatus in your sewing machine needs dusting, blow the dust out by aiming quick bursts of air from an empty squeeze bottle.

Floss the beads

Use dental floss for restringing beads.

Floss your coat

Dental floss makes a sturdy thread for securing buttons on heavy fabric.

You'll never lose a button from your winter coat again.

Magnet

Keep a magnet in your sewing box to pick up pins and needles that fall on the floor.

Memory quilts

If you've saved lots of your kids' baby clothes and blankets, here's a terrific idea for what to do with them: Make quilts for each child from pieces of their old baby clothes.

Needle sharpening

Sharpen a sewing machine needle without removing it from the machine by "stitching" through a sheet of fine-grain sandpaper.

Organized sewing

Put a lazy Susan on your sewing table to store your notions. Now, everything you need is just a spin away!

Perfect patch

When your kids' jeans require a knee patch, simply remove a back pocket, open the inside leg seam with a seam ripper, and sew the pocket over the hole. Close seam. Since the pocket has been washed as many times as the jeans, the material always matches perfectly.

Pillow stuffing

Cut clean, used panty hose in rings and use as stuffing for pincushions, pillows, or children's toys. The fabric is washable and can be easily coaxed into tight corners.

Preventive patches

When kids' pants are new, apply iron-on patches to the inside knees.

Remove that hem line

To remove the permanent press line from a hem that has been let down, dampen the crease with white vinegar and press with a piece of aluminum foil between material and iron.

Slick pincushion

An unwrapped bar of soap makes a terrific pincushion. Bonus: Needles and pins that have been in soap will glide through fabric.

Smart hem

When hemming a skirt or pants, knot the thread every 3 or 4 inches. A small break in the thread won't mean an entire rehemming job.

Stuff it with newspaper

Slip a folded newspaper through the legs or sleeves of the garment you're mending so you don't sew through both layers.

SEWING & MENDING

Thread shade

A good rule of thumb is to use a thread that is one shade darker than the fabric you are working on. Thread has a tendency of fading more quickly than solid materials.

Threading a needle

If you have trouble threading a needle, wet the end of the thread and draw it across a bar of soap. The thread will stiffen and slip right through the eye of the needle.

Threading a needle

It's easier to thread a needle if you draw the end of the thread across a wax candle first.

Washcloths

The next time you see cotton bath towels on sale, buy one and give this a try: Cut it into 8 washcloths. Either serge the edges or use a zigzag or overlock stitch on a regular sewing machine. You should be able to make loads of wonderful washcloths for a fraction of the cost of ready-made.

TELEPHONE

Ask for credit

If your phone service is interrupted for more than 24 hours, ask for a credit. You'll probably get it, especially if you nicely point out that you pay dearly for the privilege of having a telephone link to the outside world.

Audit long-distance bills

Have your phone bill audited by several long-distance providers. Some long-distance companies offer auditing services at no charge. You send them several monthly bills, and they determine what you would have paid had you used their service. If you decide to switch, make sure all fees to make the move will be waived and that you can go back if you are unsatisfied with the new service.

Beware of unfamiliar area codes

There's a message on your answering machine. It says a relative is sick or has been arrested, and you should call a phone number in the 809 area code for more information. If you don't immediately recognize the number, don't dial. Since 809 numbers are in the Caribbean and not bound by U.S. regulations, that one call, which will be treated as a 900 call, could end up costing you $100 or more.

Call corporate collect

Try it. Most large companies will accept your collect call as a matter of business. Just identify yourself as a good customer or potential client. If denied, simply call back direct. Hey, it's worth a try, and it usually works.

Call, don't drive

Let your fingers do the walking, even if it requires a toll call. It's cheaper than driving your car.

Call toll-free

You can't imagine how many companies and even individuals now have 800 numbers. Not all are listed, so be sure to ask. Toll-free directory assistance (800-555-1212) is always free, unlike local and long-distance directory assistance.

Call to remember

If there's something you absolutely have to do when you get home, just call your answering machine and leave a message for yourself. That's probably the first thing you'll check.

Cash to switch

If a competing long-distance carrier sends you a check that when cashed will automatically switch you over to their service, call your long-distance provider and tell them about it. Then ask them what they can do for you so that you won't have to switch. Expect them to match or beat the competitor's offer in order to keep your business.

Change phone numbers

When moving to a new home, call the phone company and request the former occupant's phone number. It may be available if that person did not take the number to the next residence. Because the number is already installed but inactive you may be able to bypass the usual hookup fee, which could be $50 or more. There will be some kind of transfer fee, but it will be considerably less. If you can pull this off, plan to receive calls for the previous occupant for a while. Make sure you have the new number so you can refer his or her callers. That's a small price to pay for significant savings. Contact the phone company at the earliest moment. Don't wait until you've moved in.

Directory assistance

Avoid directory assistance. It's amazing that phone companies actually charge for that, but they do. Get a phone book and use it.

Long-distance calling

If your long-distance bill is really out of control, and you are really determined to get that expense under control, take drastic measures. Instruct your phone company to block all long-distance calls. Now you will only be able to place local, toll-free, and 911 phone calls. And if you absolutely must call long distance, there's always the pay phone at the corner.

Phone service checkup

Have a phone checkup annually. Request an equipment inventory report. The phone company will send you a form listing the service for which you are charged. If you find you've been overpaying, request a retroactive refund. This would be a good time to rethink the expensive add-ons you have like Call Waiting, Call Forwarding, and phone rental fees. Annualize the amount you're paying on a monthly basis, and then decide if it's really worth it.

Send a note instead

Whenever possible write short letters or postcards instead of calling long distance. Keep a stack of stamped postcards by the phone to remind you. Buy postcards at the post office and all you pay for is the stamp. The card is free.

Six-second billing

If your present long-distance carrier does not give you 6-second billing but instead charges you to the next full minute, you may be paying more than you have to. Shop around and find a 6-second carrier, and you could save 8 to 15 percent on your long-distance calling.

Timed calls

Put an egg timer by the phone as a reminder to hang up before you talk yourself into debt.

Unlisted phone number fee

Don't pay a monthly fee to have an unlisted phone number, also called a nonpublished number in some areas. The fee for unlisted service costs anywhere from $1 to $5 a month. If for security and privacy reasons you can't let your name be published, use your pet's name or the middle name of one of your children or your maiden name instead. Your security will not be compromised because if someone calls for your pet, you'll know immediately that it is probably not someone you care to speak with.

Vacation billing

Put your phone service on "vacation" while you are out of town. The savings are modest, but every little bit helps. Call the phone company's business office.

Wrong long-distance number

Always ask for credit immediately whenever you dial a wrong long-distance number. Don't be embarrassed. It's routine. Just call your service provider and make a very quick report.

[illegible] manage the amount you're paying for a monthly base, and then [illegible] worth it.

[illegible]

Whenever possible, [illegible] of calling long distance. [illegible] keep a stack of stamped postcards by the phone to remind you. [illegible] and all you pay for is the stamp. [illegible]

[illegible] billing

If you [illegible] long-distance carrier [illegible] second billing [illegible] but instead [illegible] month [illegible] you may be paying more than you have to [illegible] second [illegible] 15 percent on your long-distance calling.

[illegible]

[illegible]

[illegible] phone number fee

[illegible] monthly fee to have an unlisted phone number, also called [illegible]

[illegible] number is somewhere [illegible] there from [illegible] a month. [illegible] and privacy [illegible] published [illegible] name [illegible] your children [illegible] instead [illegible] because [illegible] calls for your [illegible] you'll know [illegible] probably not someone you care to speak with.

Vacation billing

If your phone service [illegible] vacation [illegible] months [illegible] but every [illegible] Call the phone company [illegible]

Wrong long-distance number

[illegible] ask for a call immediately [illegible] wrong long-distance number [illegible] it [illegible] provider and [illegible] quick reports.

UTILITIES & ENERGY CONSERVATION

Air conditioners

Make sure your window air conditioner is properly sized. An oversized unit will use more energy than necessary and will not dehumidify properly. If you're in the market for a window air-conditioning unit, choose the size you need to cool one room only. Window units are not designed to cool more than one room.

Air-conditioning

To keep your air conditioner from having to work harder than it should, in the summer, cook outdoors or prepare cold meals to avoid heating your kitchen. Place heat-producing appliances such as lamps and TVs away from the thermostat. Change or clean the air-conditioning filter once a month during the peak season. Don't forget to clean the filters on window units. They're behind the front panel. Clean them with soap and water.

Air-conditioning

Set your thermostat on the highest comfortable setting. Raising the temperature just 2 degrees will reduce cooling costs by 5 percent.

Air-conditioning

If you have central air-conditioning, make sure your registers for supply and return air are not blocked by furniture or drapes.

Air-conditioning

You can reduce your air-conditioning use by preparing oven-cooked meals in the cool of the day. When it's time to eat, simply reheat the entree in the microwave or toaster oven.

Blinds and drapes

Hang blinds behind drapes to help keep the room warmer in winter, cooler in summer.

Buy winter fuel in the summer

Buy heating oil off-season. Start checking prices in the spring. Typically you should be able to take advantage of lowest prices from July to September. The same applies to firewood.

Cheap heat

During the winter daylight hours, open all windows, drapes, and window coverings on the side of your home that is receiving the most sunlight (all day on the side facing south). When the sun goes down, be sure to close all window coverings to retain the natural heat.

Check for deposits

Usually if you have been a good customer of the utility companies (gas, water, electricity, phone) for at least a year, you can arrange to have your deposits refunded or credited toward your account. You may be able to get interest, too, if you ask.

Coffeemaker

Don't leave the coffeepot warming for hours on end. Instead, transfer finished coffee to a thermos and turn that energy-sucker off.

Community aid

Take advantage of your community's free or low-cost programs for insulating your home. Check with your utility companies or community action center to see what might be available to you. You may be pleasantly surprised.

Cooking

Use as little water as possible. It takes energy to heat water. Most frozen or fresh vegetables can be cooked in no more than a ¼ cup of water. Even eggs will cook in that little water if the pan has a tightly fitting lid.

Cook topside whenever possible

Your oven uses a lot more energy than the stovetop burners.

Dimmers on lights

Add dimmers to switches on overhead lights. Soft light uses less electricity and is more flattering too.

Dishwasher

Select the "energy save" option on your dishwasher, run it only once a day (at night), and allow the dishes to air-dry rather than running that expensive heat-dry portion of the cycle.

Dryer diversion

If your home is dry inside during the winter, and you have an electric dryer (never do this with a gas dryer), you can detach the vent pipe from the outside vent, cover it with a piece of cheesecloth or nylon stocking to serve as a lint filter, and redirect that wasted heat back into your house. Come summer, return the vent to its normal position. You can buy a heat diverter attachment ($7 or $8) at your local hardware or appliance store and install it yourself. There is a lot of moisture in that diverted heat, so you need to keep an eye out for condensation and mildew. This technique is *not* advisable in areas with humid winter climates or for homes with humid indoor air.

Energy leak test

Here's how to check for air leaks. Shut the doors and windows. Move a lighted candle around the perimeters of the doors or windows. If the flame flickers you have an air leak. Plug it with caulk and weather stripping.

Flashlight always fresh

When a flashlight is stored in a drawer or glove compartment it often gets turned on accidentally, draining all the power from the batteries before you discover it. Not only are you deprived of your emergency lighting, you're out the price of the batteries. To solve the problem, always store the flashlight with the top battery turned around so it can't make contact. When ready to use, just turn the battery right side up.

Fluorescent lightbulbs

Replace incandescent light bulbs with fluorescent ones. Fluorescents cost quite a bit more but they use ¼ the energy and last 10 to 15 times longer than their incandescent counterparts. If you can't make the switch all at one time, do it gradually—one or two bulbs a month until all have been replaced.

Free firewood

If you live near one of the 155 national forests, you may have up to 6 cords of firewood free. Check with your regional office of the U.S. Forest Service. Warning: It is illegal to pick up firewood in a government-owned forest without a permit, so don't skip that part.

Heat from light bulbs

When the air-conditioning is on, turn off unnecessary lights. Much of the energy from a light bulb is heat.

Heating bills

Each degree the thermostat is set below 70 degrees knocks 2 to 3 percent off the heating bill. A well-insulated home with caulk and weather stripping makes it possible to lower the thermostat without unacceptable discomfort.

Heat pump

If your home has a heat pump, there are several things you can do to make sure it is functioning at its best and not costing you more than it should:

(1) Make sure the outside unit is not blocked by shrubs or weeds. (2) Never stack anything against the heat pump or drape anything over it. (3) Hose down the outside unit periodically to remove dust, dirt, lint, leaves, and grass clippings to make sure it is operating most efficiently. (4) Don't close off unused rooms. That reduces the efficiency of the heat pump, and the cost of replacing it will be far more than the small amount you'll save by not heating the whole house. (5) Clean and change filters and vacuum registers and returns monthly. (6) Don't block registers or air returns with furniture or drapes.

Home energy audits

Request a home energy audit from your electricity and gas companies. Typically these audits are free and will help you discover where all that energy is leaking out of the house.

Insulate your home

If you can't insulate the whole house at once, do what you can. A little insulation is better than none.

Investing in air-conditioning

Make sure your select an air-conditioning system that is efficient. Central systems are graded according to their Seasonal Energy Efficiency Ratio (SEER), and window units are measured by the Energy Efficiency Ratio (EER). The higher the number, the better. When buying a system or unit, look for a rating of 11 or higher.

Just as cozy

Substitute a fluffy comforter for your electricity-sucking electric blanket.

Kitchen

When cooking, keep as much of the surface-unit heat as possible from escaping. Use pots and pans with flat bottoms, and always use a pan that is the same size or larger than the burner.

Laundry

Wash all but the most soiled clothes in warm or even cold water, followed by a cold rinse. According to the Department of Energy, this saves the average family $50 a year without affecting the quality of the wash.

Leaky faucets

Fix leaky faucets immediately. A steady drip can waste gallons plus the energy used to heat it if it's the hot water that's leaking.

Light bulb efficiency

Put low-watt bulbs in lamps not used for reading. If you need strong light, however, one 150-watt bulb is more efficient than two 75-watt bulbs.

Light exterior colors are best

Light colors on the outside of a house reflect the sun's rays, reducing the temperature inside. If your cooling bills are higher than your heating bills, consider white or light-colored roof shingles when you must replace your roof.

Lights, on or off

When leaving the room for less than half an hour, you should leave the compact fluorescents on, and when leaving for less than 5 minutes, leave incandescents on.

Light timers

Install timers or motion detectors rather than leaving lights on all night. This will ensure that you use lights only when necessary and will greatly reduce your light bill.

Low-flow showerheads

Install a flow-controlling shower-head. The kids will never notice, but your water bill will.

Microwave and save

To conserve energy use the microwave whenever possible. A microwave oven uses 85 percent less energy than cooking on a gas or an electric range.

Money up the chimney

Don't let heat or air-conditioning escape up the chimney. Check for leaks and keep the damper closed when the fireplace is not in use.

Preheating oven

Preheat your oven only when necessary, such as when baking a cake or bread. Many foods like meats and casseroles can start out in a cold oven with no adverse effect.

Programmable thermostat

A programmable clock-operated thermostat is really worth its weight in gold. Reasonably priced, it will pay for itself in no time at all in reduced heating and cooling bills.

Radiant heat

If your home is heated with radiators, boost the efficiency by making a reflector. Cover a large piece of insulation board with aluminum foil, shiny side out. Tape the foil to the board. Slip this reflector behind the radiator to reflect heat away from the wall and into the room.

Range top

Make sure the reflector pans beneath your stove's burners are bright and clean. Shiny reflector pans help focus heat rays on the bottom of cooking utensils.

Refrigerator

Turn your refrigerator to a warmer setting when you go away for more than a day. As long as the door stays closed, food won't spoil.

Refrigerator

Vacuum the coils at the bottom or back of your refrigerator frequently to prevent dust from building up around them. Dust makes the refrigerator run more often and so does keeping it too close to the wall. Refrigerators and freezers need room to breathe or else they can get too hot and run too much.

Run it full

Run only a full dishwasher. Otherwise you're wasting precious hot water and electricity.

Save energy in the kitchen

Use small appliances like a toaster oven, electric skillet, wok, slow cooker, and pressure cooker. On average they use half the electricity of a full-size oven.

Save hot water

Don't let hot water run continuously when you're shaving or washing dishes.

Share garbage service

If neither you nor your neighbor regularly fill your garbage cans, ask if they might be interested in splitting garbage collection costs. Check to see if your city or county ordinances prohibit this. Many do not.

Take shorter showers

A bath takes many gallons more hot water than a shorter shower.

Three-way bulbs

Use 3-way bulbs. They are more efficient, provided you use the lower wattage whenever possible.

Turn it down

In the winter keep thermostats set to 65 degrees by day and 60 degrees by night unless you are elderly, in poor health, or taking certain types of medication, in which case you should consult your physician.

Turn it off while brushing

You'll save 3 to 5 gallons of water a day if everyone in the family will turn off the bathroom faucet while brushing their teeth.

Two-tier pricing

Check with your power company to see if they offer two-tier pricing. If they do, that means power used in nonpeak hours (nonbusiness hours) is charged at a lower rate. Do as much of your power-sucking tasks like dishwashing and laundry during the off-hours.

Unplug instant-on appliances

Unplug instant-on, remote-control television sets when you go away. These models continue to draw electricity even when turned off.

Use fabric wall hangings

A quilt or decorative rug will insulate interior walls, keep your room cozier, and allow you to turn down the thermostat a few degrees in the winter without a noticeable difference.

Watch batteries

If you have more than one battery-operated wristwatch, pull the stem out on the one(s) you are not currently wearing. The batteries will not run while they're sitting in the drawer. Not such a big deal until you remember what a pain it is to find a shop to replace the battery, to say nothing of the annoyance of having the battery die at the least convenient time. Turning the batteries off when not in use will keep your spare watch running well for many years.

Water check

Has the water bill got you stumped? Maybe the meter is not tracking your usage correctly. Here's how to check. Turn off all water sources inside the house and take a meter reading. Now fill a 5-gallon container 3 times and take a second reading. The meter should show a 15-gallon increase. If you see a discrepancy, call your water company's repair number and arrange for a no-cost service call.

Water heater

Match your water heater size to the needs of your family. If you are constantly heating enough water to service a family of 8 and your nest is empty, you're wasting a lot of money.

Water heater

Insulate your water heater with a blanket manufactured just for this purpose to reduce heat loss. On an electric heater, this could save $20 a year.

Water heater maintenance

Perform water heater maintenance twice a year, and you'll get many more years of service from it. Turn off the power to the water heater at the circuit breaker and drain the sediment from the bottom of the tank.

Water heater off

Turn off the water heater when your house is empty, whether it's for a weekend or a week's vacation.

Water heater timer

A $30 timer on your water heater will pay for itself in saved energy in less than a year. The unit turns the water heater off while you sleep and then back on again in plenty of time to heat water for morning showers. Also, consider taking advantage of off-peak electric rates. Call your utility company for more information.

Water saver

Insert a brick into a plastic bag and place it in your toilet tank. Its displacement will reduce the amount of water required to flush the toilet. A plastic jug filled with water will do the same.

Water-saving commode

Install water-saving toilets when you need to replace your old ones. Check with your utility company. Many offer rebates in excess of the cost of a new commode just for your trouble.

MONEY & FINANCE

BANKING

ATM safety

When using the automatic teller machine, always wait for the "Welcome" prompt to signal that your transaction is over, and then take your card. Leaving prematurely may allow the next customer to continue making transactions in your account.

Automatic banking

Arrange with your bank or credit union to have your paycheck automatically deposited, your bills paid automatically, and your savings funded automatically from your checking account. With this type of arrangement you will be handling your money less so you won't be so tempted to play games with the account. The typical bank charge is about $7 a month to handle one's money in this way—quite a bargain; at least half of that would be paid in postage alone. Your bank will be able to answer all of your questions.

Bank deposits

Before you take a check to the bank, write on the back "for deposit only" followed by your signature and account number. If the check is lost or stolen before you can get it to the bank, it cannot be cashed or deposited to any other account.

Checks direct

Don't buy checks through the bank. You can save 50 percent of what they charge by ordering through an independent source like Current, 800-426-0822, or Checks-in-the-Mail, 800-733-4443.

Credit unions

Many credit unions offer low- or no-fee checking accounts and free checks too. If there's any way you can qualify, join a credit union. Most credit unions welcome spouses, children, brothers, sisters, and parents of the member. You will enjoy federally-insured deposits and low interest auto loans. And you'll earn higher than bank interest rates on your savings accounts.

Keep the info

When you write a check to a company you haven't done business with before, jot down the address and phone number in your checkbook register so it's handy in case you need to check on your order.

New currency

Prevent newly minted paper currency from sticking together by placing bills front to front and back to back.

Personal identification numbers (PIN)

Never write your PIN number on your debit or credit card or on anything that would readily identify what it is. Instead "embed" it in a phone number under a fictitious entry in your phone book. Example: If your PIN number is 3614, make an entry of "Penelope 361-4000." Choose a PIN that can't be traced, and never select a number that can be derived from the contents of your wallet.

Second checking account

Keep a separate checking account for tax deductible expenses, and sort them every month by category, such as charitable contributions and medical and dental expenses. By year-end you'll be way ahead in the tax preparation hassle.

Shop around

Switch to a smaller, locally-owned bank. The fee structure will likely be lower and some services will actually be offered at no cost, such as free checking, free checks, etc.

CREDIT CARDS

It never hurts to ask

Request a discount whenever you pay cash in a store that honors standard bank credit cards. Since they have to pay from 3 to 7 percent of the bill to the card company on a credit purchase, they should be willing to give you at least part of the difference in the form of a discount. It won't always work, but it's worth a try. If the owner or manager thinks you are going to use credit and at the last minute you inquire about a discount for cash, you'll be more successful.

Keep making payments

As you pay off a credit card or other loan, keep making the same payments, but instead of sending them to the lender, put them into your savings account.

Never, ever

Never pay your credit card bill with a credit card.

Pay early in the month

Make credit card payments as early in the billing month as possible or make two smaller payments a month if you can't pay it all early. Most banks calculate interest on the average daily balance. The larger the payment and the sooner in the month you make it, the more of it will apply to the principal. It may not be much savings at first, perhaps a buck or two, but savings grow month after month until the card is paid off.

Plastic surgery

If you are out of control with credit cards and want to create a real turning point in your life, invite a few close friends and relatives to celebrate your plastic surgery. They'll be so curious, you know they'll show up. Of course, you intend to cut up your credit cards, then make a personal commitment to no new debt.

Stop the applications

To stop the unsolicited credit card applications from showing up in your mail, call TransUnion at 800-241-2858 and request that your name be removed from all lists that are sold or rented to retailers or others offering unsolicited credit, products, and services. You'll be asked a series of questions, including your social security number. The whole process takes about 4 minutes. In a week or so you'll receive a notice from TransUnion confirming that your name will not be included on their marketing lists. TransUnion will share your request with the other credit bureaus, and in a few months you should see a dramatic decrease in the number of applications you receive.

Wise use of credit cards

Pay entire balance during the grace period so as to never incur interest charges. Whenever you use your card, follow this practice. On the same day, as soon as you walk into the house, write a check for the full amount of purchase and deduct it from your account balance. You spent the money so it is no longer available to you. It's gone. As soon as the statement shows up, mail the full payment immediately.

You have to ask

If you receive an invitation to accept a new credit card with a remarkably lower interest rate, call your current credit card company and tell them about this competing offer. If you have a good track record with them, and they get the message that you just might leave in favor of the more attractive rate, you could receive an on-the-spot interest rate reduction. You'll wonder why you didn't call sooner.

You only need one

Accept only one credit card and make sure it has no annual fee. There's nothing virtuous about having an assortment of credit cards. One is all you'll ever need. The only thing you can do with two cards that you cannot do with one is owe more people more money.

Before you build your own

Have your head examined before you attempt to build your own home. Unless you are a developer or professional contractor, you are in for a few surprises, not the least of which is that it will take twice as long as promised and cost twice as much as estimated.

Boarders

If you have an extra room, consider taking in a boarder to help defray your costs. Post a notice at a local community college or corporation. Check with personnel offices at larger corporations in your area. Often they assist employees in locating affordable housing. Before you hand over the keys to your own house, check many references, get a credit report on the candidate, and have a written contract that includes Rules of the House.

Buying a bargain property

If you're looking for a bargain, buy the worst house in a good neighborhood. You can always fix up a house, but you can't change the neighborhood.

Impound accounts

Ask for a refund of any excess funds your mortgage lender is keeping in an escrow account. One woman discovered that her bank was collecting $100 a month more than necessary to cover anticipated property tax and insurance bills. When she asked that her monthly assessment be reduced to 1/12 of the total annual bill, the bank quickly agreed and that reduced her monthly expenditure. She also received a refund for the more than $500 excess amount that was in the fund. You have to ask.

Interest on earnest money

When purchasing a home, make sure you will earn interest on your deposit during the escrow period.

Mortgage interest rate

Inquire if the financial institution servicing your mortgage offers an interest rate reduction when payments are automatically paid from your checking account. Example: A credit union recently introduced a ¼ percent reduction for any member who authorizes automatic withdrawal.

Mortgage prepayment

Pay more than your monthly mortgage payment in the form of a second check on which you have clearly written "Principal prepayment." This is probably one of the best things you can do with extra cash. You will pay down the principal more quickly, which will result in a tremendous savings of future interest.

Negotiating trick

When negotiating the purchase or sale of a home, always ask for more than you are willing to accept—even if that is beyond your level of expectation, and you're sure they'd never agree. More than likely your opponent will meet you halfway, in essence splitting the difference. That's what makes both of you winners. You get more than you ever dreamed possible, and they didn't have to give nearly as much as they thought you expected. It's called the "art of negotiation."

Principal prepayments

Instead of paying your mortgage monthly, pay half of your mortgage payment every two weeks. You will end up making 26 half-payments, which equal 13 monthly payments. Your spending plan will absorb this additional payment with little, if any, pain, and your principal will love you. If your mortgage holder will not accept payments in this way, make your regular monthly payment as required, and include a second check equal to $^1/_{12}$ of one payment. At year-end you will have made the equivalent of 13 monthly payments with the same effect. Simply write "Principal prepayment" on the second check.

Rent control

If you rent, find an area with rent control. If the law is in place, you might as well take advantage of it and enjoy the secure feeling that your rent will not be unreasonably increased.

Selling at a loss

If you are going to sell your home at a loss, try and hold off awhile and rent it out so that you can take advantage of the tax loss when you eventually sell. Check with your accountant. If you can show it as an investment rather than a personal residence, you might be able to recoup some of the loss.

INSURANCE

Accidental death coverage

Don't pay extra for travel insurance. Statistically, it is highly unlikely you will die in an accident, and even if you do, the basic life insurance you carry should be sufficient.

Basic insurance

Make sure you have adequate protection but not excessive coverage no matter what type of insurance you are considering. By accepting higher deductibles, you can afford better coverage.

Collision insurance

Eliminate collision insurance on an older vehicle. Depending on its condition, an older car may not be worth the expense of insuring for more than liability. Conventional wisdom says that if a car is worth $2,500 or less, drop the collision. You'd be better off putting an amount equivalent to the collision premiums into an interest-bearing account and save it towards another car. Of course you should never drive without the liability coverage required by the state in which you reside.

Commute by car pool

Most insurance companies offer discounts to low-mileage drivers.

Company ratings

Make sure you are with a highly rated company of B+ or better. These days the smaller, lower-rated companies are dropping out regularly. Better safe than sorry.

Deductibles

Increase the deductible on your auto insurance and save collision insurance. If your insurance policy currently provides for say a $200 deductible, meaning you will be required to pay the first $200 of any claim, increase it to $500, and your premiums will drop dramatically. Call your insurance agent to get quotes on various deductible amounts. Just make sure that if you do have a claim, you'll be able to come up with the deductible no matter how much it is.

You'd be wise to have an amount equal to your deductible stashed in an interest-bearing account just in case, and then drive defensively to reduce the risk of ever having to use it.

Discounts

Many states offer significant auto insurance discounts if the driver has recently completed a defensive driving course. Call your insurance agent and inquire if this applies in your state. If it does, sign up!

Document with a video recording

Videotape your home inside and out for insurance records. In case of a fire, you need to have evidence of the expensive wall coverings and decorator window coverings. While you are taping, narrate aloud and describe in detail. Keep the tape in a safe-deposit box. Make sure the video date is well documented. Revideo every few years or when considerable changes are made. Tapes don't last forever either.

Don't make small claims

Too many can lead to policy cancelations or premium hikes. Insurance companies think that a frequent filer is heading for a serious accident.

Extended warranty coverage

As a general rule, extended warranty coverage on anything is a waste of money. Modern-day appliances, automobiles, and electronic equipment will operate well during the first year or 3 or whatever time the extended warranty covers. And most of these items come with some kind of a warranty anyway. You'd be better off taking that same amount of money and putting it into an interest-bearing account. That way when the item doesn't break down, you will not have thrown your money down the drain.

Health insurance

Shop your health insurance coverage regularly. With many companies the first-year premium is much less, so switching may not be a bad idea. If your employer offers a menu of coverages, check them all carefully and determine which is best for your particular situation. Never cancel one coverage until you have another fully in place.

Health insurance

If your family cannot afford full medical insurance for each member, consider the school accident insurance offered to each child at the start of each new school year. This is excellent insurance and typically pays 85 percent of medical and dental bills. It is very reasonable ($9 a year for dental, $45 a year for medical is typical)

INSURANCE

and is in effect 24 hours a day, anywhere in the world. Most kids' medical bills are the result of accidents (broken bones, knocked-out teeth, stitches, etc.) so this type of insurance makes a lot of sense.

Homeowner's insurance

Ask about home owner's insurance discounts for security systems, smoke alarms, and good driving records. Always ask! The agent or company may not volunteer the information.

Liability umbrella policy

Instead of carrying $1 million liability insurance on a single auto so as to be well protected when participating in car pools, when insuring younger drivers, etc., consider carrying a $1 million liability umbrella policy which in most cases will cover all of your cars and your principal residence. The annual premium should be around $100 if all of your policies are with the same company, if you have clean driving records, and no inexperienced operators.

Life insurance adjustments

Cut back on life insurance as your dependents become independent. Providing for a spouse alone costs less than a spouse and 8 kids.

Life insurance for kids

Don't buy life insurance for kids. It makes absolutely no sense. Insure only wage earners (including stay-home moms) whose untimely demise would create a financial hardship.

Mortgage insurance

Typically overpriced, mortgage insurance (not to be confused with private mortgage insurance [PMI] which is completely different) is like life insurance because it pays off your remaining mortgage balance in the case of your demise. But who says your spouse or heirs would want to apply insurance proceeds to pay off the mortgage, which may be the lowest interest debt you leave them? If you have this type of coverage, they'll have no choice. It is far better to buy regular term insurance. It's much cheaper and leaves your heirs with more options.

Pay annually

If possible, pay insurance premiums annually. Avoid the added costs for monthly or quarterly billing.

Private mortgage insurance (PMI)

PMI is usually required to protect the lender against the possible default of a buyer who enters into a mortgage with less than 20 percent down payment. In most situations PMI can be canceled once the equity reaches 20 percent either by paying down the mortgage or the property appreciating in value. But it will not happen automatically. You must call and get the ball rolling. Expect to be required to prove the market value of your home and that you now have at least 20 percent equity. PMI is expensive, and you could be paying $1500 or more each year in premiums. Do whatever you must to cancel it if you qualify. PMI does not protect the borrower in any way. It's for the lender all the way.

Rate reduction

Be sure to let your auto insurance company know of any changes to your driving record, such as if you have been driving to work but have recently joined a car pool, or have been commuting but quit your job to stay at home. Both of these events would result in a significant rate reduction.

Renter's insurance

If you rent, buy a tenant's policy. This is a must. Landlords are not responsible for your belongings in case of disaster.

Replacement value

Add a replacement-cost rider to renter's or homeowner's insurance. It may cost a little more, but in case of a claim, you will be glad you added the rider. Without it, the company will depreciate the value of every item, and you will be a big loser.

Shop your auto insurance every year

Make sure your agent has all of the correct information including your teenage son's good driving record and 3 years' experience. All of these things might matter.

Singles

If you're single, buy life insurance only if someone is financially dependent on you and would suffer an undue financial hardship if your income were to suddenly disappear. Most singles have no reason to carry life insurance.

Take higher deductibles

In essence, you partially self-insure by being willing to take the chance that you won't get sick, you won't crash the car, or you won't be burglarized. The higher the deductible, the lower the premium. The insurance company actually compensates the customer who is willing to share a greater portion of the risk.

INSURANCE

TV insurance offerings

Never buy life insurance from television or direct mail ads. This is a sleazy marketing ploy. The premiums are at least 400 percent too high for the coverage, and the exclusions are mammoth.

INVESTING

Certificates of deposit without penalties

This is how to get penalty-free certificates of deposit. Some banks sell CDs through investment brokers. You can buy CDs that are FDIC-insured through brokerage houses like Merrill Lynch, Gibraltar Securities, and many more. Brokers can track bank CD rates through their computers and lock in the best rates for you. One top advantage is that you can sell these CDs before maturity without paying a penalty. This is not possible with a bank. Otherwise there is no difference, no commission, and full FDIC insurance.

Guidelines for beginning investors

As a beginning investor, any plan you consider should have all the following features or you run a great risk of failure: (1) The investment must be simple to understand and easy to follow. (2) It must take very little time to administrate. (3) It should not cause you stress or anxiety. (4) It must not change your lifestyle or cause disharmony in your home. (5) You must be able to handle the investment entirely on your own. (6) It must have the advantage of liquidity (getting your money back quickly in the event of an emergency). (7) It must work equally well for the person with very little to invest as well as the wealthy investor.

IRA contribution

Try to contribute to your individual retirement account (IRA) as early in the year as possible. The difference between making your contributions each January 1 rather than December 31 of the same year can spell thousands of dollars of additional earnings in your account over the decades.

Lottery

Instead of throwing away $2 a week on lottery tickets for the next 50 years, invest that money in an aggressive growth mutual fund. Don't even think of saying that such an investment is too risky. Investing your money in the lottery is the ultimate risk, and for all practical purposes carries a percent guarantee that you'll lose your money. Remember: The lottery is a tax on the ignorant.

U.S. Savings Bonds

Here's how to earn double interest. Buy U.S. Series EE Savings Bonds on the last day of the month with money that has been earning interest in another account during the month. The bond starts accruing interest as if purchased on the first day of the month. Example: Buy a bond on June 30. When you receive the bond about 21 days later, it will be recorded as of June 1.

MONEY MANAGEMENT

Automatic payment

Arrange for your bank to pay your regular monthly bills directly from your checking account. You'll save the costs of postage, late fees, checks, and envelopes. You'll probably want to call your utility companies and request to be put on a "level pay" plan, in which your monthly amount is estimated based on past usage.

Bill-paying routine

Get into the habit of paying bills twice each month, say, on the first and fifteenth. During the month as the bills arrive, follow this routine: Open a bill and place the return portion in its return envelope and throw the rest away. Write the due date on the outside of the envelope and separate into two due-date piles: "1st of the month" and "15th of the month."

D-E-B-T

Convince yourself that unsecured debt is a 4-letter word. As soon as you teach that to yourself, teach it to your children. Banish unsecured debt from your life.

Don't carry extra cash

Take along only as much money as you expect to need each day. Impulsive purchases are difficult to

make when you have no dollars to spare.

Envelope method

Use the envelope system to handle your household money. Once a month (or as often as you are paid) withdraw a sum according to your spending plan categories, and place that specific amount of cash into each envelope marked for that purpose instead of keeping it in the checking account. This method will really help eliminate the temptations to "just write a check" for this or that. For some reason this system really keeps folks honest and forces them to spend only a set amount in each category. When it's gone, it's gone. This provides a great visual learning experience for children when they can actually observe their parents managing the money.

Free loans to the U.S. Government

Don't give the Internal Revenue Service a free loan. If you receive a large refund each year, you're losing interest on the money. It pays to lower your withholding and bank the difference. Your employer's personnel office can tell you how to arrange it.

Give up the myth

Myth: Buying things on sale is a great way to save money. Truth: Buying things on sale is a way to spend less money, but it has absolutely nothing to do with saving money.

IRS Form 1127

If you have an undue hardship such as long-term unemployment, prolonged illness, disaster, or inability to borrow, and cannot pay your federal taxes when they are due on April 15, call the IRS hotline (800-829-1040) and request Form 1127, "Extension to Pay Taxes." By filing this form, you will have until June 15 to pay without penalty. If the IRS says they've never heard of this form, be persistent. Insist on speaking with a supervisor. It does exist, it is legal, and you have every right to file it if you qualify. This is different from the form "Extension to File Taxes" in which case you must still pay any taxes owing on or before April 15.

Know what you have

Call the Social Security Administration at 800-772-1213 for a "Request for Earnings and Benefits Estimate Statement." After you mail back the completed form, you will receive a statement showing all the money you have paid into social security as well as a personalized estimated monthly benefit upon retirement. If there are errors, such as they didn't credit you one year or they have you earning the wrong amount, they can be corrected but only if you report them.

Lending to friends and family

Don't lend money to people you know. If you decide a loan is in order, make sure you can consider it an outright gift. If you happen to receive repayment, it will be an unexpected bonus.

Life motto

Be content with what you have. As much as possible, do not spend your life scheming and planning to get more things.

MONEY MANAGEMENT

Life motto

Stop spending money you do not have in your possession—today. That means no charging on credit cards, no borrowing from friends or relatives. If that sounds too radical and impossible, agree to not incur any debt just for today. Taking it one day at a time is really much easier.

Loaning money

If someone asks you for a loan, say you were just going to ask him for one. That usually ends the conversation.

Lunch out

Here's a reasonable and practical way to handle the high cost of eating lunch out every day. On Monday take $25 cash and put it in an envelope to be used only for your lunches. If it's gone before Friday, you'll have to take your lunch from home.

Money diary

Keep a money diary by writing down every expenditure no matter how small. Not only will you know where the money goes, you will automatically spend less because no one wants to write down lamebrained purchases.

Money you don't have

Stop spending more money than you have. Consciously begin today to reduce expenses so that your outgo never exceeds your income.

Newspaper subscription

If you subscribe to a newspaper, check to see if discounts are offered for paying an entire year's subscription in advance. Some papers offer a 10 to 15 percent discount. If you find you don't read the newspaper on the weekdays, change your subscription to Sunday only. You won't feel guilty, and you'll save a bundle.

Paying bills

To keep track of bills that are coming due, put the return portion of each bill in an envelope, address it, stamp it, and write the due date on the left-hand corner of the envelope. File the envelopes chronologically, and review them weekly. No more late fees.

Peer pressure

Stop trying to impress other people. If you can stop spending according to demands put on your life by others (through peer pressure or the necessity to keep up), you will see a tremendous difference in the way you spend.

Start giving

Every life well lived should be giving back regularly; then, that life will have meaning. When we are the neediest is when we should be giving the most. Financial bondage is a dead giveaway for an out-of-balance life.

When things are tight

Which payment should you pay first when things are tight and something has to take priority? Pay the rent first. Typically, landlords act quickly if you don't pay on time.

SAVING

Auto reimbursement check

Each month when you submit your expense report for the miles you put on your car and for which your employer has agreed to reimburse you, get into the habit of stashing the reimbursement checks into a special account for the sole purpose of saving for a new car. Usually the gasoline costs required to drive for job-related purposes can be absorbed into your regular monthly spending. This is a great way to force yourself into a savings plan.

Auto savings

Make arrangements with your employer to automatically deposit a certain percentage of your paycheck directly into your savings account and the balance into your checking. What you don't see you won't miss, and this is the most painless way to start saving.

Coupon stash

Many banks are opening convenient branch offices in major grocery stores. If this is true for the supermarket you frequent, open a savings account. Now when you buy groceries, write your check for the total before coupons are subtracted. Ask for your coupon savings back in cash (the equivalent of writing a check for more than the purchase amount), and make a deposit to your savings account on your way out with that cash. Also, make a point of writing your check for more than the purchase by $5 to $10 if you can manage. Stash that cash into the bank as you leave, as well. It's a painless and convenient way to save.

Don't spend coins

Collect loose change by making a personal rule not to spend it. Make it a habit to dump your pockets and purses every night into one collection receptacle. You won't miss the change, and you'll be amazed how much you can save.

Extra paychecks

If you are paid weekly and plan your bill-paying around 4 paychecks per month (that's 2 checks if you are paid biweekly), there are 4 months in each year when you will receive 5 paychecks (2 months you receive 3 paychecks if paid biweekly). Out of that fifth (or third) paycheck take only gas and grocery money for the week and put the rest into savings. You can look at the calendar and project exactly when this is going to happen. These "extra" checks could easily fund Christmas or pay for the family vacation. It's a painless way to save.

Make savings a regular bill

Once a month, or whenever you pay your bills, write a check to deposit in your money market fund or your savings account. If you can't start with 10 percent, start with less and increase the amount each month. Use automatic savings plans—let the bank take your savings out of your paycheck. You won't miss what you don't see.

Save creatively

If you find yourself borrowing back the money you've determined to save, here are some tips for how to put some space between you and the stash: (1) Keep your savings and checking accounts in different banks. (2) Open a passbook account, which will limit your access to the funds. (3) Open your savings account in a bank in another city and make all of your deposits by mail. (4) Establish an account that requires two signatures to withdraw.

Save reimbursements

When you are reimbursed for travel or other out-of-pocket expenses, save the money, put it in your savings account instead of putting it into your checking account, where it will just disappear.

School savings accounts

Open school savings accounts for your kids. Teach them how to fill out deposit slips and make their own deposits. These accounts usually have no minimum balances or service fees.

Start saving for the future

Regardless of how much in debt you are or how little money you make, saving something consistently in a special place or account is going to change your attitude. Saving even a few dollars each week helps fill the emptiness that drives some of us to spend. Something of everything you earn is yours to keep.

SAVING

Stash cash

When you write a check for groceries, round it up and take the difference in change and deposit it each evening into a change jar you have at home. Example: If the bill comes to $33.02 write the check for $34 and stash the 98 cents in change. You'll be amazed how much change you'll accumulate in a year's time.

SHOPPING

Ask for discount
Always ask for a reduction or discount if the item you desire is marked or scratched or is the floor model. You're not complaining, whining, or being obnoxious—you're negotiating, and that's smart.

Auctions
Stretch your dollars by buying things such as building materials or appliances, even gifts, at auctions. Learn how to be an impeccable inspector since all sales are final.

Barter
Whenever possible, trade goods or services instead of money: haircuts for typing, baby-sitting for landscape maintenance, or housecleaning for electrical work.

Beat the rush
If a sale starts on Thursday at 9 A.M., there's a good chance that if you walk in on Wednesday afternoon, you'll get the sale price.

Brass
If you're shopping for a brass bed, take a small magnet along. If it's real brass, the magnet won't be attracted to it. If it's brass-coated metal, the magnet will cling.

Buy gently used electronics
Before buying a new television, stereo, or other piece of electronic equipment, check with a good repair shop. Many times excellent quality merchandise has been abandoned, and the shop will sell it to you for the cost of the unpaid repair bill only.

Buy in bulk
This will cut down your trips to the grocery store and will often save 50 percent of the unit cost. Reorganize your kitchen and pantry. Find places outside the kitchen to store dry and canned goods. Repackage large amounts into small units.

Buying in bulk
Buying in bulk may not always be a money-saving activity if your family

unconsciously consumes more when they see large amounts of anything. Somehow that feeling of using just a little vanishes when the shampoo, for instance, is in a quart-sized bottle. To counteract this problem, have small containers for laundry soap, shampoo, cereal, etc., that you fill from the large bulk container, which is stored out of sight. Besides seeming that there isn't an unlimited quantity of anything, the small containers are easier to handle, and the chances of slipping and pouring out way too much are lessened.

Buying used
Check out thrift shops, but never buy just because you've found a good bargain.

Consignment stores
High-quality, previously owned clothes are sold at often 70 to 85 percent below the new price. Shop well, and you will find unbelievable bargains.

Consignment stores
Make money and save money at a consignment store. If you take in used clothing (men's, women's, and children's) that is in good to excellent condition, the owner will resell the items and send you a check for a percentage (usually 50 percent). These shops are also a great places to hunt for wonderful bargains. Find a consignment shop in an upscale neighborhood, and you've got it made.

Courtesy couponing
If you're a couponer, make sure that before you get to the store you use a bright-colored highlighting pen to mark the expiration date on each coupon you intend to redeem. Your checker will be happy and so will everyone waiting in line behind you.

Easy saving
Look through the wholesale listings in your local Yellow Pages for items that you buy frequently or in bulk, such as pet food, paper and party goods, and garden supplies. You'll find that many wholesalers do sell their wares to the public but don't advertise.

Factory direct
If you have factories in your area that manufacture things you regularly use, call to see if they have a factory outlet where they sell seconds and overruns. Try the local newspaper for roll ends of newsprint. It makes for great picnic table coverings, gift wrapping, and all kinds of crafts. Paper factories often have toilet paper and other

paper goods available. Don't confuse factory outlets of this type with the new outlet malls that are more retail than discount.

Frugal rule to live by

To spend less and save more: Make things last longer, use smaller quantities, find cheaper alternatives.

Get friendly with salespeople

They usually know when things are going to go on sale. Ask and then be willing to wait.

Get in and out

When a great sale or coupon offer sends you to a store you're not familiar with, don't spend a lot of time searching for the item. Remember, the store wants you to wander around so you'll just happen to pick up all kinds of other things you see. Instead, when you enter the store, ask an employee for the exact location, make your purchase, and get out of there as quickly as possible.

Impulse buying

Ten dollars here, 20 bucks there doesn't seem like it will make much difference in the long run. But if you buy $20 worth of impulse items each week, that's $1,040 a year. Little things do matter, and when it comes to spending impulsively, they matter a lot.

Layaway

Most stores offer layaway plans. This is a great way to purchase something over a period of time without incurring debt. As long as the store holds the merchandise until you make all of the payments it is not a debt, because you can change your mind and get a refund. Layaway forces you to save for things before you purchase them.

Learn to shop without buying

A little attitude change will allow you to thoroughly enjoy lovely things but leave them in the stores. Let someone else dust, polish, and care for them. You can visit "your" stuff whenever you like and change your mind without consequence!

Load up on loss-leaders

These are the advertised sale items that the store uses as bait to get you in the door. Buy as much as you can afford so you will have enough to last until the next time it comes on sale.

Mail-order catalogs

Never pay for mail-order catalogs, as offered in many magazines for anywhere from $1 to $6. Since most mail-order catalog companies have toll-free numbers, simply call direct and request a free catalog.

Mail-order shopping

If you love mail-order shopping and find yourself going nuts with the orders even though you've been disappointed in the past with all the junk you ordered that you neither wanted or needed, here's a tactic that could help curb the urge and actually trick yourself: Take great pains and enjoy every moment of studying your favorite catalogs. Fill out the order form, being careful to select all the items you love the most, in all the colors and sizes you desire. When you are done, prepare the form for mailing, write the total amount on the outside of the envelope and then purposely set it in a place you will see it often, then leave it there for a full week. By the time the week has passed, give yourself a little test: Without opening the order form or catalog, can you remember what you ordered? Probably not, so it doesn't matter anymore. Throw it in the trash.

Major purchases

A major purchase deserves careful planning. Break down the cost of the item into a monthly sum you can put aside over a period of time. Example: If you want to buy a new sofa, put pictures of the one you like on your refrigerator and in your checkbook. Determine the amount you will spend and how much you will put into a special account for this purpose each week or month. If your goal is firmly planted in your mind, you won't feel deprived when you give something up in order to keep making those savings deposits.

Missing the sale

If you learn the store in which you recently made a purchase is selling your purchase for a better price, make sure to stop by with your receipt. Most stores will reimburse the difference.

Planned spending

Stop shopping. Shopping often means strolling through the mall with nothing particular in mind, simply looking for great bargains and things that happen to strike your fancy. That is a very dangerous thing to do. I'm not suggesting that you never again buy anything, but that your spending should become a planned act of acquiring the goods and services you need, not spur-of-the-moment, impulsive spending.

SHOPPING

Purchase with cash

Retailers are keenly aware of the statistics that prove you will spend at least 30 percent more if you are in the store with a credit card, debit card, or checkbook. The last thing they want is a customer who carries cash. Why? Because they know how cautious and nonimpulsive the cash buyer is.

Save first, spend later

Instead of putting larger purchases on credit, save first. Once you have enough cash, make the purchase. Amazingly, by the time you save up the money, you may change your mind a dozen times. You might even decide you no longer need or want it.

Scanners

Many retail stores that are equipped with checkout scanners have store policies that say you get the item free if the price is scanned incorrectly. Stay alert and watch the prices that are scanned. If you see something that doesn't look right, speak up. Curiously, each year overall scanner errors in this country register in the millions of dollars to the benefit of the retailer.

Share magazine subscriptions

Cut subscription costs by using the buddy system. Find a friend or relative who enjoys the same kinds of magazines and newsletters that you do. Each of you pay half and share it when it arrives each month. Enlarge your group to 5: Subscription rates are split 4 ways; the fifth person receives the issues last, and instead of participating in the price, she becomes the librarian—cataloging, sorting, and storing the publications for the group.

Shopping compulsively

Break the compulsive shopping habit: Do not carry credit cards with you, put yourself on a cash diet, and throw away all junk-mail, such as mail-order catalogs, without even opening them.

Shop with cash

If you enter the store with a checkbook or credit card, you will be more apt to buy impulsively and spend far more than you intended. While it takes a lot of courage and a bit of planning, shopping with cash only is the best way to avoid expensive mistakes. If you see something that you really do need, write it down and make sure it's on your list for the next trip.

Signing contracts

Think about it for 30 days before you sign. Any purchase that requires your

MONEY & FINANCE

signature probably requires payments. You just might have a change of heart, and even if you don't, you will be confident in your decision and will hopefully avoid buyer's remorse.

Stock up off-season

Seasonal items (such as swimwear, coats, and boots) are often cleared out at phenomenal prices; so if you can handle the thought of buying snow gear in the spring, go for it.

The $100 bill trick

If you find yourself shopping compulsively—buying stuff on credit that you neither need, really want, or can even afford—try this rather unconventional tactic: Tuck away a $100 bill in a very secret place known only to you. In the future, whenever you get the urge to purchase something or feel overcome by a case of the "I wants," tell yourself, *OK, but you'll need to go home and get that $100 bill.* For some reason the urge will pass quickly. Knowing you can if you want but you choose not to has a wonderful preventive effect. Try it.

Time encourages impassivity

Do essential shopping when you don't have much time. If you have too much time to browse, you'll be tempted to buy impulsively.

Timing the market

Timing is everything. Buying clothes and seasonal stuff like snowblowers or patio furniture at full price at the start of the season is expensive. You can save a lot of money by waiting for the prices to come down. That might be towards the end of the season—or next week if you're looking at a computer system or upgrade.

Try generic

It's amazing how many brand-name products have a generic counterpart—everything from grocery items to prescription and over-the-counter drugs. You'll be surprised how close they are to the expensive brands. Think this way when buying clothes as well. Take a little time, and before you make that whopping purchase at Nordstrom, sneak into Wal-Mart and see if they don't have a very good generic.

Twenty-four-hour rule

If it costs more than a certain amount that you've set ahead of time, wait 24 hours between the time you make a decision and actually make the purchase. More times than not you will change your mind, which means you will have avoided a needless purchase.

SHOPPING

Wish list

If you struggle with the "I wants," create your own wish-list system. As you think of things you want, write them on your wish list and date the entry; keep your wish list with you at all times. The rule is that you must leave the item on the list, unpurchased, until it has been on there for 3 full months. Periodically review your list, especially when you add some new gadget to the list. Surprisingly, your level of need for most of the items diminishes to the point that you'll no longer even want it. Any item that remains after 3 months indicates something that deserves further consideration.

Work where you shop

If you are looking for a job, either primary or one to augment your present income, consider the advantage of working in a retail store, then carefully choose the store. By selecting one in which you already shop, not only will you make extra money by receiving a paycheck, you will almost always receive an employee's discount on the products you would be purchasing anyway. A 30 percent employee discount is not unusual. And remember, that's 30 percent off the lowest sale prices, too, which can translate to some healthy bargains.

TRAVEL & AUTOMOBILES

AUTOMOBILE BUYING

Automobile twins

Even if you have your heart set on a particular vehicle, remember that many cars have twins. General Motors offers many of the same cars as Chevrolets, Buicks, Pontiacs, or Oldsmobiles. Chrysler often clones its cars as Dodges and Plymouths. The Geo Prism is essentially a Toyota Corolla built in the U.S., while the Ford Probe and Mazda MX-6 are twins. The annual car issue of Consumer Reports tells you which automobiles are twins.

Buyer's Guide sticker

If you are considering buying a used car from a dealer, become familiar with the Buyer's Guide sticker posted on every used car offered for sale (for-sale-by-owner cars excluded). It was originated by the Federal Trade Commission as a consumer protection device. Before you start shopping, read the FTC pamphlet that explains the Buyer's Guide. Send 50 cents to: Consumer Information Center-F, P. O. Box 100, Pueblo, CO 81002, and request publication 440T "Buying a Used Car."

Cars shunned by thieves

Choose a car not coveted by criminals. A phone call to your local police department will reveal which cars are most likely to be stolen in your area.

Complete Car Cost Guide

The best single resource for determining what it will cost to own a particular vehicle is The Complete Car Cost Guide, about $45, available from Intelli Choice, Inc., 800-227-2665. This book evaluates depreciation, gas consumption, insurance costs, and frequency of repairs to derive the average 5-year cost of operating each car.

Contract scrutiny

Before signing a final auto purchase or lease agreement, check it with a magnifying glass. The folks who write up the final agreement often make mistakes. Occasionally the agreed-upon price gets listed incorrectly, or extras you crossed off get added back in, or a higher financing charge than the one you settled upon finds its way back into the deal. Give the contract a brutal examination.

Dealer add-ons

Factory-installed options are good buys, but think twice about any option the dealer wants to add, such as a stereo or sunroof. Typically, specialty shops do better work and charge half the price.

Dealers' fiscal year

If you are in the market to buy a new car, wait until the end of March. December is not the end of most dealers' fiscal year as most would like you to believe, but March is.

Delivery of new car

Insist on a test drive of your new car before you accept delivery. Never take delivery at night, because you want to examine the car carefully in full daylight. Make sure there's been no damage in transit and that the car has not been repainted. Telltale signs of repainting are paint traces on the rubber striping or trim, mismatched colors, and misfitting panels.

Do it yourself

The dealer fabric protection offered as an option when purchasing or leasing an automobile amounts to a can of Scotchguard sprayed on the upholstery. At about $200 it's not a very good buy. Skip the option, pick up a can of Scotchguard, and do it yourself.

Don't divulge your bottom line

Don't tell a dealer you can afford, say, a $300 monthly payment. Tell him what you can afford, and he'll gladly increase the interest rate or lengthen the terms until it exactly matches what you can afford. Either way, you lose. In the privacy of your home figure out what you can afford, but don't reveal your secret at the dealership. Dicker for the lowest rate you can get.

Get it in writing

If you want something fixed on the car you are buying, get it in writing the moment it is offered or agreed upon. Do not expect to have the dealer pay for something you did not get in writing.

Inspect for hidden damage

Looking for a used car? Look for repaired accident—damage on a used car. Vehicles that have been banged up and reconstructed will have telltale signs. Check under the hood to make sure the fender seams haven't been sprayed over with paint. Have someone drive behind the car to see if the back wheels align with the front, and look for water marks in the trunk. Most importantly, have the car checked by your mechanic.

Insurance
Check on insurance rates before you make a decision to purchase a particular car. Call your agent with a couple of choices and get quotes.

Lightweight
If economy is your first priority, buy the smallest car you can live with. Weight is the biggest enemy of fuel economy.

New car account
If you use your car for work and get reimbursed for mileage, deposit the reimbursement check directly to a credit union account or bank account set up specifically for the purpose of saving for a replacement.

New car test
When you finally take a new car home, give it a long and thorough test-drive. Take the car back immediately if you detect a major problem. The courts have upheld demands for a refund when the car was returned within the first few days.

Night test drive
Before making a final decision, test drive the car you are considering at night. You want to make sure the headlights are powerful enough for your comfort and that everything else that's supposed to light up, does.

Old is OK with low mileage
Old cars with relatively low mileage are choice buys. Age pushes the value down, but the mileage is more representative of the vehicle's true age. A properly maintained car with 50,000 miles on it is likely to have the same kick regardless if it is 3 years old or 8. The 8-year-old car, however, will be much cheaper.

One point at a time
When shopping for a car, negotiate one point at a time: the price of the car, then the dealer add-ons you want eliminated, the trade-in value of a used car, then financing. If you allow the negotiations on all these points to comingle, you'll be so thoroughly confused you'll lose your leverage.

Operation costs
Keeping your old car instead of buying a new one can save you a lot of money over the years. Example: A 4-year-old, 4-door American sedan driven 15,000 miles per year on average

will cost $7,642 to operate over another 4 years. Under the same conditions a new car would cost $14,036 to operate for the same 4 years.

Research prices for 30 days

Before you shop for a used car, be it from a dealer or private seller, know the general value of cars you're shopping for. Study a month's worth of classified ads to learn what your dream car goes for on the private market.

Safest colors

In the market to purchase a car? Insurance actuarials say that if you're interested in safety, you should drive a greenish-yellow color car if you do not want to be accidentally hit by another vehicle. The next safest colors are cream, yellow, and white—in that order. The least safe colors are red and black. Light-colored, single-tone cars stand out from their surroundings, making them easier to see and avoid.

Skip antirust option

Rustproofing as a dealer option is not advisable. Cars are rustproofed at the factory, and unless you live in an area that goes heavy-duty on the wintertime salt, contemporary automobiles don't need extra protection. It isn't uncommon today to find new cars coming with five-, seven-, or even ten-year rust protection warranties. In many cases this option will invalidate any rust-warranty that came with the car from the manufacturer.

Sunroof increases head room

If you've found the perfect car except for one thing—your hair touches the ceiling—consider ordering it with a sunroof; or if it's a used car, you could have this installed. A sunroof typically will give you another inch or two.

Trailer hitch

Don't consider buying a used car that has a trailer hitch. Trailer towing represents severe service, and you'll be happier with a car that has been gently used, not possibly abused.

Transferable warranties

If the seller says the vehicle is still under the original manufacturer's warranty or any dealer service contract, double-check that these benefits can be transferred from the original owner. Take no one's word for it—read the contracts.

Turn the stereo off

When you are test driving a used car, turn the radio or tape player off. The stereo system can mask other car sounds that a conscientious buyer should be listening for and creates a false sense of euphoria about the car. Listen to the stereo after you have completely evaluated other areas of operation.

Ultimate test drive

If you are in the market for a new car, rent 1 or 2 of your choices for a weekend when the rental rates are at their lowest. Drive it under a variety of conditions and for long periods of time. A 5-minute test drive with a hovering dealer sitting in the seat next to you may not give you a true representation of the car's performance and comfort the way a few days on your own will.

Used car mileage

The mileage on a typical car is 12,000 to 15,000 a year. If you see, say, a 6-year-old car that has only 6,000 miles on it, be suspicious. It's possible that the odometer has been tampered with or has reached the 100,000 mark and started over again.

VIN matchup

Never buy a used car without seeing the ownership documents. Match the car's Vehicle Identification Number (VIN) on the driver's side of the dashboard with the VIN on the title and registration.

When to buy

The best time to buy a new car is winter when salesmen are hungry, and the population is financially strapped, preparing for or recovering from Christmas.

Willing to walk

As a consumer, one of your greatest strengths when negotiating to buy a new car is your willingness to walk away from it. Unless a salesperson believes you will walk away, you are not likely to get the best deal.

VIN matching

TRAVEL & AUTOMOBILES

AUTOMOBILE CARE & REPAIR

Aluminum mag wheels

If your car has aluminum mag wheels, check with the manufacturer to see if they are protected by a clear-coat finish. If yours are protected, as most are, do not use a brush to scrub them. This will scratch the clear coat and give the wheels a fuzzy look instead of the brilliance you paid for. Use only a mild, nonabrasive cleaning wax or polish.

Battery terminals

Pour club soda on the battery terminals. It's a great way to quickly clean and neutralize the acid residue at the battery terminals. In a pinch, even a cola will do.

Battery terminals

A car's starting problems are frequently related to corroded battery terminals. Clean the battery terminals occasionally with a paste of baking soda and water, and then reduce the corrosion problem by smearing them with a thin coating of petroleum jelly.

Big oil filter

The most effective way to immortalize your car is to install the largest oil filter that will fit under the hood. Be sure to change the oil and filter very often.

Black like new

When black rubber or plastic trim on your automobile fades or gets ugly white spots, apply black paste shoe polish. It will look like new again.

Brakes

Have your brakes replaced before the rotors have to be turned. You'll save hundreds of dollars. Your mechanic should check for free and tell you how much of the pad is remaining. Don't push it past 5 percent.

Car polish to avoid

The car polishes to avoid are any that contain abrasives and those that seal too well, because they close the pores of the paint. If the can says the product has a mild abrasive cleaner or seals the finish, stay away from it.

Clean interior

Clean a car's vinyl upholstery with a damp cloth dipped in baking soda. Follow with a mild solution of dish-washing liquid and water. Rinse thoroughly.

Clutch first

On standard or manual-shift cars, get into the habit of always pushing in the clutch before starting the engine regardless of whether the car is in gear. Besides being an obvious safety practice, holding the clutch in while starting the engine lets it turn over just a bit more easily, lessening the power required from the battery and starter motor.

Coolant, always

Always keep a mix of equal parts antifreeze and water in your car's cooling system, even if you live in a mild climate where it never freezes. Not only will it keep your cooling system functioning well, antifreeze contains valuable rust inhibitors.

Correct gasoline is best

Make sure you use the octane grade gasoline recommended in your car's owner's manual. Using a more expensive higher-octane gas than recommended will deliver no benefit, and a lower-octane gas than recommended could damage the engine.

Dealer parts

As a rule, car dealers go for greed and charge 30 to 70 percent more for auto parts than auto-parts stores do. Make a habit of checking auto-parts stores first before running to the dealer. And don't overlook the auto-wrecking yards. They're the best deal going if you don't need a new part. Unfortunately, many parts are available only through the dealer, so in some situations you're stuck.

Debug

To remove stubborn bugs from a windshield, sprinkle surface with baking soda and scrub gently with a wet sponge.

Don't drive like a turtle

Don't poke along in city driving. The slower you go doesn't mean the slower the car will wear. Actually the opposite is true. Slow, turtle-like driving costs you miles per gallon and also increases engine deposits. Keep your city speed in the economical 35 to 45 mph range when possible. Most cars reach their maximum mileage potential in this range, so this practice not only insures top miles per gallon in the city but also promotes longer engine life.

AUTOMOBILE CARE & REPAIR

Downshifting—don't
If your car is a stick shift, don't downshift as a standard alternative to braking. Downshifting uses more gas and wears out the clutch and transmission. Generally it's cheaper to replace worn brakes than a worn clutch.

Drain and replace
Drain and replace your car's radiator fluid every other year. The anticorrosion elements of coolant are spent in about 2 years.

Dryer sheets
Use fabric softener sheets to clean and de-static your car's dashboard, upholstery, and carpeting. Hide the sheet under the seat and enjoy the subtle fragrance.

Emergency fan belt
Panty hose can come through as an emergency fan belt if your car fan breaks. Cut the panty portion away and twirl both legs into a rope; wrap the strong nylon rope around your car engine pulleys; make 2 knots and cut off the loose end. Start your car and drive slowly for several miles to a gas station or telephone.

Garage it
If you have a garage or carport, don't be guilty of the cardinal sin of being too lazy to pull the car in. Those few seconds you spend putting the car away could literally mean years of extra life for your vehicle.

Gas mileage
If you'd like to increase your gas mileage, avoid roof and trunk racks. These things ruin aerodynamics and significantly reduce gas mileage.

Gas mileage
Don't carry more than you need. A light load gets much better gas mileage. Clean out heavy items from the trunk, and leave only the spare tire and safety equipment. Don't make your car a mobile warehouse for stuff you can just as easily leave in the garage.

Gas mileage
Save gasoline and contribute to the long life of your car's engine by taking advantage of "right turn on red" laws. After coming to a complete stop, if the way is clear, turn right on that red light and keep moving. Unnecessary idling time spent at red lights wastes your fuel and that of the cars behind you. Cut idle time and you cut carbon and sludge buildup.

Like 500 miles of wear
You drive home and leave the car parked out front. Later you put it

away for the night by starting the engine and putting it in the garage. Because 90 to 95 percent of engine wear occurs in the first 10 seconds after starting the engine, by merely driving the car into the garage you have accomplished the equivalent of 500 miles from the viewpoint of mechanical engine wear—the actual removal of metal that occurs when engine parts are temporarily devoid of lubrication and metal meets metal.

Oil bargains

Stockpile oil, oil filters, and air filters when they go on sale. Unopened bottles of oil don't have a shelf life problem.

Oil, top it off

Don't wait until the oil is a quart low before adding. There is no law saying you can't add half a quart and put the other half away for later use. A full crankcase guarantees the engine will have the maximum amount of oil available to it at all times. Each time you add even a small amount of fresh oil, you are recharging the entire lubricating system with fresh additives. Forty percent of the engine is directly dependent upon the oil to cool it.

Park on pavement

Try to always park on pavement, even at home. Don't park in the alley when you can park on the paved street. You'd be surprised how much dirt and dust can be sucked into your car's engine compartment when it is parked in dusty areas. Abrasive wear caused by grit, dust, and dirt is one of the major causes of engine failure. Keep away from dirt and dust-producing areas, and you will enhance your car's chances for longevity.

Pepper in the radiator

Put a teaspoon of ground black pepper into your auto's radiator to seal a pin hole. Sounds a little wacky but nonetheless ingenious. It may take more than a teaspoon, but start with that. If you use too much pepper over time, however, you run the risk of clogging the heater core and losing your heat during cold weather. Consider this pepper trick a temporary measure to tide you over until you can afford a more permanent repair.

Poor quality oil

Be very cautious if you are tempted to buy oil at a quick-service mart or food store. Many of these outlets sell only cheap brands of oil. If only SA- or SB-rated oil is available, know that it is practically worthless if you are planning to put it into a 1968 or newer model car. Unless you have an oil burner, stay away from these light-service oils. Look for an oil that carries the designation "API Service SG."

Radial tires

When buying tires, choose radials over bias-ply. You'll pay more up front but will save in the long run. Radials deliver better mileage because they have less rolling resistance. More importantly, they last 15 to 20 percent longer.

Reconditioned parts

If at all possible use reconditioned or secondhand parts for repairs, especially if you are nursing an old car and you don't expect to drive it more than 2 more years.

Retreads okay

Consider buying retreads or blemished tires, particularly for an older car. You can save up to 50 percent of the cost of new tires, and the law requires that they be safe.

Revving engine

Do not race your engine out of gear or in neutral. Revving an engine while the car is not moving can only do harm; it will never help. Many people like to rev the engine a few times just before putting it to bed. The old theory held that the extra revs pumped extra oil through the cylinder walls and made the next start easier. Actually, the opposite is true. Those high rpm's allow unburned fuel to dilute the oil, wash away protective cylinder coatings, and contribute to sludge buildup and oil contamination.

Rotate those tires

Rotate your tires every 6,000 to 9,000 miles. The goal of rotation is to get the tires to wear out uniformly. Check your car manual for the recommended rotation scheme, because there is a right way—and therefore a wrong way—to do that.

Rust

To loosen rusty nuts and bolts, pour club soda over them.

Secret warranties

Some automakers issue special warranties on certain aspects of the auto that are kept quiet and secret from the automobile owner. To find out if your car has secret warranties, send the year, make, and model along with a large self-addressed, stamped envelope to the Center for Auto Safety, 2001 S Street NW, Washington, DC 20009. They will respond with a description of all secret warranties on your car.

Short trips in cold weather

If at all possible, don't take your car on very short trips of 5 miles or less on days when the outside temperature is below freezing. If a bus is available, take it, or if you can accomplish your goal with the telephone instead of going in person, do it.

Slippery oil

Consider using an additive that increases the slipperyness of the engine's oil. Your local auto-parts store owner will gladly make a recommendation. If your driving is not regularly on long freeway trips, inquire about fuel additives that reduce carbon buildup as well.

Specialists

Need a brake job, muffler repair, or front-end alignment? Head for the shops specializing in these jobs. They offer lower prices than the dealers, and polls show they deliver better customer satisfaction.

Spotting tire wear

Uneven tire wear often is easier to spot with your fingers than with your eyes. Run hands from side to side and up and down the tread. Uneven wear could indicate misalignment or loose chassis parts. Beware of pieces of steel belting or metal embedded in the tire that could cut your hand.

Student mechanics

If your car has a ding, dent, or bent fender, check out the auto body department of a local vocational school or community college. You may be able to have your car repaired by the students—while under the watchful eye of the instructors. All you will be charged is the cost of parts. There is typically no labor charges under these circumstances.

Tanker truck at the gas station

Don't buy gas while a tanker truck is filling up the stations' tanks. The gas going into the underground tanks could stir up any sediment present, which could end up in your tank.

Tar and tree sap

A little dab of butter, margarine, or even mayonnaise is great for removing sap or tree pitch that has not yet hardened from the surface of your car.

Tire plugs

Always carry a tire-plugging kit with your car's spare tire. This is nothing more than a few small rubber plugs and a screwdriver for inserting the plugs. It is so simple to use, even a child could learn. A damaged tire can be sealed and plugged right on the vehicle.

Tire pressure

Check the pressure of your tires frequently. Underinflation increases rolling resistance, which increases tire wear and gas consumption by as much as 5 percent.

Touch-up paint

Liquid Paper (white correction fluid available at an office supply store) makes a great touch-up paint for white cars. It covers beautifully, dries to a hard finish, and holds up well through weather and washing. To apply, either use the built-in applicator or tear a match from a book of matches and use the nonmatch torn end as a tiny paintbrush. If and when it wears away, simply reapply.

Ugly wax marks

Car wax can be removed from automobile trim with ammonia that has been carefully applied with a rag or a cotton swab.

Unplug for engine's sake

Unnecessary use of electrical devices, such as headlights in the daytime (unless required for safety), or anything plugged into the cigarette lighter like a cell phone, fax machine, hair dryer, curling iron, or electric shaver will actually make an engine work harder by making it more difficult to turn the alternator.

Vinyl dashboard and upholstery

The greatest enemy of your car's vinyl dashboard and interior is the sun's heat and ultraviolet rays. Here's what you can do to slow down vinyl deterioration: First clean the vinyl upholstery and dashboard. Dry well and apply sunscreen lotion with the highest UV factor you can find. Just rub it in as you would on your skin. When the sunscreen has had time to soak in, buff off any excess and apply a commercial vinyl protectant, which will help seal it in.

Walk and save

When driving into a parking lot, take the first available space you see, and don't be afraid to walk the extra distance. Slow, stop-and-go driving is the most gas-consuming; so be willing to walk a little, and you'll save a lot.

Wash floor mats

Some carpet floor mats will fit into your regular washing machine and come out really clean with a regular wash in warm water with mild detergent. Lay them out to air-dry.

Windows closed
Drive with the windows closed. Open windows mess up aerodynamics and cost you more in gas mileage than running the air conditioner.

Wiper blades
To get a few more month's use out of windshield wiper blades, lightly sand the edge of the rubber blade with sandpaper. Be sure to carefully remove all traces of sand from the blades, reattach, and they'll work like new.

Wiper blades
Before you toss out those windshield wiper blades, try cleaning the rubber part with rubbing alcohol. You may be pleasantly surprised to find they were not worn out at all—just gunked up.

AUTOMOBILE SMARTS

Accident-prepared

Carry a disposable camera, pad of paper, and pen in the glove box of your car. In case of an accident you'll have what you need to collect information and take on-the-spot photos. Be sure to draw a map and record all the details while they are still fresh in your mind.

Always prepared

Store a sweatsuit, sneakers, and a pair of old socks in the trunk of the car next to the spare tire. This way, if there's a flat tire, throw the sweats on over your good clothes, and kick off your shoes and change to sneakers. Change the tire without having to worry about getting dirty. Another plus: If the car simply breaks down, the sneakers will get you to the nearest gas station faster.

Auto gadget caddy

A large handbag or other kind of handled tote with its many zippered compartments makes a dandy storage system for the trunk of your car. Fill the pockets with battery cables, flashlight, first aid kit, maps, window cleaner, paper towels, and a plastic window scraper.

Automatic transmission

Give your automatic transmission a little break by learning how to help it shift. Ease up slightly on the accelerator when you feel the transmission begin its shift. This increases engine vacuum and helps the transmission into a smooth, effortless shift.

Auto stereo

In cold weather it's wise to wait until the car's interior warms up before using the radio or cassette player. These units should be warm, especially the cassette player, before they are turned on. Be patient and allow the heater to warm the interior, and your expensive sound system will work better longer.

Baby wipes

Keep a box of baby wipes in the car to clean your hands after pumping gas.

Being-followed test

A great way to avoid a possible carjacking is to be aware of what's going on around you. If you think someone is following you, make 4 right turns, which will in essence have you driving in a circle. If that suspicious car makes the same turns, immediately drive to the nearest police station, busy store, or service station to seek help.

Big ice scraper

Scrape snow from car windows with a plastic or rubber dustpan. It won't scratch the glass.

Bumper stickers

Remove a decal or bumper sticker by first softening the adhesive with a hair dryer. Use a medium heat setting for a few seconds until the adhesive softens and the annoying sticker starts to peel. Continue with the heat until the entire sticker peels off easily.

Car registration

Never leave your car registration in the glove compartment. It gives a car thief automatic proof of ownership. Keep it with you.

Cat litter for traction

In winter weather carry a heavy bag of clay-based litter in your trunk, and the extra weight will help keep the vehicle stable. If you are stuck in snow or ice, clear the area around your drive wheels, pour litter in front of the tires in the direction you want to go, and then drive away slowly. Clay does not contribute to corrosion. And it is heavy. So once the danger of snow is past, remove it from your trunk to encourage better gas mileage.

Chrome

Briskly scrub rust spots on car bumpers with a piece of crumpled aluminum foil, shiny side up. Also works well on the chrome shafts of golf clubs.

Condensation on car windows

To take care of the condensation that builds up on the inside car windows during the cold winter months, leave the air-conditioning on with the temperature in the heat position, and windows will clear like magic. Or carry an ordinary chalkboard eraser in the car. Simply erase the condensation away.

Dangerous times

Statistics say the most dangerous time to drive your car is late afternoon to early evening on Friday. The safest day is Sunday. The most dangerous month is November; the safest is March.

Deodorizer

To keep your car smelling fresh, put some of your favorite potpourri in a mesh bag and tuck it under the front seat. No more dangling pine trees.

Don't be predictable

A car that's always parked in the same place for the same amount of time each day or night lets thieves know where to look for it and gives them plenty of time to figure how much time they'd need to make off with it.

Drive for 5

Drive for 5 drivers: yourself, drivers in front, drivers at both sides, and the driver behind you. Be prepared at all times for at least 4 of them to do the unexpected.

Driving shoes

Keep a pair of driving shoes in the car. Sharp heels and sport shoes wear holes in the carpet. Use a carpet sample or remnant under the pedals to prolong the life of your vehicle's carpet.

Engine idle time

It is more economical to turn the engine off rather than let it idle if the idle time exceeds 30 seconds, according to EPA tests. If the engine is going to idle less than 30 seconds, leave it on because it takes more gas to restart it than 30 seconds of idling will use. Not only will this practice prove beneficial to your mileage rating, it will also help reduce deposit buildup and wear directly attributable to prolonged engine idling.

Fifth gear

Don't use overdrive or fifth gear until the car has warmed up sufficiently—approximately 10 minutes under normal driving and weather conditions. The rear axle and transmission fluids must be adequately warmed for these units to work properly and efficiently.

Fill up early in the day

Fuel your gas tank early in the morning, and you'll get 5 percent more gas for the same price. The heat of the afternoon sun causes gasoline to expand in the station's fuel tank so less pumps out as the day wears on. The average early bird will spend up to $50 a year less on fuel.

Flat tire

If a tire goes flat, drive slowly to the nearest safe place to change it. The farther you drive, the higher the odds of ruining your tire. Don't, however, be dollar foolish by changing the tire in a dangerous place.

Floor mats to the rescue

If your car gets stuck in the snow, slip one or more of the floor mats under the stuck tire(s) to provide traction you need to get out. Don't forget to run back and get the mats unless to do so would place you and your passengers in harm's way.

Gas cap replacement

If you've ever left your gas cap at the gasoline station, you won't be surprised to know that many others have too. The next time you're capless, ask the station attendant if you might look through their lost-and-found gas cap assortment. You're sure to find one that fits, and they'll be happy to have you take one off their hands.

Gas cap return

An address sticker securely attached to the inside of your gasoline cap may get it returned to you if you accidentally leave it behind at the pump.

Hands off

Don't drive with your hand resting on the gear shift. It may feel good, but adds unnecessary wear to the transmission selector forks.

Improve the dipstick

Save the guesswork when checking your car's oil by making the dipstick easier to read. Drill tiny holes at the lines that read "full" and "add" so they'll never get obliterated.

Left-footed driving

If your car has an automatic transmission you may be tempted to brake with your left foot. Bad habit. Left-footed braking leads to riding the brakes, which results in a slew of problems: poor gas mileage, reduced engine life, and worn-out brakes.

Overheating first aid

At the first sign of your car's overheating, shut off the air conditioner and open the windows to decrease the load on the engine and help it cool down. If the car is still overheated, turn on the heater and blower to transfer heat from the engine to the interior. If you are stopped in traffic, shift into neutral and rev the engine a little to speed the water pump and fan. The increased circulation should help to cool things off.

Retrieving hubcaps

With a permanent marking pen, write your name, address, and phone number on the inside of your car's hubcaps. This way, if one goes flying you have a chance of having it returned. Include the word "reward," and you will greatly increase the likelihood of a return. Even if it costs you 20 percent of the price of a replacement, you'll be 80 percent ahead.

Snow chains caddy

Start with an old pair of jeans. Cut off the legs to make short shorts. Sew the legs shut. Drop one chain into each "leg" compartment, and the tools required for installation fit easily into the pockets. Attach handles for easy carrying.

Stopped on a hill

When stopped on a hill always use your parking or foot brake to hold the car still. Don't hold it by applying gas to the accelerator or, in the case of a standard transmission, by riding the clutch and applying gas. These bad habits accelerate wear of the engine, clutch, and transmission. Use your brakes. That's what they're there for.

Sunglasses storage

Keep sunglasses handy when driving by storing them right on your car's sun visor. Attach the case to the visor by gluing self-adhesive fasteners to each. Your shades will always be within easy reach.

Windshield ice

You won't have to scrape snow and ice from your windshield if you place a large, plastic, cut-open trash bag over the windshield; secure the bottom edge under the windshield wipers and close the sides in the car doors.

Pulling on the way ... your gas mileage ... of a stand age, such as by ri...
you have a chance of getting at ... ng clutch and applying ... the
least ... Inside the wind ... ed, ... can cause accelerated wear of the
tires, you will greatly improve the mile- ... engine, clutch, and transmission. Use
age of your car. Even if it costs ... your brakes. That's what they're there
you 25 percent of the price of a ... for.
replacement, you'll be 80 percent
ahead.

Sunglasses storage

Keep sunglasses handy when driving ... to put them right on your ears ... son visor. Attach the case to the visor ... with self-adhesive fasteners ... and your shades will always be within easy reach.

Snow chains handy

... with an old pair of jeans. Cut ... of the legs to make short bags, sew ... the legs shut. Drop one chain into each leg ... trunk compartment ... the tools required for installation ... into the pockets ... which handles ... for easy carrying.

Windshield fix

You won't have to scrape snow and ice from your windshield if you place ... over the windshield ... under the wipers and close the ends in the car doors.

Stopping on a hill

When stopped on a hill, always use ... pedal ... to hold ... the car will ... gas to hold ... in the car doors.

TRAVEL & AUTOMOBILES

AUTOMOBILE TRIPS

Avoid the crowds

Before visiting popular tourist sites, call ahead to find out when the tour buses usually arrive. Dozens of tourists arriving at the same time can flood attractions with crowds that result in long lines and slipshod service. Buses usually run on fixed schedules, so you should be able to count on the information you receive.

Best routes

If you prefer leisurely car trip vacations, take the business or truck routes through cities. You'll find the good motels that were bypassed by the Interstates. These can be very nice and quite inexpensive.

Camera bag

Fill a small fabric bag with dried beans or rice to keep in your camera bag. When you want to take a time exposure and need to hold the camera very still, simply set the beanbag on a steady surface, place the camera on the bag, line up the shot, and shoot. The camera stays perfectly still because it is securely cradled on the beanbag. This is also a perfect solution for when you want to get into the photo, too. Just securely position the camera on the beanbag, set the timer, and run like crazy.

Car organizer

A pocket shoebag hung over the back of the front seat can hold small toys, crayons, and other loose items in the car.

Clothespins

Toss some clothespins into your baggage. They'll turn any hanger into a makeshift clothes dryer.

Coke in a pinch

Corroded battery terminals can leave you stranded. Quick fix: Pour a cola drink or other carbonated beverage over the terminals. This is a temporary measure to get you where you need to go without a tow.

Coping with travel stress

Whether you're on a business trip or a family vacation, when things start to get a little tense, pretend there's a video camera filming your every action. Once you see the playback in your mind, you'll be glad you can tell yourself to "cut" and start again.

Crayon tote

Metal bandage containers make great on-the-road crayon holders. Small enough to carry in your bag, you can pull them out any time you want to keep little hands busy.

Cross-country driver

Consider driving someone else's car. Auto-transport companies (listed in the Yellow Pages) are often looking for good drivers to move cars from one part of the country to the other. Typically you pay only for gas, and they'll even get you started with a full tank.

Disappearing ink

A disappearing-ink marking pen, available at the fabric store, is great for marking maps. In a day or so, your marks will fade, and your map is all ready for the next trip.

Give and take

At the start of a trip give each child a handful of dimes. If they ask "How much farther?" or any other tiresome questions, they forfeit a dime. Let them keep what's left.

Group security

When checking into a hotel, get a hotel business card for each family member to carry in case of accidental separation.

Renting a car

If you rent a car, reject offers of additional optional coverage if you currently carry auto insurance on the car(s) you own. Be prepared for some heavy-handed tactics to get you to accept it. Salespersons get hefty bonuses if you can be persuaded. Call your insurance agent to check on rental car coverage ahead of time.

Save on hotel rates

On any given day, hotels can have many different rates depending on occupancy. Always call the hotel desk instead of the 800 reservation number. Ask about weekend rates, holiday and seasonal specials, or discounts for affiliations you might have, such as the Automobile Club of America.

Single bag

If an overnight stop is on your car trip itinerary, pack a small bag with one change of clothes for each family member and basic toiletries. Instead of unpacking the whole car, all you'll need to take into the motel is one bag.

Washington, D.C.

The family dream-come-true vacation spot is Washington, D.C. All government-run museums and monuments—including the Air and Space and American History Museums—are admission-free. Go visit your tax dollars at work.

PLANE TRAVEL

Airplane seating strategy
When only middle seats are available, ask the gate agent to put you in the empty seat between a couple with the same last name. Chances are good you'll get that aisle or window seat when they ask if you'd like to switch so they can sit together.

Airport peace and quiet
If you need to find a quiet place in an airport to either sleep or work, and you don't belong to one of those expensive elite clubs, go to a gate where the plane has just taken off. It will be deserted for a while, and when another scheduled flight moves in on you, find another just-departed location.

Airport rental cars
Car rental companies with desks in the airports are generally more expensive than off-site renters. It costs these companies a lot of money to lease airport desk space. And guess who gets to make up the difference?

Back-to-back booking
Since flights that involve weekend stays are less expensive than those that don't, on some routes it's cheaper to buy 2 round-trip tickets and throw away half of each.

Be persistent
If you are dealing directly with the airline reservation desk and are unable to book the flight you want, hang up and call a second time. If you get a different ticketing agent you may get what you want. Go figure.

Bereavement fares
Most airlines offer radically reduced fares in time of bereavement. When you call for a reservation under these circumstances, explain your situation and ask for their bereavement fare. Don't be offended if a cooperating airline requires verification of funeral arrangements.

Bump on purpose
If you want to get bumped from your airline reservation because you have

the time and wouldn't mind that round-trip ticket that most airlines offer in exchange for giving up your seat and taking a later flight, let the gate agent know that you are willing to give up your seat if needed when you check in.

Bump-proof

When flying, if you do not want to get bumped from a flight that's been overbooked (most are these days), get to the gate an hour before departure and be the first to check in. When a flight is oversold and no passengers volunteer to be bumped, the last ones to check in are the first to be denied boarding.

Car parking habit

If you travel a lot and leave your car at the airport, park it in the same spot every time. When you return dead tired, you'll have one less thing to think about.

Carry-on bags

When boarding a plane, don't wait until you arrive at your seat to store your bags. Stow them in the first overhead compartment available after you pass through the first-class cabin. Many of these compartments will be empty. You won't have to carry them to your seat or back to the front when you exit the plane.

Cheaper flights

An airline flight that makes a stop between your departure city and your destination can sometimes be significantly cheaper than one that makes no stops. You may have to spend an extra hour or two on the ground, and you risk additional delays, but the savings may be worth it.

Companionship

When traveling with a companion, each should pack some clothes in the other's luggage to lessen the impact if one bag is lost or detained.

Curbside check-in

Skip the curbside luggage check-in facility if at all possible and go directly to the ticket counter. Your luggage is more likely to be handled correctly, and you won't be expected to tip. If you must use airport curbside check-in, remember these are airport—not airline—employees. Double-check their work, especially the 3-letter destination code on your bags' tags. If you want to see your bags at the other end of your trip, tip these handlers.

Dental surgery and flying

Never fly if you have had dental surgery within the past 12 hours. The change in air pressure will cause severe pain and possibly bleeding.

PLANE TRAVEL

Exit-row seating
On most planes the spacing is wider in an exit row, which means more legroom. On domestic flights if you sit in an exit row, you must speak English and be able and willing to open the emergency door. You will need to get to the gate early if you want to get one of these highly sought-after seats, since airlines do not assign them in advance.

Fare wars
If you purchase an airline ticket and before you use it the airlines have a big fare war, you may be able to receive a refund for the difference. Check with your airline for the specific rules and regulations, and don't wait for them to call you. They won't.

First flight
Book the first flight of the day. When flights are delayed, they affect other connections. The earlier you leave, the more options you have. Avoid taking the last flight of the day if you must be at your destination the next morning. If that flight is canceled, you're stuck.

Flight strategy
Avoid flying on Fridays. Instead book your flight for a Tuesday or Wednesday if you can. Midweek travel is less crowded. Avoid flights that depart or arrive between 7:00 and 9:00 A.M. or 4:00 and 7:00 P.M. at any major airport. These are the busiest times of the day.

Insurance for lost luggage
If you lose your luggage, and it is not recovered, the airline's limit of liability is up to $1,250 of the depreciated value of the bag and its contents. If your loss exceeds this amount, your household insurance policy may pick up the difference.

Itinerary
Write the dates of your stay and where you want lost luggage to be delivered in the city you'll be visiting. Attach this abbreviated itinerary to the outside of your luggage.

Just business
Put your business address and phone number on your luggage tags. Your home address and information may suggest to potential thieves that your house will be vacant. Make sure to put the same information inside each piece of luggage too.

Know the rules
If a flight is diverted, causing departure delays, most air carriers will give you a meal voucher. If you need to

stay overnight because the airline has a problem, most will pay the hotel bill plus the cost of ground transportation. But you must ask, so don't be timid.

Know your planes

L-1011s have tiny overhead storage bins so check all the luggage you can. 757s have one difficult-to-navigate, long, narrow aisle. 737s generally have less legroom. Both 737s and 757s have the fewest restrooms per capita. The most comfortable planes are 767s, 747s, MD-11s, and MD-80s.

Locked luggage

Lock your bags. This won't guarantee the contents will be kept safe, but it will definitely discourage a dishonest baggage handler.

Missing bags

If your bag does not show up on the luggage carousel, make sure you fill out a claim form and get a receipt before you leave the airport.

Oddball luggage

Checked bags frequently go astray because they look alike and someone walks off with one that looks like yours. Buy brightly-colored luggage, put a colorful luggage strap around your bag or use neon-colored stickers to make your bag stand out in a crowd. Tacky luggage is also a less likely candidate for theft.

Priority handling

Attach bright, neon-colored tags to your luggage that have been printed with the word "Priority" and laminated at a local printing company. Your bags will attract the attention of baggage handlers and will usually be the first to come off the plane. As a bonus, your luggage will stand out in a sea of look-alike baggage.

Rebooking shortcut

You're at the airport when you learn, that your flight has been canceled. Don't rush to the ticket counter where you will have to wait in line with everyone else on the canceled flight. Instead find a phone and call the airline's reservation number. Ask to be rebooked on the next scheduled flight.

Reduce delays

When booking a flight, remember that the more times you land, take off, or change planes the more you increase the chance of delays. If you cannot avoid making connections, look for a flight that has stopovers at small airports. Reduced traffic reduces delays. Allow at least an hour for connections.

Remove luggage tags

Remove all tags from luggage that are left over from previous trips to avoid confusing the baggage handlers and scanning devices.

Rule 240

If your flight is delayed due to mechanical or scheduling problems, don't fret. Rule 240 requires most airlines to put you on another flight if it can get you there sooner than the flight they have picked out for you, even if the flight is with a different airline. A copy of Rule 240 is available at every airline gate. If the employees are hesitant to grant your request, mention Rule 240 and things should change dramatically.

Seat assignments

Ask for your seat assignment when you book a flight. If you wait until you check in, you're less likely to get the seat you want. Most airlines won't assign seats more than 30 days in advance, so make a note to call back if you're booking far in advance.

Seating strategy

When 2 people are traveling together on a plane with 3-abreast seating, one should request an aisle and the other a window. This maximizes the chances of the seat in the middle remaining empty. If someone does sit there, and you want to sit next to your companion just ask the person if they'd like the window or aisle instead of the annoying middle seat.

Ticket agents

Never yell at a ticket agent. An old Chinese proverb says, "If you are patient in a moment of anger, you will escape a hundred days of sorrow."

Volunteer rewards

Airlines often overbook flights to insure a full plane. If more people show up than there are seats, the airline will ask for volunteers to take a later flight in exchange for travel coupons or vouchers. If you aren't on a tight schedule, volunteering could earn you a free round-trip ticket good for one year to any city to which that airline flies.

TRAVEL TRICKS

Home time

If you are taking medications when you travel, take an extra watch and keep it always set on home time. You'll never have to wonder when to take your medicine.

Leaks in the suitcase

Make sure the bottles of shampoo, lotions, and makeup in your suitcase don't leak all over your clothes. Put a bit of cotton inside each bottle cap before closing it.

Lights on timers

Before you go away on vacation, put new light bulbs in all the lamps connected to timers. You want to be sure that when the timers go on, so will the lights. Save the light bulbs you replaced for using when you'll be home.

Packing earrings

Pierced earrings won't get lost if you poke them through a handkerchief or cotton socks or into a bar of soap.

Packing list

Toss the checked-off packing list you used to prepare for the trip into your suitcase. Use it to recheck when gathering everything at the end of your stay.

Packing pants

Roll slacks around a mailing tube to keep them from wrinkling in your suitcase.

Photocopies just in case

Whenever you travel, make two photocopies of everything in your wallet (credit cards, driver's license, medical insurance card, passport, etc.). Put one copy in your luggage, and leave the other at home.

Plants on vacation

Before leaving on vacation put your plants in a small, plastic children's swimming pool. Fill the pool with about 3 inches of water. The plants will survive for at least 1 week. Make sure the pool is in an area that will not get direct sunlight during the days you're gone.

TRAVEL TRICKS

Shampoo your clothes

Don't bother packing laundry detergent. The shampoo you bring or you find in your hotel room is great for washing blouses and underwear. Caution: Shampoos formulated for oily hair are more alkaline and should not be used on delicate fabrics like silk, as they can cause fading.

Stains on the road

Pack a laundry stain pretreatment in your luggage, and use it on stains before they can set. This way, stains will wash out easily once you're home and get to the laundry.

Suitcase

Store an opened, fragrant bar of soap in a suitcase to prevent musty odor from forming during storage.

Take the tape

When traveling, always take a roll of cellophane tape. It removes lint, seals bottles, and even temporarily mends cuffs and hems. Duct tape works well, too, particularly where stronger mending is needed, like for shoe repair or suitcase patches.

Test the weight

After packing for a trip and just before leaving the house, pick up your bag and carry it around for a full 5 minutes. If you're out of breath, it's too heavy. Eliminate what you can or pack 2 smaller, lighter-weight bags instead of one heavy one.

Train travel

When traveling on Amtrak, take your own blanket. While the train supplies pillows for passengers, a blanket will cost $8.

Travel iron

A hair dryer can double as a travel iron. Dampen the creased garment and spread it on a flat surface. Set the dryer on warm and hold it in one hand while smoothing the item with the other.

Travel ready

To keep everything organized when you pack for a trip, group all the small essentials into large plastic zippered storage bags. When you get to the hotel, put your bedside bag (travel alarm clock, flashlight, nightlight) on the night table; the toiletries bag (powder, deodorant, toothbrush, hair essentials, makeup) on the bathroom shelf. Everything's together, easy to use, ready to go in a moment's notice, and you probably won't find yourself leaving things behind.

TRAVEL TRICKS

Travel size

Save 35mm film containers for holding face cream, laundry detergent, and other travel supplies you need in small quantities while traveling.

Traveler's aid

Do-it-yourself remedy for traveler's . . . uh . . . (how do I say this delicately?) dysentery: In a glass mix 8 ounces fruit juice, ½ teaspoon honey, and a pinch of salt. In a second glass mix 8 ounces purified water and ¼ teaspoon baking soda. Alternate sips from each glass until you've finished both.

Vacationing pets

Have a special ID tag for any pet that's traveling with you. Include the name and telephone number of someone who will be able to get in touch with you while you're away.

ABOUT THE ILLUSTRATOR

Joel Barbee, a master when it comes to connecting his pen with his reader's funny bone, has enjoyed an illustrious career working with the best, including Disney, Warner Bros., Golden Books, *Freedom Papers, Los Angeles Times,* and numerous advertising agencies. Ask Joel, an avid saltwater angler, what he does to keep busy these days and he's likely to hand you a stack of current publications like *South Coast Sportfishing, Western Outdoors, Pacific Fisherman, Salt Water Sportsman,* and *Outdoor News*—where his work shows up regularly. And right on top of the stack would be the current issue of *Cheapskate Monthly,* which, Joel contends, is his all-time favorite account. Joel and Arlene, the true love of his life for 40 years, have two grown children and live in San Clemente, California, where their home sits high atop a bluff overlooking the Pacific Ocean.

A FINAL WORD

There's a good reason why this book is not titled *The Complete Tiptionary.* That's because as far as I am concerned, *Tiptionary* will never be complete.

As long as people like you keep discovering new ways to do things more cheaply, better, and faster there will always be another great tip right around the corner. And as long as I live and breathe, I'll be out there searching for it.

I'm certain that as you have dined on this *Tiptionary* smorgasbord, dozens of tips came to your mind. Would you share them with me? I'd love to hear from you. Please understand that it's not possible for me to respond to you personally. But you can be sure that if your tip meets my rather loose criteria as described in the Introduction and hasn't already been submitted—somewhere, sometime—your tip will be immortalized within the pages of *Tiptionary.* And then you will find how much fun it is to share a great tip and have someone come back at you with a big smile and the sentence that always makes my day, "Wow! What a great idea!"

I can't wait to hear from you.

Mary Hunt
P. O. Box 2135
Paramount, CA 90723-8135

WHAT IS SOILOVE?

Soilove is a very inexpensive, very effective laundry stain pretreatment product, a bottle of which I found hidden in the back of a shelf at my grocery store many years ago. Little did I know when I bought that bottle for less than a buck (60 percent cheaper than anything else on the shelf), I was about to discover the best all-around stain treatment product on the face of the earth. I use a spritz of Soilove for just about any kind soil problem I run into. Unfortunately, Soilove continues to be hidden on the shelves in some California and Arizona stores.

The company got so tired of hearing me whine that my *Cheapskate Monthly* readers couldn't get Soilove where they live that several years ago they made it available by mail order. If you'd like to try Soilove, give America's Finest Products a call at 800-482-6555. Tell them you read about Soilove in *Tiptionary.* (Tip: Soilove does not come in a spray bottle, so pour it into your own to allow for more judicious use.)

A SPECIAL OFFER

Cheapskate Monthly is a 12-page newsletter published 12 times a year, dedicated to helping those who are struggling to live within their means to find practical and realistic solutions to their financial problems. *Cheapskate Monthly* provides hope, encouragement, inspiration, and motivation to individuals who are committed to financially responsible and debt-free living and provides the highest quality information and resources possible in a format exclusive of paid advertising. You will find *Cheapskate Monthly* filled with tips, humor, and great information to help you stretch those dollars till they scream!

How to Subscribe to *Cheapskate Monthly*
Send check or money order for $18 to:
Cheapskate Monthly
P. O. Box 2135
Paramount, CA 90723-8135
(562)-630-8845 or (562)-630-6474

INDEX

B

INDEX

INDEX

INDEX

INDEX

INDEX

INDEX

INDEX

INDEX

INDEX

INDEX

INDEX

INDEX

INDEX

INDEX

INDEX

INDEX

INDEX

INDEX

INDEX

INDEX

INDEX

INDEX

INDEX

INDEX

INDEX

INDEX

INDEX

INDEX

INDEX